# Public Policy

# AMERICAN GOVERNMENT AND HISTORY INFORMATION GUIDE SERIES

Series Editor: Harold Shill, Chief Circulation Librarian, Adjunct Assistant Professor of Political Science, West Virginia University, Morgantown

*Also in this series:*

AMERICAN EDUCATIONAL HISTORY—*Edited by Michael W. Sedlak and Timothy Walch*

AMERICA'S MILITARY PAST—*Edited by Jack C. Lane*

IMMIGRATION AND ETHNICITY—*Edited by John D. Buenker and Nicholas C. Burckel*

PROGRESSIVE REFORM—*Edited by John D. Buenker and Nicholas C. Burckel*

PUBLIC ADMINISTRATION IN AMERICAN SOCIETY—*Edited by John E. Rouse, Jr.*

SOCIAL HISTORY OF THE UNITED STATES—*Edited by Donald F. Tingley*

U.S. CONSTITUTION—*Edited by Earlean McCarrick*

U.S. CULTURAL HISTORY—*Edited by Philip I. Mitterling*

U.S. FOREIGN RELATIONS—*Edited by Elmer Plischke*

U.S. POLITICS AND ELECTIONS—*Edited by David J. Maurer*

URBAN HISTORY—*Edited by John D. Buenker, Gerald Michael Greenfield, and William J. Murin*

WOMEN AND FEMINISM IN AMERICAN HISTORY—*Edited by Elizabeth Tingley and Donald F. Tingley*

---

The above series is part of the

## GALE INFORMATION GUIDE LIBRARY

The Library consists of a number of separate series of guides covering major areas in the social sciences, humanities, and current affairs.

General Editor: Paul Wasserman, Professor and former Dean, School of Library and Information Services, University of Maryland

Managing Editor: Denise Allard Adzigian, Gale Research Company

# Public Policy

## A GUIDE TO INFORMATION SOURCES

*Volume 13 in the American Government and History Information Guide Series*

### William J. Murin

*Associate Professor of Political Science*
*University of Wisconsin-Parkside*

### Gerald Michael Greenfield

*Associate Professor of History*
*University of Wisconsin-Parkside*

### John D. Buenker

*Professor of History*
*University of Wisconsin-Parkside*

*Gale Research Company*
*Book Tower, Detroit, Michigan 48226*

**Library of Congress Cataloging in Publication Data**

Murin, William J
    Public policy.

    (American government and history information
guide series ; v. 13) (Gale information guide library)
    1. Policy sciences—Bibliography.
    I. Greenfield, Gerald Michael, joint author.
II. Buenker, John D., joint author.  III. Title.
IV. Series.
Z7161.M967  [H61]  016.3616'1    80-25872
ISBN 0-8103-1490-8

To the Women in Our Lives

# VITAE

William J. Murin currently serves as the director of University of Wisconsin-Parkside's Master of Public Service Administration program and its Institute for Local Government and Human Services. He received his B.A. from Kent State University, an M.P.A. from Maxwell School of Syracuse University, and a Ph.D. from the University of Maryland in 1971. His teaching and research have focused primarily in the areas of urban politics, transportation policymaking, and urban administration and management. His writings include MASS TRANSIT POLICY PLANNING (Lexington Books, 1971), URBAN POLICY AND POLITICS IN A BUREAUCRATIC AGE, with Clarence N. Stone and Robert K. Whelan (Prentice-Hall, 1979), and a book of readings, CLASSICS IN URBAN ADMINISTRATION, POLICY, AND POLITICS (Moore Publishing Company, forthcoming).

Gerald Michael Greenfield is associate professor of history at the University of Wisconsin-Parkside. He received his B.A. from the State University of New York at Buffalo, an M.A. from Brooklyn College, and a Ph.D. from Indiana University, Bloomington, in 1975. A specialist in Latin America and comparative urbanization, his articles have appeared in the LUSO-BRAZILIAN REVIEW, JOURNAL OF LATIN AMERICAN STUDIES, SOUTH ATLANTIC URBAN STUD-IES, and ESSAYS CONCERNING THE SOCIO-ECONOMIC HISTORY OF BRAZIL AND PORTUGUESE INDIA.

John D. Buenker is professor of history at the University of Wisconsin-Parkside. He holds a Ph.D. from Georgetown University and has previously taught at Prince Georges College and Eastern Illinois University. He is the author of URBAN LIB-ERALISM AND PROGRESSIVE REFORM (Scribner's, 1973) and coauthor of PRO-GRESSIVISM (Schenkman, 1977), IMMIGRATION AND ETHNICITY: A GUIDE TO INFORMATION SOURCES (Gale, 1977), and PROGRESSIVE REFORM: A GUIDE TO INFORMATION SOURCES (Gale, 1980). He has also contributed essays to ESSAYS ON ILLINOIS HISTORY, THE STUDY OF AMERICAN HIS-TORY, KENOSHA COUNTY IN THE TWENTIETH CENTURY, RACINE: GROWTH AND CHANGE IN A WISCONSIN COUNTY, and FLAWED LIBERATION: AMERI-CAN CULTURE. He has written articles and reviews for the JOURNAL OF AMERI-CAN HISTORY, the AMERICAN HISTORICAL REVIEW, the NEW ENGLAND QUARTERLY, the HISTORIAN, MID-AMERICA, ENCYCLOPEDIA AMERICANA, the DICTIONARY OF AMERICAN BIOGRAPHY, ROCKY MOUNTAIN REVIEW, and the state historical journals of Illinois, Indiana, Ohio, Pennsylvania, New York, Connecticut, New Jersey, and Rhode Island. He is the recipient of the William Adee Whitehead Award of the New Jersey Historical Society and the Harry E. Pratt Award of the Illinois Historical Society and of fellowships from Newberry Library, the American Philosophical Society, and the Wisconsin Alumni Research Foundation. He was a Guggenheim Fellow in 1975-76.

# CONTENTS

# INTRODUCTION

The transdisciplinary nature of this guide will hopefully make it useful to practitioners, teachers, and students in a wide variety of disciplines. In addition to those individuals who are interested in aspects of public policy at a general level, we hope that persons with specific interests in transportation, housing, civil rights, welfare, and other substantive policy areas will find this guide of use.

To be truly representative of the literature in this rapidly growing field would require several volumes. In the transportation field alone, there is one bibliographic source with more than fifty thousand entries. Thus selectivity, not comprehensiveness, became a guiding principle in our work.

In compiling this list, we consulted a variety of recognized secondary sources with extensive bibliographic information. Some of these sources include PUBLIC ADMINISTRATION ABSTRACTS, URBAN STUDIES ABSTRACTS, both published by Sage Publications; ABC POL. SCI., CURRENT CONTENTS IN THE SOCIAL AND BEHAVIORAL SCIENCES, and the numerous new journals devoted to policy issues and problems. POLICY SCIENCES, POLICY ANALYSIS, PUBLIC POLICY, and the POLICY STUDIES JOURNAL are used extensively.

In order to maintain control over the size of the volume, it was necessary to ignore several potentially useful sources of materials. The compilation is almost exclusively devoted to public policy within the American political system. There is virtually nothing included of a comparative or other perspective. This does not reflect our judgment about the worth of materials in these areas, but rather it reflects the limitations of space. Also omitted is any systematic treatment of government documents that deal with policy-related issues. Again, while there are thousands of possible citations published by government sources, space limitations forced us to leave out this entire area.

Our organizational scheme tries to reflect some of the major component parts of the public policy field. The last chapter, dealing with policy issues, attempts to reflect the diverse and heterogeneous nature of public policy, policy analysis, and policy sciences as a field of study. While we have tried to include many of the classical works in public policy, the majority of the entries are contemporary. Unfortunately, the rapidly changing nature of the field makes the bibliography dated almost as soon as it appears. For those readers interested in yet newer material, we recommend the Sage abstracts in public administration and urban studies, ABC POL. SCI., CURRENT CONTENTS IN THE SOCIAL AND BEHAVIORAL SCIENCES, and POLICY STUDIES JOURNAL. The latter is especially useful as it often includes bibliographies in specific policy areas, policy relevant papers from conferences, and government documents.

# Chapter 1
# THEORIES AND CONCEPTS

## THEORIES AND CONCEPTS

1    Abert, James G. "Defining the Policy Making Function in Government:
An Organizational and Management Approach." POLICY SCIENCES 5
(September 1974): 245-55.

> Abert advances a "definitional approach" as a necessary step
> in organizing and managing the policymaking process. He
> defines five functions--planning, analysis, research, demon-
> stration, and evaluation--and shows how these functions and
> their management interact over several years of policymaking.

2    Abt, Wendy Peter. "Design Issues in Policy Research: A Controversy."
POLICY ANALYSIS 4 (Winter 1978): 91-122.

> Abt makes the following points: better ways are needed to
> evaluate the risks and benefits of nonexperimental design in
> policy research; a key to successful policy research is in
> understanding the organizational content within which it occurs;
> and greater guidance must be given to government leaders who
> commission research and to those who do the research.

3    Adelman, Leonard; Stewart, Thomas R.; and Hammond, Kenneth R.
"A Case History of the Application of Social Judgment Theory to Policy
Formulation." POLICY SCIENCES 6 (June 1975): 137-60.

> Social judgment theory provides a theoretical framework for
> understanding the origin of policy quarrels and methods for
> their resolution. Social judgment theory claims that disputes
> in policy are often cognitive in origin. In most cases, judg-
> mental aids are necessary to clarify the sources and causes
> of disagreement.

4    Anderson, Andy B. "Policy Experiments: Selected Analytic Issues."
SOCIOLOGICAL METHODS AND RESEARCH 4 (August 1975): 13-30.

> Policy experiments represent a tool for testing the consequences
> of planned social programs. There are several ways to or-
> ganize and administer policy programs, and different con-
> figurations may have great differences in costs, efficiency,
> and effectiveness. By increasing the number of research
> objectives, the cost, complexity, and inefficiency of an ex-
> periment are usually increased.

# Theories and Concepts

5    Anderson, Charles W. "Comparative Policy Analysis: The Design of Measures." COMPARATIVE POLITICS 4 (October 1971): 117-32.

Anderson outlines a role for comparative politics in the area of policy analysis related to public choice. He calls for the construction of procedures to unravel complex problems and the crafting of instruments to meet the problems.

6    Archibald, Kathleen. "Three Views of the Experts' Role in Policy-making: Systems Analysis, Incrementalism, and the Clinical Approach." POLICY SCIENCES 1 (Spring 1970): 73-86.

This paper compares three approaches to improving policy-making: systems analysis, incrementalism, and the clinical approach. Systems analysis and incrementalism are compatible, and systems analysis has in large part accepted the incrementalists' view of the policymaking process. This acceptance has not strengthened policy analysis as much as it has increased awareness of its weaknesses. The clinical approach, with its focus on organizational change, promises to strengthen policy analysis. The potential contributions of the clinical approach are considered as well as the eventual synthesis of the three approaches.

7    Bailey, John J., and O'Connor, Robert J. "Operationalizing Incrementalism: Measuring the Muddles." PUBLIC ADMINISTRATION REVIEW 35 (January-February 1975): 60-66.

Incrementalism has been employed as a general concept to describe policymaking, but several difficulties have arisen in its application to budgeting. The work of several authors is examined to illustrate what happens when the distinctions between process and output are not observed.

8    Bell, Daniel. THE COMING OF POST-INDUSTRIAL SOCIETY. New York: Basic Books, 1973. 507 p.

Bell identified changes taking place in our society. The singular feature of the post-industrial society is the "codification of theoretical knowledge." Bell offers a picture of a "knowledge society" which is emerging out of corporate capitalism.

9    Best, Michael H., and Connolly, William E. "Market Images and Corporate Power: Beyond the Economics of Environmental Management." In PUBLIC POLICY EVALUATION, edited by Kenneth M. Dolbeare, pp. 41-74. Beverly Hills, Calif.: Sage, 1975.

Best and Connolly concern themselves with wide-ranging academically oriented policy research. They point to a set of factors that have been taken for granted and built into existing research. Their preference is for a more inclusive approach, but with a large number of variables.

10   Blume, Stuart S. "Policy as Theory: A Framework for Understanding the Contribution of Social Science to Welfare Policy." ACTA SOCIOLOGICA 20, no. 3 (1977): 247-62.

This paper is based on the view that since social science is concerned with the generation of codified knowledge of the social world, its impact should be seen as principally upon other sets of ideas. It suggests that social policy may be conceptualized as an evolving sequence of concepts, theories, and problems comparable with the cognitive development of science.

11    Bothun, Douglas, and Comer, John C. "The Politics of Termination: Concepts and Processes." POLICY STUDIES JOURNAL 7 (Spring 1979): 540-53.

This article attempts to clarify some of the theoretical issues relevant to the idea of termination of public policies. It distinguishes between functional and structural termination. The authors find that few programs are terminated. Efforts at termination occasionally lead to an expansion of resources.

12    Bozeman, Barry. "Social Science and Social Indicators; Problems and Prospects." MIDWEST REVIEW OF PUBLIC ADMINISTRATION 8 (April 1974): 99-110.

This paper classifies and reviews literature on agenda setting in social indicators research and reviews and evaluates suggestions for a research, theoretical, and political activity phase of social indicators movement.

13    Braybrooke, David, and Lindblom, Charles E. A STRATEGY OF DECISION. New York: Free Press, 1963. 268 p.

This book attempts to explain how consensus is reached in developing public policy. It fully develops the now familiar idea of incrementalism or disjointed incrementalism. Braybrooke and Lindblom devote space to policy analysis and evaluation from an ideal or classical perspective, reality as seen by the authors, and utilitarianism.

14    Brock, Bernard. PUBLIC POLICY DECISION MAKING: SYSTEMS ANALYSIS AND THE COMPARATIVE ADVANTAGES DEBATE. New York: Harper and Row, 1973. 176 p.

This book is a systems approach to comparative advantages analysis. It provides a theoretical base for new procedures in policymaking. General systems theory is the recommended pattern of analysis for public policy decision making.

15    Bryant, Coralie, and White, Louise G. "The Calculus of Competing Goals: Planning, Participation, and Social Change." GROWTH AND CHANGE 6 (January 1975): 38-43.

The article reviews three approaches to citizen participation in planning: (1) consensus paradigm, a collaborative search for the public good; (2) feed different interests of different groups into process, not gloss over them, a conflict approach; and (3) economic theory, no common goal, each individual decides whether to participate or not based on costs and benefits.

# Theories and Concepts

16    Buchanan, James, and Tullock, Gordon, eds. THEORY OF PUBLIC
      CHOICE. Ann Arbor: University of Michigan Press, 1972. 329 p.

      This study illustrates an economic theory for making positive
      decisions about the allocation of resources via the govern-
      mental process and for analyzing alternative incentive schemes
      on public choice. Essays concern: military draft, monopoly
      control, socialized medicine, organization of education, and
      others.

17    Bunker, Douglas R. "Organizing to Link Social Science with Public
      Policy Making." PUBLIC ADMINISTRATION REVIEW 38 (May-June
      1978): 223-32.

      Discusses the difficulties scientists and public policymakers
      have in getting together for mutual exchange of information
      and help in formulating government policies. The author
      offers three structural innovations he feels will help in or-
      ganizing for improved knowledge utilization: (1) internal re-
      search centers for each policy field; (2) subunits of these
      centers charged with the cultivation and coordination of net-
      works of policy research capacity for their area; and (3)
      cognate extramural institutes funded to pursue programmatic
      studies.

18    Campbell, Vincent N., and Nichols, Daryl G. "Setting Priorities
      Among Objectives." POLICY ANALYSIS 3 (Fall 1977): 561-78.

      The art of setting priorities is still in its infancy. Different
      problems call for different analytic structures and clients
      vary greatly in their attitudes toward decomposition and
      quantifications. Analysts must deal openly and honestly
      with the uncertainties of estimates and quantitative formulas.

19    Chandler, Marsha; Chandler, William; and Vogler, David. "Policy
      Analysis and the Search for Theory." AMERICAN POLITICS QUAR-
      TERLY 2 (January 1974): 107-18.

      Purpose of this essay is to move the discussion of policy
      analysis away from simple typologies toward general applica-
      tions. It integrates elite and mass involvement measures.
      This integrative theory-building exercise has exposed a wide
      range of alternative patterns of political conflict.

20    Clarke, James W. "Environment, Process and Policy." AMERICAN
      POLITICAL SCIENCE REVIEW 68 (December 1969): 1172-82.

      Purpose of the study is to examine the variables which are
      related to the consideration and adoption of new political forms.
      The analysis deals with the correlates of political change on
      the local level. The hypothesis is that variations in social,
      economic, and political characteristics of communities are
      associated with the decision to keep or alter local government
      structures. Data from forty-three Pennsylvanian cities pro-
      vide the analytical base.

21    Cobb, Roger W., and Elder, Charles D. "The Politics of Agenda-
      Building: An Alternative Perspective for Modern Democratic Theory."
      JOURNAL OF POLITICS 33 (November 1971): 892-915.

      The article seeks to reformulate and extend one aspect of
      contemporary democratic theory. The authors argue that
      recent research and classical theories of democracy are
      lacking in a descriptive and prescriptive sense. They suggest
      a perspective that takes into account recent research and is
      consonant with classical concerns. It focuses on the pro-
      cesses of agenda building at the systemic and institutional
      levels. The importance of popular participation may extend
      well beyond the simple act of voting to the actual shaping
      of the substantive issues of public policy.

22    Cowart, Andrew T. "Expanding Formal Models of Budgeting to Include
      Environmental Effects." POLICY AND POLITICS 4 (December 1975):
      53-66.

      Different properties of the environment are relevant for
      different types of governmental activities. Models derived
      from this conceptualization allow properties of environmental
      stress to enter the decision calculus. Environments have
      been conceptualized in terms of properties thought to operate
      across a range of public activities, per capita personal income,
      levels of education, and degree of industrialization. Fewer
      than half of the budgetary decisions studied were responsive
      to environmental conditions, but substantial change in environ-
      mental stress does have budgeting effects.

23    "Current Problems of Policy Theory: A Symposium." POLICY
      STUDIES JOURNAL 3(Spring 1975): 225-92.

      This study includes nine articles dealing with conceptual
      premises in the study of policy, governing urban space,
      meta-models and policy studies, empirical research and
      policy studies, and others.

24    Cutt, James. "Policy Analysis: A Conceptual Basis for a Theory of
      Improvement." POLICY SCIENCES 6 (September 1975): 223-48.

      Cost-benefit analysis and cost-effectiveness analysis in
      resource allocations decisions is "microanalytical," but policy
      analysis requires a "macroanalytical" framework. An ana-
      lytical system is proposed incorporating the following steps:
      (1) an objective function must be established for national
      policy, and a corresponding set of indicators and weights
      must be established for particular programs; (2) a set of
      analytical parameters must be developed which are comparable
      and consistent with the national objective function; (3) a general
      analytical framework of cost-benefit analysis and cost-effective-
      ness analysis must be developed; and (4) an analytical frame-
      work must be established for the measurement of tradeoffs
      or opportunity costs for alternative policies.

25    Dahl, Robert A., and Lindblom, Charles E. POLITICS, ECONOMICS, AND WELFARE: PLANNING AND POLITICO-ECONOMIC SYSTEMS RESOLVED INTO BASIC SOCIAL PROCESSES. New York: Harper Torchbooks, 1953. 556 p.

Dahl and Lindblom assess the political and economic techniques whereby nations and smaller social groups attempt to maximize the attainment of their goals. The book ties together both political and economic theory by comparing policymaking according to polyarchy, hierarchy, bargaining, and market systems.

26    DeWoolfson, Bruce H., Jr. "Public Sector MBO and PPB: Cross Fertilization in Management Systems." PUBLIC ADMINISTRATION REVIEW 35 (July-August 1975): 387-95.

Management by objectives (MBO) and planning-programming-budgeting (PPB) are not mutually exclusive or contradictory approaches to complex management situations in the public sector, but are complimentary types of management systems. Conceptual models of the key features of both systems are developed, with the caveat that system characteristics vary from setting to setting. The key features are then compared and contrasted to identify possible ways of improving upon present and future management systems efforts.

27    Dillon, G.M. "Policy and Dramaturgy: A Critique of Current Conceptions of Policy Making." POLICY AND POLITICS 5 (September 1976): 47-62.

Policymaking and policy analysis have been rationalist in their conceptualization of the policy process, in their prescriptions for its reform, and in the rhetoric employed to promote and legitimate both existing policy and policy changes. Little attention has been given to the dramatic and symbolic effects that are generally characteristic of policymaking. It is suggested that the more substantive preoccupations of the rationalist mode are themselves best understood as dramatic and symbolic devices.

28    Draper, Frank D., and Pitsvada, Bernard T. ZERO-BASE BUDGETING FOR PUBLIC PROGRAMS. Washington, D.C.: University Press of America, 1978. 148 p.

The book examines in detail the concept of ZBB. More specifically: what is ZBB? how does it work? what are its benefits and costs? how does it fit in with other budget innovations? and, what are the problems and prospects for ZBB? The book begins with an exploration of public budgeting from historical and theoretical perspective and then discusses where ZBB fits in with theory and practice. One chapter is devoted to the mechanics of ZBB, another to the benefits and costs of ZBB, and the final chapter discusses the problems and prospects of ZBB.

29    Dror, Yehezkel. "From Management Sciences to Policy Sciences."
In MANAGEMENT AND POLICY SCIENCE IN AMERICAN GOVERN-
MENT, edited by Michael J. White, Michael Radnor, and David A.
Tansik, pp. 267-95. Lexington, Mass.: D.C. Heath, 1975.

Management sciences constitute a great advance in human
capability to handle some types of problems. Nearly all
broader policy problems are beyond the control of management sciences in their present form, and most of the sub-
components of policy problems cannot be dealt with. One
of the most serious dangers posed by management sciences
when applied to complex issues is that they will improve some
subdecisions without penetrating to the main policy choice.
Policy sciences constitute an attempt to achieve a central
role for rationality and intellectualism in human affairs and
to increase significantly the capacity of humanity to direct
its future.

30    _____. "Some Features of a Meta-Model for Policy Studies." POLICY
STUDIES JOURNAL  3 (Spring 1975):  247-55.

Social science research is judged by accepted criteria of
validity and reliability. These are based on a consensus
of a community of scholars concerning the acceptable approxi-
mations of "truth." The appropriate criterion for policy
studies should be "preferization." The first yardstick to be
applied to any improvement-directed policy study is the quality
of the relevant policies as they are or would be without that
study. If the study can improve policy results so they will
be "preferable" to those otherwise achieved, then the "preferization" test is met and the policy study should be judged
acceptable. The preferization criterion implies many guidelines for the advancement of policy studies, such as search
for time-compressing research methods and for reality-
debugging investigatory techniques. More important, it raises
the question of how to provide institutional support and incentives for a scientific and professional endeavor that must
be judged, at least in part, by a criterion strange and probably suspect to conventional academic culture. Because of
its far-reaching implications, the preferization feature is an
especially critical dimension of policy research methodology.

31    Edelman, Murray. THE SYMBOLIC USES OF POLITICS. 2d ed.
Urbana: University of Illinois Press, 1967. 201 p.

Edelman tries to discover the symbolic processes that tie
officials to their followings and that underlie political claims,
political quiescence, and the winning of benefits. He examines
the symbolic ties organized groups have to public officials and
he considers how the responses of the mass of political spec-
tators influence the ability of the organized to win benefits
through government.

32    Gergen, Kenneth J. "Assessing the Leverage Points in the Process of
Policy Formation." In THE STUDY OF POLICY FORMATION, edited
by Raymond A. Bauer and Kenneth J. Gergen, pp. 182-204. New York:
Free Press, 1968.

This essay proceeds on two fronts: (1) It develops a three-dimensional model for the identification of leverage points in the policymaking system; "leverage points" can be equated to power and influence. (2) The model is then used to examine a number of major methods used to identify those occupying primary positions of leverage.

33    Gershuny, J.I. "Policymaking Rationality: A Reformulation." POLICY SCIENCES 9 (June 1978): 295-316.

This paper proposes a reformulation of the concept of rationality in public policymaking. Comprehensive rationality is unfeasible as a practical policymaking strategy, so it suggests that a modified concept could provide a suitable "ideal criterion" for the assessment of policymaking strategies. Adopting this "limited rationality" criterion emerges as a basic prescription for the conduct of public policymaking.

34    Gilbert, Charles E. "Shaping Public Policy." ANNALS OF THE AMERICAN ACADEMY OF POLITICAL AND SOCIAL SCIENCE 426 (July 1976): 116-51.

This is a special issue dedicated to "Bicentennial Conference on the Constitution: A Report to the Academy." Gilbert identifies ten tendencies that are going to be fundamental in shaping policy in the next century. He concludes that the ways of shaping policy are as subject to constructive change through public participation as through legislative actions of constitutional amendments.

35    Godwin, Kenneth R., and Shepard, Bruce W. "Political Process and Public Expenditures: A Re-Examination Based on Theories of Representative Government." AMERICAN POLITICAL SCIENCE REVIEW 70 (December 1976): 1127-35.

Studies attempting to predict public tax expenditures using political variables have generally incorrectly assumed that political variables function as determinants of policy levels and types. In the absence of knowledge of whether public services are being oversupplied or undersupplied in relation to citizen demands, the effect of political variables can better be tested by moving beyond single equation regression models. A better way of examining the impact of political variables is to integrate them with conventional theories of political representation. This leads to the concept "translation error," and ways of examining relationships between this variable and political variables are explained.

36    Goodin, Robert, and Waldner, Ilmar. "Thinking Big, Thinking Small, and Not Thinking at All." PUBLIC POLICY 27 (Winter 1979): 1-24.

Incrementalists argue that by thinking small and constantly reacting to feedback, they can muddle through without recourse to any theoretical understanding of the system. This article distinguishes three varieties of incrementalism, showing that each requires a theoretical base and that none necessarily supports small scale social interventions in preference to large scale ones.

37     Greenberg, George D., et al. "Developing Public Policy Theory: Perspectives from Empirical Research." AMERICAN POLITICAL SCIENCE REVIEW 71 (December 1977): 1532-43.

> Theoretical efforts to date have not demonstrated adequate recognition of the distinctive qualities of the dependent variable in the development of theories of public policy formation. Public policy is a troublesome research focus because of an inherent complexity--the temporal nature of the process, the multiplicity of participants and of policy provisions, and the contingent nature of theoretical effects. This article shows how complexity makes it essentially impossible to test apparently significant hypotheses.

38     Hage, Jerald, and Hollingsworth, J. Rogers. "The First Steps Toward the Integration of Social Theory and Social Policy." ANNALS OF THE AMERICAN ACADEMY OF POLITICAL AND SOCIAL SCIENCE 434 (November 1977): 1-23.

> The authors present a framework for understanding certain types of policy outcomes. It allows coding most existing policy studies and offers potential for developing generalizations that transcend specific policy sectors.

39     _____. SOME PROBLEMS IN THE STUDY OF SOCIAL POLICY. Discussion Paper, No. 438-477, Madison: University of Wisconsin, Institute for Research on Poverty, 1977. 46 p.

> One of the problems confronting the study of public policy is communication among those involved in policy analysis. This paper develops a set of variables for coding policy studies that permits policy analysis across time and societies.

40     Halachmi, Arie. "Policy Analysis: A Review and a Suggestion." JOURNAL OF POLITICAL SCIENCE 4 (Fall 1976): 1-11.

> Current approaches to policy analysis tend to concentrate on the ways policies are made or ought to be made and on the character of their impact on reality. These are important concerns but they do not assure a continuous application of knowledge for improvement of policymaking. This paper suggests that a use of the methodological basis of evaluation research, coupled with due consideration of contextual factors, is capable of leading to a better policymaking, one that brings policymakers and polity closer to desired goals.

41     Hambrick, Ralph S., Jr. "A Guide for the Analysis of Policy Arguments." POLICY SCIENCES 5 (December 1974): 469-78.

> Using the 1973 State of the Union Address as an example, the paper discusses a set of interrelated propositional types for the design and critique of public policy.

42     Head, J.G. "Public Goods and Public Policy." PUBLIC FINANCE 17, no. 3 (1962): 197-219.

This article examines the meaning of the public good concept as it appears in the theory of Paul Samuelson and relates it to the more familiar Pigovian and Keynesian theories of public policy. The goal of the article is to show the place of the concept of public good in a general prescriptive theory of public policy.

43 Heisler, Martin O., and Peters, B. Guy. "Toward A Multidimensional Framework for the Analysis of Social Policy." ANNALS OF THE AMERICAN ACADEMY OF POLITICAL AND SOCIAL SCIENCE 434 (November 1977): 58-70.

This article argues that conceptual models of the policy process are too simplistic in that they have relied upon single factor explanations of policy outcomes. What is needed is a more complex conceptualization of the policy process giving special attention to the factors of time, policy area, level of government, and action.

44 Hennessey, Timothy M., and Peters, B. Guy. "Political Paradoxes in Post-Industrialism: A Political Economy Perspective." POLICY STUDIES JOURNAL 3 (Spring 1975): 233-40.

There is a paradox in the literature on post-industrialism: the forces of post-industrialism will render politics rather unimportant, while at the same time these forces will create the conditions in which politics will become more decisive. The provision of public goods can only be determined by reference to the preferences of citizens. If jurisdiction over specific goods is removed further and further from the citizens, information costs and uncertainty will increase, and citizens will forego participation in local affairs. When such costs become prohibitive to a large number of citizens, the government's capacity to deliver goods and services at their proper cost is impaired and error proneness increases.

45 Hettich, Walter. "Bureaucrats and Public Goods." PUBLIC CHOICE 21 (Spring 1975): 15-25.

The research of William Niskanen has demonstrated that bureaus do not necessarily produce too much output. This paper suggests that Niskanen fails to devote sufficient attention to the sponsor's motivation and decision making. In addition, the bureau's position depends on the political mechanism through which demand is expressed. The relation between bureau and sponsor should be further explored, with the hope that future development would result in integration of the theory of public demand and public production.

46 Hurst, Willard. "Consensus and Conflict in Twentieth Century Public Policy." DAEDALUS 105 (Fall 1976): 89-102.

Hurst offers a reflection on the values expressed in American law that have become influential today. While public policy in the past emphasized the dignity of individual life, Hurst points to a "heightened concern for the commonwealth" which has modified the value that the law has traditionally placed on active will. He sees the 1950s as important when the nation became aware of the unsolved problems of social and economic privilege. The resulting conflict has challenged the legitimacy of the society.

47   Jaffe, Louis L. "The Illusion of the Ideal Administration." HARVARD LAW REVIEW 86 (May 1973): 1183-1200.

Finding fault with various ideas of "ideal" administration, Jaffe emphasizes the political forces which affect agency decision making. From that perspective he critiques two beliefs: that agencies function best when under some broad, vague delegation; and that agencies may be taken to task for failure to achieve some concept of the public interest.

48   Kerr, Donna H. "The Logic of 'Policy' and Successful Policies." POLICY SCIENCES 7 (September 1976): 351-63.

There are three features essential to any policy: (1) someone must intend to act in accord with some imperative; (2) someone must perceive as likely that certain conditions will occur more than once or a restricted number of times; and (3) someone may substitute or employ discretionary behavior under certain established conditions.

49   Kramer, Fred A. "Policy Analysis as Ideology." PUBLIC ADMINIS-TRATION REVIEW 35 (September-October 1975): 509-17.

Policy analysis employs scientific techniques and gives the appearance of objectivity. The data is presented as value free, and analysts claim that these data should take precedence over qualitative concepts. Analysis also can be thought of as political ideology. Policy analysis is still an art in which the creativity and skill of the practitioner are of prime importance, for policy analysts should take off the "mask of objectivity" and develop "theoretical self-consciousness." They should become aware of their own perspectives and publicly elaborate and defend all factors which sustain their theories.

50   Lasswell, Harold D. "From Fragmentation to Configuration." POLICY SCIENCES 2 (1971): 439-46.

The emergence of policy science has important consequences for the modern world. Civilization has moved from a high level of homogeneity to a new configurative outlook.

51   Lerner, Daniel, and Lasswell, Harold, eds. THE POLICY SCIENCES. Stanford, Calif.: Stanford University Press, 1951. 344 p.

Seventeen social scientists contributed to this effort to determine how problems of human relations can be investigated and measured by scientific methods, and how policymakers can benefit from the policy sciences. Psychology, anthropology, sociology, political science, history, and economics are discussed and the contributions show how data from their fields can be used in policy formation.

52    Lindblom, Charles E. THE INTELLIGENCE OF DEMOCRACY. New
York: Free Press, 1965. 352 p.

An examination of bargaining and other forms of mutual adjustment in policy formation. The book picks up where Dahl and
Lindblom's POLITICS, ECONOMICS, AND WELFARE (no. 25)
stops. The end of the book presents a valuable four-page
summary of Lindblom's arguments.

53    _____. THE POLICY-MAKING PROCESS. Englewood Cliffs, N.J.:
Prentice Hall, 1968. 122 p.

This is a succinct account of Lindblom's description of governmental policymaking. The process is viewed as complex,
analytical, and "systemic, with no clearcut beginning or end."
The major section of the book deals with the network of power
influence on policymaking.

54    Lowi, Theodore J. "American Business, Public Policy, Case Studies,
and Political Theory." WORLD POLITICS 16 (July 1964): 667-715.

This is an essay that has become highly influential in the policy
literature. Lowi seeks to develop a new framework for policy
study. He suggests that the kind of policy (distributive, redistributive, regulatory) involved in a situation shapes the nature
of the policymaking process.

55    _____. THE END OF LIBERALISM: IDEOLOGY, POLICY AND THE
CRISIS OF PUBLIC AUTHORITY. New York: W.W. Norton and Co.,
1969. 321 p.

Modern democracy in the United States has failed because it
has confused expectations about democratic government,
demoralized government since justice cannot be achieved, and
weakened the capacity of government to live by democratic
formalisms.

56    _____. "Four Systems of Policy, Politics and Choice." PUBLIC
ADMINISTRATION REVIEW 32 (1972): 298-310.

Beginning with the assumption that policies determine politics,
Lowi develops a four-part politically relevant policy taxonomy
to guide the theoretical and applied study of public policy.
The four types of policy are distributive, constituent, regulative, and redistributive.

57    _____, et al. POLISCIDE. New York: Macmillan, 1976. 306 p.

The authors provide case studies from several perspectives
of the social, economic, and political impacts of the location
of an atomic accelerator in the village of Weston, Illinois.

58    Lyday, James M. "An Advocate's Process Outline for Policy Analysis:
The Case of Welfare Reform." URBAN AFFAIRS QUARTERLY 7
(June 1972): 385-402.

Lyday considers the policy process as an iterative series
of nine steps from goal determination through enactment and

subsequent to adjustment of policy. The author describes the process as broad, eclectic, descriptive, and chronological providing a framework in which numerous techniques, disciplines, and viewpoints can be complementary rather than conflicting. The author believes that policy outcomes would be improved by the adopting of such a system.

59    McIntosh, William Alex, et al. "Theoretical Issues and Social Indicators: A Societal Process Approach." POLICY SCIENCES 8 (September 1977): 245-67.

There are several kinds and levels of social indicators and the theoretical definitions of social indicators must take these levels into account. The article suggests and provides examples for the output and distribution of "well being," the effect of policy manipulatable and nonmanipulatable inputs, and the secondary consequences of inputs.

60    MacRae, Duncan, Jr. "Policy Analysis as an Applied Social Science Discipline." ADMINISTRATION AND SOCIETY 6 (February 1975): 363-88.

MacRae reviews the creation of new schools of policy analysis, their curricula, and the needs for different kinds of graduates from the programs.

61    Majone, Giardomenico. "On the Notion of Political Feasibility." EUROPEAN JOURNAL OF POLITICAL RESEARCH 3, no. 3 (1975): 259-74.

In a positive approach to policy analysis, the examination of the conditions of public policy feasibility assumes great importance. "Political feasibility" tends to be an imprecise term. This paper considers three groups of political constraints: those due to limits of available political resources, those due to the limits imposed by costs and benefits of a policy, and those imposed by the institutional framework.

62    _____. "The Role of Constraints in Policy Analysis." QUALITY AND QUANTITY 8 (January 1974): 65-76.

Majone gives a preliminary exploration of the role and use of constraints in policy analysis. Majone distinguishes among logical, empirical, and policy constraints. The distinctions, he feels, also shed light on the role of deductive reasoning, empirical research, and political insights in policy evaluation.

63    Martin, Ben L. "Experts in Policy Processes: A Contemporary Perspective." POLITY 6 (Winter 1973): 149-73.

Experts and expertise are viewed as relative and not absolute phenomena. "Expertness" is present when clients, citizens, or others accept one as an expert. A more equitable relationship develops when experts are viewed this way and not as "wearing fine scientific garments."

64   Mitroff, Ian I., and Pondy, Louis K. "On the Organization of Inquiry:
     A Comparison of Some Radically Different Approaches to Policy Analysis."
     PUBLIC ADMINISTRATION REVIEW 34 (September–October 1974):
     471–79.

        Argues for some new directions in policy analysis and organi-
        zation theory. A fundamental aspect of all organizations is
        the kinds of inquiring or information activities in which they
        typically engage and support. It calls for an integrated whole
        systems perspective with respect to a program of research
        on organization theory and its relation to policy analysis.

65   Nagel, Stuart S., ed. POLICY STUDIES AND THE SOCIAL
     SCIENCES. Lexington, Mass.: Lexington Books, 1975. 315 p.

        This volume includes twenty-six essays from the POLICY
        STUDIES JOURNAL covering multiple disciplinary approaches
        to policy studies. Included are views from sociology and
        social work, economics, psychology and education, anthro-
        pology, geography, history, social philosophy, mathematics
        and the natural sciences, law, and political science.

66   Nagel, Stuart, and Neef, Marian. "Finding an Optimum Choice Level
     or Mix in Public Policy Analysis." PUBLIC ADMINISTRATION REVIEW
     38 (September–October 1978): 404–12.

        This essay discusses some general considerations concerning
        how to arrive at an optimum choice, level, or mix when
        confronted with alternative public policy decisions, especially
        decisions relating to the legal process. The paper does not
        present much hard data, but the authors feel that the concepts
        and formulas can be helpful in providing a framework for
        thinking about solutions to public policy problems.

67   Nelson, Richard R. "Intellectualizing About the Moon-Ghetto Metaphor:
     A Study of the Current Malaise of Rational Analysis of Social Problems."
     POLICY SCIENCES 5 (December 1974): 375–414.

        Examines the intellectual traditions of analysis of why some
        programs are successful while others fail. The purpose of
        the essay is to examine these intellectual traditions and see
        what lessons can be learned regarding how to make analysis
        more useful.

68   _____. THE MOON AND THE GHETTO: AN ESSAY ON PUBLIC
     POLICY ANALYSIS. New York: W.W. Norton and Co., 1977.
     159 p.

        Nelson examines three traditions that have dominated the
        thinking about the causes and solutions for social problems:
        rational analysis, systems analysis, and the research and
        development tradition. Case study application of the ap-
        proaches includes the federal government's role in day-care
        centers, the SST, and nuclear breeder reactors.

69   Peters, B. Guy. "Types of Democratic Systems and Types of Public
     Policy." COMPARATIVE POLITICS 9 (1977): 327–55.

A typology of democratic political system can be drawn by associating elite behavior with political culture (homogeneous or fragmented). Similarly, a typology of public policies can be drawn by associating decisional system with demand pattern. When these two typologies are synthesized, a new typology is produced in which depoliticized systems are associated with redistributive policies, centrifugal systems with distributive policies, consociational systems with regulative policies, and centripetal systems with self-regulatory policies.

70    Price, Don K. THE SCIENTIFIC ESTATE. Cambridge, Mass.: Belknap Press of Harvard University Press, 1967. 323 p.

Although technical expertise has come to play an important role in the policymaking process, the fear that the new powers created by science may be beyond the control of constitutional processes is unjustified.

71    Radnor, Michael. "Management Sciences and Policy Sciences." POLICY SCIENCES 1 (December 1971): 447-56.

The paper reviews the claims made by policy science advocates of the revolutionary and unique nature of the field. The potential contributions of policy science are analyzed and related to management science perspectives. Radnor seeks cooperation between the two instead of competition.

72    Randall, Ronald. "Influence of Environmental Support and Policy Space on Organizational Behavior." ADMINISTRATIVE SCIENCE QUARTERLY 18 (June 1973): 236-47.

The conceptual framework of market theory from private organizations is used in public organizations. Environmental support and policy space are used to explain the development of a human resources development program by district offices in the Wisconsin State Employment Service in relation to employing organizations and other organizations in their districts.

73    Ravenal, Earl C. "Policy Relevance and Policy Models." POLICY STUDIES JOURNAL 2 (Spring 1974): 219-26.

Ravenal seeks to find out why decision makers do not "buy" the products of social science research. He defines the key elements as "policy relevance" which includes a correct understanding of the role of the decision maker and the decision-making process.

74    Reagan, Michael D. "Policy Issues." POLITY 1 (Fall 1968): 35-51.

Reagan, like many of his professional peers, is unhappy with the state of political science. This essay argues that too much time and concern has been devoted to the process of policymaking, and too little to the product. Also, there has been an excess of science and a deficit in concern for the relevant.

75    Redford, Emmette S.   DEMOCRACY IN THE ADMINISTRATIVE
      STATE.  New York:  Oxford University Press, 1969.  211 p.

      An examination of the role of administration in the policy
      process, together with concern for the democratic control
      of administration.

76    Rein, Martin.  "Equality and Social Policy."   SOCIAL SERVICE
      REVIEW   51 (December 1977):   565-87.

      Rein distinguishes between traditional definitions of social
      policy (redistribution of wealth and increased equality) and
      economic policy (distribution of wealth and increased output).
      He adds that more and more the two are interrelated and
      welfare systems must be developed in conjunction with concern
      for both economic and social policy.

77    Rein, Martin, and White, Sheldon H.   "Can Policy Research Help
      Policy?"  PUBLIC INTEREST, no. 49 (Fall 1977), pp.   119-36.

      The long standing problem-solving model is in large part
      a myth:   research may solve problems but it also has three
      other important functions--identifying problems as a step
      toward putting issues on the agenda, mobilizing government
      action, and confronting and settling dilemmas and trade-offs.
      Whether research solves problems or not, it does help those
      involved in the making of policy to decide what are the prob-
      lems.

78    _____.  "Policy Research:  Belief and Doubt."  POLICY ANALYSIS
      3 (Spring 1977):   239-71.

      Rein and White discuss belief and doubt about the usefulness
      of social research in shaping government decisions.  They
      then look at the ways in which social research is actually
      used in government decision making.  They conclude that most
      of the use is disreputable and they conclude that what is
      needed is a different conception of the research-policy alliance.

79    Ripley, Randall B., et al.  "Policy-Making:  A Conceptual Scheme."
      AMERICAN POLITICS QUARTERLY  1 (January 1973):   3-42.

      The authors develop a conceptual scheme of the policy arena
      and attempt to show its usefulness for research and applied
      activities.  The policy arena has three interrelated elements:
      environmental concepts, structural concepts, and policy re-
      sponse concepts.  They argue that institutional structure is
      a major source of independent variables and suggest that policy
      successes and failures are measured using the stated intentions
      of the policymakers as goals.

80    Rittel, Horst W.J., and Webber, Melvin M.  "Dilemmas in a General
      Theory of Planning."  POLICY SCIENCES  4 (June 1973):  155-69.

      The search for scientific bases for confronting problems of
      social policy is bound to fail, because of the nature of these
      problems.  Policy problems cannot be definitely described.
      Moreover, in a pluralistic society there is nothing like the

undisputable public good; there is no objective definition of equity; policies that respond to social problems cannot be meaningfully correct or false; and it makes no sense to talk about optimal solutions to social problems unless severe qualifications are imposed first. There are no solutions in the sense of definitive and objective answers.

81    Rourke, Francis E. BUREAUCRACY, POLITICS, AND PUBLIC POLICY. Boston: Little, Brown and Co., 1969. 186 p.

Rourke's central concern is the role of the bureaucracy in the policymaking process. He asserts that much of our policy is made via bargaining, negotiation, and conflict among appointed and not elected officials. Rourke examines how bureaucracies and bureaucrats get their power, how they use it, and the processes of policymaking in bureaucracies.

82    Rule, James B. INSIGHT AND SOCIAL BETTERMENT: A PREFACE TO APPLIED SOCIAL SCIENCE. New York: Oxford University Press, 1978. 205 p.

Rule's book explores the relationship between the study of social conditions (social problems) and ameliorative steps to improve them (public policy). This is not a primer on procedures or techniques in policy analysis. Rather, Rule takes stock of epistemological and analytical questions that should be entertained before the formulation of a specific policy recommendation. Rule asks the question: does a better understanding of social conditions lead ipso facto to their improvement? For Rule, the answer is "not much" and certainly not right away.

83    Samuels, Warren J. "Approaches to Legal-Economic Policy and Related Problems of Research." In POLICY STUDIES AND THE SOCIAL SCIENCES, edited by Stuart S. Nagel, pp. 65-73. Lexington, Mass.: D.C. Heath, 1975.

Policy scientists could contribute several things of great value to legal-economic analysis. These include: models of legal-political and economic interaction; objective, positive, empirical studies of government and studies of economic activity as both an input and an output of political-legal process; and endeavors to wed both theoretical and empirical analyses toward a self-consciously objective, positive comprehension of law and economics.

84    Schaefer, Guenther F. "A General Systems Approach to Public Policy Analysis." POLICY AND POLITICS 2 (June 1974): 331-46.

General systems theory is not a scientific theory in the usual sense of the word; it lacks a concrete substantive content. When the systems approach and its terminology were introduced to political science, it quickly became fashionable to talk of political systems and their characteristics; but these initial interpretations have little if anything to do with general systems theory. Despite a large number of unresolved questions and issues, the proposed approach demands conceptualization and requires accurate description of the intricate network of transactions and interdependence that characterizes the interaction between governmental and other social actors. Such an approach would include the time dimension, so frequently ignored, and deals at a relatively simple level with the concept of policy impact.

85    Schaefer, Guenther A., and Rakoff, Stuart H. "Politics, Policy, and Political Science: Theoretical Alternatives." POLITICS AND SOCI-ETY 1 (November 1970): 51-78.

The comparative state politics literature has generally con-cluded that social and economic variables were of greater importance in determining policy output than were political variables. Political science's response has been to question the methodological accuracy of these findings. This essay suggests that these findings are due to the selection of a model that is not accurate, reliable, or precise. It is further concluded that the choice of this model, when com-bined with characteristics of the current academic environ-ment, produced these types of findings.

86    Schneider, Mark. "The 'Quality of Life' and Social Indicators Research." PUBLIC ADMINISTRATION REVIEW 36 (May-June 1976): 297-305.

The use of social indicators in policy decision-making systems as well as more descriptive analysis of societal well-being is investigated in this essay. The concept of quality of life as a tool of comparative social indicators research is analyzed. The article concludes with observations on the implications that this distinction has for the use of the concept of quality of life in future social indicators research.

87    Schoettle, Enid C. Bok. "The State of the Art in Policy Studies." In THE STUDY OF POLICY FORMATION, edited by Raymond A. Bauer and Kenneth J. Gergen, pp. 149-81. New York: Free Press, 1968.

This essay describes how contemporary social science theory analyzes the processes of policy formulation and execution. The analysis proceeds on two levels: upon the participant in the policymaking system and upon the system of policy formulation.

88    Schulman, Paul R. "Nonincremental Policy-Making: Notes Toward an Alternative Paradigm." AMERICAN POLITICAL SCIENCE REVIEW 59 (December 1975): 1354-70.

Much policy and public administrative literature is dominated by incremental and divisible goods paradigms. This essay asserts the existence of a class of nonincremental indivisible policies. Such policies display a unique set of political and administrative characteristics. They are examined in connec-tion with manned space exploration policy.

89    Shapiro, Martin. "From Public Law to Public Policy, or the 'Public' in Public Law." PS 5 (Fall 1972): 410-18.

This paper is concerned with the distinction made by political scientists with respect to public versus private law. The essay focuses on the evolution of the term, why political scientists are so concerned with it, and suggests that the profession eliminate the public limitation and follow a policy-oriented analysis of law.

90    Simmons, Robert H., et al. "Policy Flow Analysis: A Conceptual Model for Comparative Public Policy Research." WESTERN POLITICAL QUARTERLY 27 (September 1974): 457-68.

Governments are placed under an ever increasing strain as the environments they serve continue to change. This piece develops a model focusing on the changed role of political actors in the policy process, with the goal of showing the importance of values in the determination of public policy.

91    Spadaro, Robert N. "Role Perceptions of Politicians vis-a-vis Public Administrators: Parameters for Public Policy." WESTERN POLITICAL QUARTERLY 26 (December 1973): 717-25.

Seeking an enlarged understanding of the public policy process, this study develops an operationalized role perception of politicians and public administrators toward each other. Both sets of actors generally agree on broad policy areas and role responsibilities; there is sufficient mistrust so that maximally effective policy planning is not occurring.

92    Stene, Edward O. "The Politics Administration Dichotomy." MIDWEST REVIEW OF PUBLIC ADMINISTRATION 9 (April-July 1975): 83-89.

Arguing that the death of the politics-administration dichotomy is overdue, Stene reviews the rejection of the reformers' notion that politics and administration are distinct. The key to understanding the conceptual distinction lies in understanding the definition of politics. For Stene, politics is the game of acquiring power, while administration is the game of instilling expectation, scientific and factual consideration into decision-making processes at all levels.

93    Stonecash, Jeff. "Politics, Wealth and Public Policy: The Significance of Political Systems." POLICY STUDIES JOURNAL 7 (Summer 1979): 670-75.

The argument of this essay is that the role of politics and wealth as "determinants" of public policy has been misconceived theoretically and misspecified in empirical analyses. Politics and wealth have been regarded as sufficient causes of policy variations, while their role is as facilitators or inhibitors of the extent to which preferences become policy. These differences and their implications for equation specification and empirical analyses are developed.

94    Trinkl, Frank H. "Solving Opposed Judgments in Resource Allocation Decisions." POLICY SCIENCES 3 (December 1972): 421-34.

This article considers several approaches for obtaining consensus among two groups of policymakers making resource allocation decisions. A theory of cooperative games is used by the author in his framework.

94A   Tullock, Gordon, and Wagner, Richard, eds.  POLICY ANALYSIS AND DEDUCTIVE REASONING.  Policy Studies Organization Series, no. 15.  Lexington, Mass.:  Lexington Books, 1978.  201 p.

The ten essays examine and illustrate the application of deductive reasoning in the analysis of public policy.

95   Van Dyke, Vernon.  "Process and Policy as Focal Concepts in Political Research."  In POLITICAL SCIENCE AND PUBLIC POLICY, edited by Austin Ranney, pp. 23–39.  Chicago:  Markham Publishing Co., 1968.

Van Dyke reviews some of the contributions of Arthur F. Bentley, Harold Lasswell, and David B. Truman on the use of process and policy as concepts in political research.  He asks that clearer meanings of the concepts and an assessment of their usefulness and limitations as focal concepts in political research be undertaken.

96   Walker, Jack L.  "Performance Gaps, Policy Research, and Political Entrepreneurs:  Toward a Theory of Agenda Setting."  POLICY STUDIES JOURNAL  3 (Autumn 1974): 112–16.

Agenda setting has long been an area of interest to political scientists.  This paper investigates the early stages of the policy-making process when problems and issues are first surfacing.  Two basic questions are briefly treated:  how do problems present themselves for treatment, and under what conditions will changes be proposed and policy innovations enacted.

97   Williams, Bruce A.  "Beyond 'Incrementalism,' Organizational Theory and Public Policy."  POLICY STUDIES JOURNAL  1 (Summer 1979): 683–89.

This article suggests that a closer analysis of bureaucratic organizations' role in the public policy process may aid in resolving the debate between advocates of incremental policy models and advocates of rational policy models.  The authors argue that organizational theory suggests that both rational and incremental decision-making may take place within organizations.  They define two different modes of policymaking—diachronic and synchronic—which conform generally to the rational and incremental policy models.

98   Wilson, James Q., and Banfield, Edward C.  "Public Regardingness As a Value Premise in Voting Behavior."  AMERICAN POLITICAL SCIENCE REVIEW  58 (December 1965):  876–87.

The authors examine the nature of the individual's attachment to the body politic and with the value premises underlying the choices made by certain classes of voter.  Some classes are more disposed than others to rest their choices on some conception of the public interest. Some classes tend to be more public than private regarding electoral and policy choices.

99    Zeckhauser, Richard, and Schaefer, Elmer. "Public Policy and Normative Economic Theory." In THE STUDY OF POLICY FORMATION, edited by Raymond A. Bauer and Kenneth J. Gergen, pp. 27-102. New York: Free Press, 1968.

This chapter concerns itself with making choices among competing desires--the allocation of scarce resources among competing ends. The chapter evaluates several techniques for normative economic methods for dealing with economic problems.

## METHODS AND MODELS

100    Albritton, Robert B. "Cost-Benefits of Measles Eradication: Effects of a Federal Intervention." POLICY ANALYSIS 4 (Winter 1978): 1-21.

This study applies time-series experimentation methods in estimating cost and benefits of measles eradication efforts conducted by the Center for Disease Control beginning in 1966. Application of an integrated moving average model, in an interrupted time-series design, facilitates estimation of reductions in measles cases attributable to federally sponsored eradication efforts and provides a basis for applying cost-benefit standards to this public policy.

101    Albritton, Robert B., and Bahry, Donna. "Effects of Public and Private Sector Decisions on Health Care Costs." POLICY STUDIES JOURNAL 7 (Summer 1979): 762-70.

This paper sets out to test the impact of Medicare and Medicaid using two complementary methods. The first involves an interrupted time-series design (ARIMA) meant to isolate the effects of government intervention. The second involves a five-equation path model that seeks to explain changes in health costs. Neither set of results indicates a direct link between the introduction of medicare-medicaid and rising costs. Yet, there is some evidence that the influx of funds had an indirect effect by contributing resources to upgrade the quality of medical services.

102    Allen, T. Harrel. NEW METHODS IN SOCIAL SCIENCE RESEARCH: POLICY SCIENCES AND FUTURES RESEARCH. New York: Praeger, 1978. 157 p.

This book tries to solve social problems via policymaking that results from new advances in social science methodology. The first three chapters create the groundwork for embarking on novel approaches to social science methodology that must be developed if the social science disciplines are to analyze social problems successfully. The second half of the book is devoted to spelling out the new methodologies for accomplishing effective policymaking.

103 Ashford, Douglas E. COMPARING PUBLIC POLICIES, NEW METHODS AND CONCEPTS. Sage Yearbooks in Politics and Public Policy, vol. 4. Beverly Hills, Calif.: Sage, 1977. 266 p.

> Ten original articles in comparative policies studies and methods for further developing the field are presented. The volume is divided into four parts: logic of comparison; institutions and comparisons; economic theory and comparison; and policy as a determinant of politics.

104 Auld, Douglas A.L. "Social Welfare and Decision-Making in the Public Sector." CANADIAN PUBLIC ADMINISTRATION 16 (Winter 1973): 604-12.

> Auld presents an examination of the measurement of social welfare. Traditional quantitative methods of socioeconomic evaluation may give society misleading answers about the impact of public policy and achievement of social objectives. Social indicators as an approach to policy evaluation are discussed and the paper concludes by showing how social indicators may complement traditional socioeconomic measures.

105 Baer, William C., and Fleming, Skye M. "Counterfactual Analysis: An Analytical Tool for Planners." JOURNAL OF THE AMERICAN INSTITUTE OF PLANNERS 42 (July 1976): 243-52.

> Counterfactual analysis consists of substituting a hypothesized event or policy for a real one at a point in the past and tracing out the consequences against a known historical backdrop. By posing alternatives and their consequences, counterfactuals permit users to judge which option they prefer. While hypothesis testing can determine whether or not a sequence of events is causally related, it can say nothing as to whether it is good or bad, socially significant or unimportant.

106 Behn, Robert D.,and Vaupel, James W. "Quick Analysis." POLICY STUDIES JOURNAL 6 (Spring 1978): 325-32.

> This article describes a series of rudimentary analytical techniques that can be performed quickly and inexpensively. Taken as a group, they are characteristic of an eclecticism in methods that is part of policy studies.

107 Berk, Richard A. "Performance Measures: Half Full or Half Empty." SOCIAL SCIENCE QUARTERLY 54 (March 1974): 762-69.

> This article is a set of observations on the articles in the Symposium on Urban Agency Output and Performance presented at the annual meeting of the American Political Science Association, in New Orleans, September 1973. Berk's comments focus on the data bases and methodology used in the article. The essence of the argument is that the quest for methodological purity tends to hamper needed policy-related research, so while good data are necessary, this need should not cause undue timidity in pursuing policy research.

108 Bernstein, Samuel J.,et al. "The Problems and Pitfalls of Quantitative Methods in Urban Analysis." POLICY SCIENCES 4 (March 1973): 29-39.

> Claiming that the use of quantitative methods in urban analysis is a complicated and risky undertaking, the authors discuss conceptual-technical, administrative, and societal problems in urban analysis. They define and list quantitative techniques and associated problems and assess the organizational factors necessary for implementing successful urban analysis programs.

109 Blair, John P., and Maser, Steven M. "Axiomatic vs. Empirical Models in Studies." POLICY STUDIES JOURNAL 5 (Spring 1977): 282-89.

> Literature on the determinants of public activity reveals inadequacies of policy analysis in the absence of statistical models. Without a general model it is difficult to generalize from purely statistical tests. Most researchers have a conceptualization of the research which could be formalized to build the model. Implications derived from a standard set of assumptions are cumulative and can be refined by other investigators. Policy development requires predictive models to estimate policy impacts.

110 Blair, John P., and Maser, Steven M. "A Reassessment of Axiomatic Models in Policy Studies." In POLICY ANALYSIS AND DEDUCTIVE REASONING, edited by Gordon Tullock and Richard E. Wagner, pp. 3-17. Policy Studies Organization Series, no.15. Lexington, Mass.: Lexington Books, 1978.

> Two methodological trends are diverging within policy studies. One approach is motivated by the increased emphasis on action-oriented research. The other reflects efforts toward the development of axiomatic models of social choice. This essay argues for the use of rigorous deductive theory in policy studies. In the final assessment the time each analyst devotes toward a priori theorizing will reflect his anticipation of return from this activity. Reduction of the theoretical exercise to secondary status is inappropriate. The perspective offered here is one of balance.

111 Borcherding, Thomas E., and Deacon, Robert T. "The Demand for the Services of Non-Federal Governments." AMERICAN ECONOMIC REVIEW 62 (December 1972): 891-901.

> The authors develop a model of public spending from the received theory of collective decision making and test the significance of several variables of the theory. Marginal cost and urbanization fail to explain demand levels for certain local government functions, especially education and highways.

112 Boruch, Robert F. "Randomized Experiments for Evaluating and Planning Local Programs: A Summary on Appropriateness and Feasibility." PUBLIC ADMINISTRATION REVIEW 39 (January-February 1979): 36-40.

This paper presents some research findings on the appropriateness of using randomized field experiments as a method of planning and evaluating local programs. It provides a justification for such efforts and points out the shortcomings and pitfalls of such approaches.

113    Brunner, Ronald D., and Brewer, Garry D. "Policy and the Study of the Future: Given Complexity, Trends, or Processes?" In their POLITICAL DEVELOPMENT AND CHANGE, pp. 327-44. New York: Free Press, 1975.

Both timeliness and accuracy are important criteria for policy analysis and forecasting. The major advantage of the chartist approach is timeliness, and the major advantage of the fundamentalist approach is greater potential accuracy. However, the empirical limitations of model-building are significant. Modeling is not a panacea although, when intelligently intermixed with other techniques, it is often better than might be anticipated. Harold D. Lasswell has proposed a decision seminar, designed to track and measure social events. If we are unable to build entirely accurate scientific models, at least we can try to recognize and rectify our errors through techniques such as the decision seminar.

114    Brunner, Ronald D., and Liepelt, Klaus. "Data Analysis, Process Analysis, and System Change." POLITICAL DEVELOPMENT AND CHANGE, edited by Garry D. Brewer and Ronald D. Brunner, pp. 487-514. New York: Free Press, 1975.

Among students of comparative politics, there exists a growing interest in change as an approach to the understanding of political systems. While this development promises conceptual payoffs and suggests the reorientation of data and techniques, it also sharpens the contrast between a data analysis viewpoint and a process viewpoint regarding the nature of political systems.

115    Chen, Milton M.; Bush, J.W.; and Patrick, Donald L. "Social Indicators for Health Planning and Policy Analysis." POLICY SCIENCES 6 (March 1975): 71-90.

Applying measured social values to the distribution of the population among a set of levels-of-well-being, a function status index summarizes the level-of-well-being of a population at a particular point in time; in addition, a quality-adjusted life expectancy can be computed that approximates a comprehensive social indicator for health. These indicators possess the statistical properties required for time series and interpopulation comparisons.

116    Cook, Thomas J., and Scioli, Frank P., Jr. "Policy Analysis in Political Science: Trends and Issues in Empirical Research." POLICY STUDIES JOURNAL 1 (Autumn 1972): 6-10.

After briefly reviewing the literature suggesting that socioeconomic variables have a greater impact on policy output than do political variables, the authors explain three limitations of the policy output literature. They also suggest that a potentially fruitful area of future research is the study of the impact of public policies.

117 _____. "Resources for Public Policy Analysis." POLICY STUDIES
JOURNAL 1 (Winter 1972): 61-63.

> In listing the kinds of empirical research methods and
> sources available to policy researchers, the authors include
> research centers, journals and periodicals, funding sources,
> and data sources.

118 Cook, Thomas, et al. "Empirical Research Methods." In POLICY
STUDIES IN AMERICA AND ELSEWHERE, edited by Stuart S. Nagel,
pp. 17-35. Lexington, Mass.: D.C. Heath, 1975.

> The comparative study of public policy has both great pros-
> pects and difficult problems. However, in time, the problems
> would seem to be largely surmountable. Researchers in the
> areas studied earliest, particularly social welfare and economic
> development, have progressed the farthest in defining the
> problems and exploring them in terms of more sophisticated
> theoretical frameworks and methodological techniques. Perhaps
> the most provocative questions--dealing with allocations of
> resources among competing publics, the distribution of the
> burden of financing public goods, and the relationship between
> various policy domains--have been barely explored.

119 Coulter, Philip B. "Comparative Community Politics and Public Policy."
POLITY 3 (Fall 1970): 22-43.

> This is a wide-ranging treatment of shortcomings of then
> current (1970) methodological approaches to the study of public
> policy. Coulter calls for greater sophistication in the use of
> quantitative tools and a more alert appreciation of their limita-
> tions. He detects seven weaknesses in community policy
> studies: (1) inattention to linkages and inattention to process
> variables; (2) public expenditures as policy outputs; (3) failure
> to differentiate policy types; (4) inadequate quantitative analysis;
> (5) political ethos; (6) regionalism; and (7) governmental in-
> stitutions as intervening variables.

120 Dye, Thomas R., and Pollack, Neuman F. "Path Analytic Models in
Policy Research." POLICY STUDIES JOURNAL 2 (Winter 1973):
123-30.

> Path analysis provides an opportunity to develop and test
> causal models which can help in understanding precisely how
> social, economic, or political forces shape public policy or
> precisely how public policies impact the social, economic, or
> political environment. Ideas are portrayed in diagrammatic
> fashion. Assumptions of path analysis are that relationships
> are additive and linear; that the residual "error" terms are
> uncorrelated; that the causal paths involve no reciprocal causa-
> tion; and that the causal arrangement is appropriate.

121 Edward, George C. III. "Disaggregation in Policy Research." POLICY
STUDIES JOURNAL 7 (Summer 1979): 675-83.

> Disaggregation has gained considerable prominence in policy
> research, but it is sometimes flawed by invalid and unreliable

measures of policy and improper inferences derived from policy data. This research examines examples of policy studies which disaggregate within a level of analysis; between levels of analysis; or within a level of analysis, making inferences between levels of analysis.

122  Fennessey, James. "Improving Inference for Social Research and Social Policy: The Bayesian Paradigm." SOCIAL SCIENCE RE-SEARCH 6 (December 1977): 309-27.

This paper reviews some data interpretation difficulties associated with many social projects and suggests that the Bayesian paradigm offers a number of advantages for overcoming the problems. The Bayesian paradigm is proposed as a highly promising vehicle through which social researchers and policymakers may work and communicate more effectively.

123  Firestone, Joseph M. "The Development of Social Indicators from Content Analysis of Social Documents." POLICY SCIENCES 3 (July 1972): 249-63.

Social indicators indicate or measure only within the context of a theory of social change, and theories of social change that deal only with social conditions, behavioral interchanges or transactions, and the material environment, are likely to be unsuccessful because they ignore the mental side of life.

124  Gergen, Kenneth J. "Methodology in the Study of Policy Formation." In THE STUDY OF POLICY FORMATION, edited by Raymond A. Bauer and Kenneth J. Gergen, pp. 206-37. New York: Free Press, 1968.

This essay is concerned with the availability of reliable data for theory building in the social sciences. It outlines a set of methods by which data can be obtained concerning the behavior, thoughts, feelings, and perceptions of a decision maker in an on-going decision-making process.

125  Gordon, Kenneth F., and Sands, Gary. "Development of a Simulation Model of the Detroit Housing Market." POLICY SCIENCES 4 (September 1973): 365-78.

The key inputs to the Detroit model are census tract data describing specific attributes of the households, dwelling units, and neighborhoods in the city. The model can provide forecasts of future levels of demand for housing with the specified structural and locational attributes. By operating the model under varying assumptions concerning public actions, it is possible to simulate the effects of the public policies being considered.

126  Hall, Owen P.,Jr. "A Policy Model Appraisal Paradigm." POLICY SCIENCES 6 (June 1975): 185-95.

The current direction in policy modeling has revealed a gap between model builders and decision makers, a gap that increases with the size and complexity of the model being constructed. While there was some similarity in the relevance

of the policy context, differences occurred with respect to
the amount of self-appraisal. There exists a need for additional efforts in developing and applying appraisal criteria.

127     Holsti, Ole R. "The Baseline Problem in Statistics: Examples from
        Studies of American Public Policy." JOURNAL OF POLITICS 37
        (February 1975): 187-201.

        Holsti discusses one type of statistical abuse, selection of
        an unrepresentative baseline from which to convey false
        impressions about trends. Illustrations are drawn from
        Joyce Kolko and Gabriel Kolko's THE LIMITS OF POWER
        (1972) and an essay by W. Glenn Campbell about the inade-
        quacies of U.S. defense budgets. ("Assuring the Primacy
        of National Security." In NATIONAL SECURITY, edited
        by David Abshire and Richard Allen. New York: Frederick
        A. Praeger, 1967).

128     Horowitz, Irving L. "Social Science Mandarins: Policy-Making as a
        Political Formula." POLICY SCIENCES 1 (Summer 1970): 339-60.

        The customary sequence of events starting with science and
        ending with policymaking lacks empirical confirmation. Certain
        factors in the structure of government make the teleological
        model central to the understanding of policymaking.

129     Johnson, Ronald W. "Research Objectives for Policy Analysis." In
        PUBLIC POLICY EVALUATION, edited by Kenneth M. Dolbeare, pp.
        75-94. Beverly Hills, Calif.: Sage, 1975.

        Selection of methods is in part a reflection of research ob-
        jective. In addition, the paper is a conveniently organized
        review of policy research as of 1975.

130     Jun, Jong S., ed. "Management by Objectives in the Public Sector."
        PUBLIC ADMINISTRATION REVIEW 36 (January-February 1976):
        1-45.

        Seven articles covering the issues related to the application
        of MBO in the public sector. Topics included are: MBO and
        public management; results to be expected from using MBO;
        program and policy objectives in using MBO; MBO in state
        government; MBO at the federal budget level; and MBO and
        program evaluation.

131     Kramer, Fred A. "Policy Analysis as Ideology." PUBLIC ADMINIS-
        TRATION REVIEW 35 (September-October 1975): 509-17.

        Analysis--primarily economic analysis of social policies--is
        often presented to nonanalyst decision makers as if it were
        purely objective. The methods and perspectives of such
        analysis are products of an ideology that has political effects.
        Many analysts fail to see the limits of their techniques.

132     LaPorte, Todd R., ed. ORGANIZED SOCIAL COMPLEXITY: CHAL-
        LENGE TO POLITICS AND POLICY. Princeton, N.J.: Princeton
        University Press, 1975. 373 p.

The editor presents the methodological and theoretical concerns of nine contributors about the problems which increasing
social complexity poses for politics and policy analysis.

133 Lewis-Beck, Michael S. "The Relative Importance of Socioeconomic
and Political Variables for Public Policy." AMERICAN POLITICAL
SCIENCE REVIEW 71 (June 1977): 559-66.

A dominant issue in the quantitative study of public policy
has been the relative importance of socioeconomic and political
variables for determining policy outcomes. Past efforts have
been unsatisfactory largely because they relied on inadequate
statistical techniques. The comparison of "effects coefficients,"
derived from path analysis (as distinguished from coefficients
derived from zero-order correlation, partial correlation, or
multiple repression techniques), is offered as the preferred
means of evaluating independent variables.

134 Maciariollo, Joseph A. "Dynamic Benefit Cost Analysis: Policy Evaluation in a Dynamic Urban Simulation Model." SOCIAL-ECONOMIC
PLANNING SCIENCES 9 (June 1975): 147-68.

Originally the author's Ph.D thesis, this is an attempt to
illustrate a dynamic procedure for cost-benefit analysis. He
argues that many social problems are amenable to study through
dynamic and nonstatic techniques. He applies a simulation
methodology to a central city area to illustrate a comparative-
dynamic procedure for benefit-cost analysis.

135 Meehan, Eugene J. "Social Indicators and Policy Analysis." In
METHODOLOGIES FOR ANALYZING PUBLIC POLICIES, edited by
Frank P. Scioli Jr., and Thomas J. Cook, pp. 33-46. Lexington,
Mass.: Lexington Books, 1975.

At present, the most that can be said for the social indicators
movement is that it provides an opportunity for social scientists
to discover the bounds of an adequate social science.

136 Nagel, Stuart S. "Choosing Among Alternative Public Policies."
In PUBLIC POLICY EVALUATION, edited by Kenneth M. Dolbeare,
pp. 153-76. Beverly Hills, Calif.: Sage, 1975.

This article introduces a basic methodology which can be used
for testing the effects of alternative public or legal policies.
The methodology depends mainly on whether the legal policies
involve (1) making an activity legal or illegal, or (2) deciding
how to allocate government funds.

137 Neiman, Max. "Policy Analysis: An Alternative Strategy." AMERICAN
POLITICS QUARTERLY 5 (January 1977): 3-26.

Data from fifty-one American cities are used to test aspects
of a model of political communications. Several hypotheses
are tested and conclusions drawn.

138    Obler, Jeffrey M.  "The Odd Compartmentalization:  Public Opinion,
       Aggregate Data, and Policy Analysis."  POLICY STUDIES JOURNAL
       7 (Spring 1979):  524-40.

       This article examines some of the assumptions underlying
       the use of aggregate data in policy analysis.  It explores
       the assumption of antagonistic attitudes between haves and
       have nots on social welfare policy.

139    Ostrom, Elinor.  "The Need for Multiple Indicators in Measuring the
       Output of Public Agencies."  POLICY STUDIES JOURNAL  2 (Winter
       1972):  85-92.

       In the public sector it is difficult to conceptualize and measure
       either the physical output of a public agency or the appropriate
       dollar value of the output.  The Workshop in Political Theory
       and Policy Analysis (University of Indiana, Bloomington) has
       recently embarked on a major research effort for the RANN
       Division of the National Science Foundation.  The major focus
       of this project is the development of multimode measurements
       of three municipal services:  street light, street repair, and
       urban recreation facilities.  Those areas were chosen since
       a physical measure can be developed or has been developed
       for each of them.  For each of the areas studied, what kinds
       of relationships exist between the physical measures of service
       output and citizen perceptions and evaluations of that output
       will be ascertained.  In addition, the relationships between
       internal records and public officials' estimates of services,
       physical measures, and citizens' perceptions and evaluations
       of service levels will be examined.

140    Pack, Howard, and Pack, Janet Rothenberg.  "The Resurrection of
       the Urban Development Model."  POLICY ANALYSIS  3 (Summer 1977):
       407-27.

       Widespread failure or limited application characterized the
       earliest use of urban development models.  Case studies of
       eleven models using regional planning agencies indicate that
       land-use models are being successfully developed and incor-
       porated into analytic work.  Model simulations are performed
       almost exclusively for the analysis of comprehensive regional
       plan alternatives; specific policy simulations are rare.  Models
       are currently more useful for impact analysis than for com-
       prehensive planning; they are supposed to bring greater ob-
       jectivity, precision, and the ability to consider alternatives
       to planning and policy analysis.  However, this has not been
       the case.  Many users lack real understanding of the theoretical
       structure underlying the estimated relationships or of the im-
       plication of the estimating procedures themselves.  The impact
       of model misuse is great.

141    Procos, D., and Harvey, A.S.  "Modeling for Local Planning Decisions."
       EKISTICS  44 (November 1977):  257-66.

       Most models concerned with the prediction of future urban
       growth are deductive and have been built on aggregate data
       on factors such as employment and population.  They have
       attempted to forecast small-scale outcomes on the basis of

broad projections. Critics attack the crudity of the system's modeling and note that this system fails to address the small planning scale in terms of policy and physical planning. In-ductive forecasting--predicting for the whole on the basis of individual instances of behavior and activity, obtained in the form of disaggregate data--can remedy these deficiencies. Data collection for an in-depth understanding of urban en-vironments "need not cover the entire population at the ex-pense of detail because of crudely perceived financial limita-tions." A small variable size sampling of conditions and of change within particular areas often can serve the purpose of the study just as well. Selection of the sample will, in some cases, be a matter of statistical confidence limits and, in others, will be a matter of the particular phenomena to be modeled. The selection should, in all cases, "lead to a departure from the attitudes of the past toward a policy approach to complex and interlocked urban systems."

142   Riader, Melvyn C. "Installing Management by Objectives in Social Agencies." ADMINISTRATION IN SOCIAL WORK  1 (Fall 1977): 235-44.

This article offers a four-phase approach for installing management-by-objectives (MBO) in social agencies. The first phase of implementing MBO is to conduct an in-depth self-study. Indicators of potential difficulty with MBO are specified to enable administrators to determine whether or not MBO is appropriate to their agency. The second phase consists of developing a strategy for implementing MBO. Planned change strategies promoting commitment to MBO are discussed. The third phase is concerned with designing an MBO system appropriate to the agency. Guidelines for tailor-ing MBO to social agencies are identified. The fourth phase focuses on approaches that will institutionalize MBO into the culture of the agency and assure long-lasting commitment to the system. These approaches include flexibility, personal growth, and ways to provide frequent two-way feedback.

143   Roos, Leslie L.,Jr.; Roos, Noralou P.; and McKinley, Barbara.  "Im-plementing Randomization." POLICY ANALYSIS  3 (Fall 1977):  547-60.

Many difficulties confront the evaluation researcher in his/her efforts to implement randomization of subjects for treatment groups and control groups. A case study of a hospital evalua-tion highlights these problems. The authors' experiences are summarized in a series of suggestions for facilitating the acceptance of randomized experimental designs.

144   Said, Kamal E. "A Policy-Selection/Goal-Formulation Model for Public Systems." POLICY SCIENCES  5 (March 1974): 89-100.

The author shows that private sector optimization models are not adequate to handle the complexity of the decision-making process in public policy analysis. He creates a model which claims to lessen the ideological debate over goal selection by formulating goals and policy simultaneously. The principal feature of the model is that it acknowledges the political nature of public policymaking.

145    Saltman, Juliet. "Housing Discrimination: Policy Research, Methods and Results." ANNALS OF THE AMERICAN ACADEMY OF POLITICAL AND SOCIAL SCIENCE 441 (January 1979): 186-96.

> The U.S. Department of Housing and Urban Development has conducted a nationwide audit to determine the extent of racial discrimination in housing. The audit is a quasiexperimental field survey. Its operation is described and the policy changes sought to strengthen fair housing laws are discussed.

146    Scioli, Frank, Jr., and Cook, Thomas J. METHODOLOGIES FOR ANALYZING PUBLIC POLICIES. Lexington, Mass.: Lexington Books, 1975. 171 p.

> Thirteen articles, some of which originally appeared in POLICY STUDIES JOURNAL (Winter 1973) appear here. The methodological categories include measurement, design, and analysis.

147    Shakun, Melvin F. "Policy-Making Under Discontinuous Change: The Situational Normativism Approach." MANAGEMENT SCIENCE 22 (October 1974): 226-35.

> Policymaking under conditions of discontinuous change is discussed in terms of situational normativism, a descriptive normative approach to policymaking systems. Norms and values play a key role in the adaptation of the system. The nature of these norms and values is discussed, and the implications for system adaptation are explored by the use of a model. Aspects of policy, strategy, and systems design are considered. A behavioral model for purposeful research and adaptation under discontinuity is presented. At the policy level, a referral process (between operational and non-operational goals and norms) is described which allows for change with respect to the set of operational goal variables.

148    Shepard, W. Bruce, and Godwin, R. Kenneth. "Policy and Processes: A Study of Interaction." JOURNAL OF POLITICS 37 (May 1975): 576-82.

> Reliance on recursive models sacrifices more than the capabilities of detecting feedbacks from policy and process interactions. Recursive models might superficially appear adequate for the study of the determinants of public policies, but their use for the study of even this part of the interaction relationship can be misleading.

149    Sullivan, John. "A Note on Redistributive Politics." AMERICAN POLITICAL SCIENCE REVIEW 66 (December 1972): 1301-5.

> This is a response to Fry and Winters and adds an additional six socioeconomic variables to the original list. Sullivan's findings are the opposite of Fry and Winters's ("The Politics of Redistribution." AMERICAN POLITICAL SCIENCE REVIEW 54 [June 1970]: 508-22. To prevent the addition of more and more variables, Sullivan develops two criteria for selecting independent variables: the size of the zero-order correlations and the degree of multicolinearity among the independent variables. Using these criteria, and utilizing

three political and three socioeconomic variables, the results are again inconsistent with Fry and Winters's.

150    Trinkl, Frank H. "Allocations among Programs Having Counteractive Outcomes." POLICY SCIENCES 3 (July 1972): 163-76.

Difficulties have been encountered in applying cost-benefit analysis to the problem of determining resource allocation among social programs, especially when there are multiple outcomes associated with each of the programs. A model which promises to be useful in resolving this problem is presented in this article. Two steps are required for the use of the model: (1) values need to be assigned to the various objectives that the program is designed to accomplish, and (2) probabilistic functions relating resources to program outcomes need to be specified.

151    Tullock, Gordon, and Wagner, Richard E. "Rational Models, Politics, and Policy Analysis." POLICY STUDIES JOURNAL 4 (Summer 1976): 408-15.

Political science models are not as empirically validated as economic models; thus the tools of economics are being applied to noneconomic phenomena, especially to politics and public policy issues. The conceptual base of the economic models is utility maximization--the aim of politicians is to increase their wealth and power. The use of economic models in political science began with Anthony Downs in 1957 and has since grown.

152    Van Meter, Donald, and Asher, Herbert. "Causal Analysis: Its Promise for Policy Studies." POLICY STUDIES JOURNAL 2 (1973): 103-9.

The authors argue that there is a need for a more causal approach to theorizing and data analysis in the field of policy analysis. Even where actual causal estimation techniques cannot be used, they feel that a causal style of thinking is still beneficial for theory building and hypothesis generation.

153    Wilson, James Q., and Banfield, Edward C. "Political Ethos Revisited." AMERICAN POLITICAL SCIENCE REVIEW 65 (December 1971): 1048-62.

This study was an effort to test the existence and correlates of the "unitarist" and "individualist" political ethos in a sample of 1,059 mostly male Boston homeowners in 1967. Respondents displayed each attitude or two or more attitudes in the predicted ethnic, religious, income, and educational attributes.

154    Wilson, John Oliver. "Social Experimentation and Public Policy Analysis." PUBLIC POLICY 22 (Winter 1974): 15-38.

Social experimentation is the latest attempt by social scientists to contribute to the understanding of public policy. This paper examines the nature of social experimentation undertaken by the federal government; illustrates how the characteristics of social experimentation differ from other types of public policy analysis; and some of the problems involved in social experimentation.

155     Winthrop, Henry. "Social Systems and Social Complexity in Relation to Interdisciplinary Policymaking and Planning." POLICY SCIENCES 3 (December 1972): 405-20.

> This article argues that models for planning and policymaking must be more of the multiloop, nonlinear types and must incorporate unconventional technologies.

156     Yarwood, Dean L., and Alexander, Thomas B. "History and Policy Studies." POLICY STUDIES JOURNAL 7 (Summer 1979): 803-11.

> This article deals with actual and potential contributions of history to policy studies. Some historians have attempted to influence specific policies through their writings, others have held policy-relevant positions in government agencies, while others have functioned in roles that have made them official preservers of the past. The authors discuss a number of ways in which history is relevant to policy studies.

## TEACHING POLICY STUDIES

157     Ashford, Douglas E. "Political Science and Policy Studies: Toward a Structural Solution." POLICY STUDIES JOURNAL 5, special issue (1977): 570-83.

> Policy studies could become an independent effort to understand major political changes in the modern state. To do this, policy studies would depart from the prevailing modes of policy analysis, which are mainly derived from economics and its close relation in political science.

158     Bednarski, Mary W., and Florczk, Sandra E. NURSING HOME CARE AS A PUBLIC POLICY ISSUE. Learning Packages in Policy Issues, PI 4. Croton-on-Hudson, N.Y.: Policy Studies Associates, 1978. 62 p.

> As the proportion of aged in the total population grows, nursing home care becomes an increasingly important public policy issue in the United States. This package describes the policy environment for nursing home care, the key actors, possible legislative and other policy changes, and alternatives to nursing home placement. Through a series of exercises students learn from experience how to conduct interviews and gather information in other ways on nursing conditions and patient loads and how to evaluate public policy proposals for dealing with nursing home problems and alternatives to nursing home placement.

159     Bunker, Douglas R. "A Doctoral Program in the Policy Sciences." POLICY SCIENCES 1 (March 1971): 33-42.

> Bunker explains the Ph.D program in policy sciences at State University of New York-Buffalo. He describes the products of the program as hybrid research-scientists-practitioners.

160   Cohen, Larry J., and Rakoff, Robert M.  "Teaching the Contexts of Public Policy: The Need for a Comparative Perspective."  POLICY STUDIES JOURNAL  6 (Spring 1978): 319-24.

An imbalance exists in the teaching of policy studies because the social, political, and economic context in which policies evolve is not adequately explored.  Comparative studies is a most effective way to introduce the context of policy.

161   Coplin, William D.  INTRODUCTION TO THE ANALYSIS OF PUBLIC POLICY FROM A PROBLEM-SOLVING PERSPECTIVE.  Learning Packages in the Policy Sciences, PS 6.  Croton-on-Hudson, N.Y.: Policy Studies Associates, 1975.  40 p.

This is one learning package published by the Policy Studies Associates to help students develop policy analysis skills and techniques and apply them to important policy issues.  This particular package is designed to introduce students to the tasks necessary to study public policy from problem solving perspective.

162   _____, ed.  "Symposium on Teaching Policy Studies."  POLICY STUDIES JOURNAL  6 (Spring 1978): 302-92.

Coplin collects thirteen articles grouped under "what," "how," and "where" of the teaching of policy studies in the university.

163   Corning, Peter A.  "Toward a Survival Oriented Policy Science."  SOCIAL SCIENCE INFORMATION  14, no. 5, (1975): 59-86.

With the era of abundance at an end and the time of scarcity with us, we are caught up in the politics of survival.  Political science can make a contribution to the study of survival and assist policymakers who have to deal with the harsh realities.

164   Coulter, Philip.  "Policy Science:  The Perspective of Policy Research Institutes."  POLICY STUDIES JOURNAL  6 (Winter 1977):  238-45.

Coulter reviews policy science education from the perspective of the Policy Science Institutes.  There were fifty institutes surveyed, thirty-four responses on the question of preferred education for the policy scientist were received.  Conclusion is that economics, public administration, and sociology are the highest regarded academic training areas for policy scientists, but that most important is expertise in analytical techniques, policy substance, or policy process.

165   Dror, Yehezkel.  "Institutional Growth of Policy Sciences."  POLICY STUDIES JOURNAL  1 (Winter 1972): 56-60.

This is an attempt to review the nature and rate of institutional developments within the general field of the policy sciences.  Dror identifies research institutes, university programs, publications, conferences, foundation activities, government units, and consultants as examples of institutional growth.

166     Dye, Thomas R.  "Policy Analysis and Political Science:  Some Problems at the Interface."  POLICY STUDIES JOURNAL  1 (Winter
1972):  103-6.

> Responding to Yehezkel Dror's call for "the application of
> political science to important policy problems," Dye outlines
> several questions about the relationship between political
> science and policy studies.  The issues involve differences
> in normative values, the appropriate role of political scien-
> tists in the policymaking process, problem-oriented versus
> theory-oriented research, and the relative amateurism of
> political scientists in interdisciplinary research.

167     _____.  "Political Science and Public Policy:  Challenge to a Discipline."  In POLICY VACUUM:  TOWARD A MORE PROFESSIONAL
POLITICAL SCIENCE, edited by Robert N. Spadaro, Thomas R. Dye,
Robert T. Golembiewski, Murray S. Stedman, and L. Harmon Zeigler,
pp. 31-54.  Lexington, Mass.:  D.C. Heath, 1975.

> Policy analysis is political science.  Graduate and research
> programs should emphasize the training of empirical skills
> and interdisciplinary expansion by way of policy analysis,
> since subdisciplinary areas presently are self-limiting.
> Existing models and theories are not sufficient for descriptive
> policy analysis.  The separation between the real world and
> the academic must be eliminated to prevent political science
> from becoming extinct.

168     _____.  "Politics vs. Economics:  The Development of the Literature
on Policy Determination."  POLICY STUDIES JOURNAL  7 (Summer
1979):  652-62.

> This essay describes some of the issues in the politics versus
> economics debate, and asserts that ideological positions have
> influenced conceptualization, methodology, and findings in
> research on causes of public policy.  Specifically, it is argued
> that pluralist ideology has directed attention to political com-
> petition and participation as causal variables.  It is argued
> that if political science is to become a policy science, then
> political scientists must discard narrow definitions of what is
> political and examine the full range of forces shaping public
> policy.

169     Elkin, Stephen L.  "Political Science and the Analysis of Public Policy."
PUBLIC POLICY  22 (Summer 1974):  399-422.

> This essay reviews some of the policy analytic traditions
> offered by political scientists.  He notes a tradition that
> describes most of the policy analysis work done by political
> scientists:  output studies, process studies, administrative
> studies, and political economy approaches.  It is suggested
> that through the political economy approach political scientists
> can make their largest contribution to policy analysis.

170     Engelbert, Ernest A.  "University Education for Public Policy Analysis."
PUBLIC ADMINISTRATION REVIEW  37 (May-June 1977):  228-36.

This essay concerns itself with the origins of the field of policy analysis, the major tracks of study, the approach and content of subject matter, the developing relationships to the public service, and some unresolved education issues in the field.

171    Frank, James E., and Smith, Richard A. "Social Scientists in the Policy Process." JOURNAL OF APPLIED BEHAVIORAL SCIENCE 12 (January-March 1976): 104-17.

A number of normative models of participation are developed which differ in prescribing the types, range, and timing of inputs by social scientists into the policy process. The models presented are seen as inadequate because they fail to account fully for the political nature of the policy process and the conditions under which social science knowledge may be needed but not demanded.

172    Fritschler, A. Lee, and Fritz, Dan. "A View from the Top: Comprehending the Public Policy Process through Simulated Internships." TEACHING POLITICAL SCIENCE 3 (July 1976): 427-34.

This article relates the experiences of developing a one-week program for private sector executives to show the environment in which high-level government officials make and implement public policy; influences affecting public policy decisions; the relationships among federal, state, and local officials in making policy; interrelationships between elected and non-elected officials in making policy; and the management technologies used by public officials.

173    Froman, Lewis A., Jr. "The Categorization of Policy Contents." In POLITICAL SCIENCE AND PUBLIC POLICY, edited by Austin Ranney, pp. 41-52. Chicago: Markham Publishing Co., 1968.

Froman discusses how political scientists might attempt to arouse pressing public policy questions. He argues that potentially interesting topics on subfields within the discipline have been left unexplored.

174    Fry, Brian R., and Tompkins, Mark E. "Some Notes on the Domain of Public Policy Studies." POLICY STUDIES JOURNAL 6 (Spring 1978): 305-12.

This is an article presented in a symposium on teaching policy studies. Despite the recent growth in policy studies programs, no consensus has yet developed on what is appropriate training in the field. Authors propose the development of a four-part framework that defines the domain of policy studies as individual, small group, organizational, and systems levels of analysis.

175    Hambrick, Ralph S., Jr., and Snyder, William P. THE ANALYSIS OF POLICY ARGUMENTS. Learning Packages in the Policy Sciences, PS 13. Croton-on-Hudson, N.Y.: Policy Studies Associates, 1976. 69 p.

Designed to equip students to better understand, evaluate, and develop policy arguments, this package requires students to identify the common forms of policy arguments, distinguish between policy and program issues, identify the principal kinds of arguments used in policy arguments, and evaluate the effectiveness of policy arguments.

176    Lazarsfeld, Paul F. "The Policy Science Movement (An Outsider's View)." POLICY SCIENCES 6 (September 1975): 211-22.

The paper focuses on the roles that policy scientists assign to themselves in the decision-making process. Four characteristics of the policy scientist's self-image are discussed: his work should include a reassessment of the problem's goals; he represents a new type of professional; he cannot be expected to contribute to the general knowledge of specific academic disciplines; he is concerned with making recommendations that are acceptable to his sponsor.

177    Lewis, Joseph H. "Policy Sciences and the Market." POLICY SCIENCES 2 (June 1971): 287-300.

The most recent response of universities to the urban crisis has taken the form of new graduate programs in the policy sciences. They are widely diverse in course content, teaching methods, measures to assure experiential inputs and devices for survival in the standard discipline-oriented university climate, but all have the common purpose of improving the quality and enlarging the quantity of both public policy practitioners and analysis. What has so far received relatively little attention is the nature of the decision universe in which the products of these programs, the graduates, will need to perform if they are to have impact. In this paper that universe and the relationship of the university to it are characterized in simple market terms. Doing so suggests that the most pressing problems for policy science lie on the demand, not the supply, side of the market. It will take the best efforts of policy scientists to address them successfully.

178    Melanson, Philip H. "The Political Science Profession, Political Knowledge and Public Policy." POLITICS AND SOCIETY 2 (Summer 1972): 489-501.

The analysis presented here examines the internal processes of the American political science profession and its links to the American political system. Given the lack of reliable knowledge available to the profession, it should be wary of making pseudoscientific assertions as though they were irrefutable.

179    Mosher, Frederick. DEMOCRACY AND THE PUBLIC SERVICE. Public Administration and Democracy Series, no.1. New York: Oxford University Press, 1968. 219 p.

First in a series under the general editorship of Roscoe Martin, this volume focuses on the role of a nonelective public service in a democratic society. Central to the analysis is the impact of education, professionalism, and collective organizations in the public service. It concludes with an essay on merit, morality, and democracy.

180    O'Leary, Michael K., and Coplin, William D.  "Teaching Political Strategy Skills with PRINCE."  POLICY ANALYSIS  2 (Winter 1976): 145-60.

The PRINCE political accounting system (programmed international computer environment) was developed for use with a computer simulation model of foreign policy. Instructors devote one to two weeks to introducing students to the system, which is then applied to a public policy issue. Instructors have found the system useful in mid-career training programs in which policy analysis skills constitute a major set of educational goals.

181    Price, Don K.  "1984 and Beyond:  Social Engineering or Political Values?"  In AMERICAN PUBLIC ADMINISTRATION:  PAST, PRESENT, FUTURE, edited by Frederick C. Mosher, pp. 233-52.  University: University of Alabama Press, 1975.

The analysis and development of policy and the execution of policy decisions are inseparable functions, and the public administrator must be concerned with both. Another dilemma is general and specialized education. It is necessary to take people who have started as professional specialists and add to their specialized knowledge both the capacity for comprehending its relationship with broader interests and a dedication to the general purposes of government and society. This calls for a pattern of career development that puts a high premium on going beyond a particular specialty. A third dilemma is caused by the need to choose between encouraging an elite meritocracy or a participatory democracy.

182    Radin, Beryl A.  "On Teaching Policy Implementation."  POLICY ANALYSIS  4 (Spring 1978):  261-70.

This essay discusses the content of a course in policy implementation at the LBJ School of Public Affairs at the University of Texas, Austin. Radin concludes that even though no precise definition of policy implementation exists in the literature, such a course can be taught. This course includes readings, class exercises, guest lecturers, and the assignment of a series of five "well-defined" papers. The papers enable each student to construct an implementation study of a federal policy or program.

183    Ranney, Austin, ed.  POLITICAL SCIENCE AND PUBLIC POLICY. Chicago:  Markham Publishing Co., 1968.  287 p.

The essays in this volume all attempt to discuss what political science as a discipline can contribute to the content of public policy. The central question is whether studies of policy content are as important as political process studies in the discipline of political science.

184    Salisbury, Robert H.   "The Analysis of Public Policy:  A Search for
       Theories and Roles."   In POLITICAL SCIENCE AND PUBLIC POLICY,
       edited by Austin Ranney, pp. 151-75.  Chicago:  Markham Publishing
       Co., 1968.

       This essay attempts several tasks.  It explains the political
       scientist's definition of public policy (i.e., while political
       scientists have traditionally been concerned with policy, their
       concern has been limited to constitutional policy); it develops
       models and typologies of substantive policy; and finally, it
       raises the question of the way in which political scientists
       can employ their credentials as professional analysts of
       political systems and processes to affect policy outcomes.

185    Seidman, Larry.  "A Course in the Economics of Public Policy Analysis."
       POLICY ANALYSIS  1 (Winter 1975):  197-215.

       A course in the economics of policy analysis was given to
       thirty-five students at the Graduate School of Public Policy
       at the University of California.  Covering ten policy topics
       in twenty weeks, the course began with a review of first
       principles but focused immediately on the efficiency-equity
       issue.  Graded, weekly problem sets ensured that the students
       interacted with the material.  The divergent economic back-
       grounds and skills of the students became a dilemma.  It
       would be preferable to offer two courses.

186    Uphoff, Norman.  "Integrating Policy Studies into Political Science."
       POLICY STUDIES JOURNAL  1 (Summer 1973):  252-57.

       One of the concerns with the rapid growth of policy studies
       is what is its proper relationship to political science, the
       parent discipline.  Two approaches are possible:  it can be
       seen as a sub-field of the discipline or as a possible sub-
       field that threatens to declare its independence from the
       parent discipline.  This article reports on Cornell Univer-
       sity's attempts to resolve the problem.  Their solution has
       been to view the "place" of policy studies as part of yet
       beyond, the bounds of political science, an interdisciplinary
       field of study.

187    Winthrop, Henry.  "Policy and Planning Programs as Goals of Scien-
       tific Work:  Interdisciplinary Training for Social Planning as a Case
       Study in Applied Social Science."  AMERICAN JOURNAL OF ECONOMICS
       AND SOCIOLOGY  34 (July 1975):  225-48.

       Policy and planning have become a series of new professions
       in and out of academic life as each of the specialized social
       and behavioral sciences is applied to the problems of society.
       Specialization tends to develop theoretical constructs which
       have little relation to reality.  To transcend these limitations,
       interdisciplinary training is proposed and developed for one
       area, social policy and social planning.

188    Wolf, Charles, Jr.  "Policy Sciences and Policy Research Organizations."
       POLICY SCIENCES  2 (March 1971):  1-6.

The author, an employee of RAND Corporation at the time of this article, seeks to determine if policy research organizations like RAND have a role to play in contributing to the supply of policy research analysts via advanced teaching and training programs.

189    Yates, Douglas T., Jr.  "The Mission of Public Policy Programs: A Report on Recent Experience."  POLICY SCIENCES  8 (September 1977):  363-74.

This paper is a report of a Ford Foundation-sponsored meeting on graduate education and research programs in public policy held in 1975.  Numerous individuals representing such universities as Harvard, Duke, Stanford, Yale, Princeton, Berkeley, Carnegie-Mellon, and Michigan were present.  The paper discusses- development in public policy programs, patterns of curriculm development, governance issues, the demand for policy analysts in governments, methodological issues in policy analysis, and the impact of substantive policy research.

## TEXTBOOKS: GENERAL AND MISCELLANEOUS

190    Ahern, William R.  "Applying Principles of Policy Analysis to an Off-shore Oil Leasing Decision."  POLICY ANALYSIS  1 (Winter 1975): 133-40.

The article presents three principles of policy analysis and illustrates them with examples from an analysis of a resource development decision.  The principles are:  (1) all major possible outcomes of the decision should be identified; (2) all outcomes should be predicted using explicitly stated assumptions and explicitly stated uncertainties; and (3) net outcomes should be predicted in context.

191    Ashford, Douglas E.  "The Structural Analysis of Policy: Or Institutions Really Do Matter."  In COMPARING PUBLIC POLICIES:  NEW CONCEPTS AND METHODS, edited by Douglas E. Ashford, pp. 81-98.  Sage Yearbooks in Politics and Public Policy, vol. 4.  Beverly Hills, Calif.:  Sage, 1978.

The author provides illustrations of the problems that the comparative analysis of policy raises.  Inertial raises the basic choice between growth and stability.  Scale poses a choice between the liberal's view that small units of government enhance democratic life and the increasing awareness that individual participation has limited impact in the modern state.  The third, and possibly the most promising start for comparative policy studies, is substitutability, or the diverse ways that governments accomplish very similar things.

192    AuClaire, Philip A.  "Informing Social Policy:  The Limits of Social Experimentation."  SOCIOLOGICAL PRACTICE  2 (Spring 1977):  24-37.

A commitment to "experiment for reform" has several implications for those concerned with emerging roles within sociological practice. One is the degree to which the interests and needs of the "targets" of public policy, as well as policymakers, are met. An argument is developed pointing to the need for policy advocacy within sociological practice.

193 Balk, Walter L. IMPROVING GOVERNMENT PRODUCTIVITY: SOME POLICY PERSPECTIVES. Sage Professional Papers in Administrative and Policy Studies, no. 03-025. Beverly Hills, Calif.: Sage, 1975. 70 p.

The deterioration of the environment and the costs of government and social programs have made productivity a matter of continuing concern to all policymakers. Productivity improvement is the public agency process of obtaining more yield out of allocated resources. Productivity consists of a set of two control relationships—efficiency and effectiveness. Political and social constraints will be particularly important in public agencies. Attention must be given to improving quality as well as to increased output.

194 Beckman, Norman, ed. "Policy Analysis in Government: Alternatives to 'Muddling Through.'" PUBLIC ADMINISTRATION REVIEW 37 (May-June 1977): 221-63.

The editor presents six articles on policy analysis, defined as the application of analytical skills to the solution of public problems. The articles deal with policy analysis as myth or reality, university education for policy analysis, policy analysis for Congress, analysis in states and communities, the nongovernmental policy analysis organization, and a piece dealing with issues "beyond analysis."

195 Bower, Joseph L. "Descriptive Decision Theory from the 'Administrative' Viewpoint." In THE STUDY OF POLICY FORMATION, edited by Raymond A. Bauer and Kenneth J. Gergen, pp. 103-48. New York: Free Press, 1968.

This essay surveys the administrative theory literature to find a theory that will provide a simple picture of how an organization works and a basis for improving the performance of organizations. Such a theory is not found.

196 Clotfelter, James. "Policy Studies and Regional Studies." POLICY STUDIES JOURNAL 4 (Winter 1976): 188-92.

This is a short piece suggesting that some aspects of regional studies might have application for students of policy studies. It is suggested that regional studies might prove valuable in cases where there are successful models of interdisciplinary research, thereby making complicated research tasks more manageable.

197 Dalton, Thomas R. "Citizen Ignorance and Political Activity." PUBLIC CHOICE 32 (Winter 1977): 85-89.

A major assumption of this paper is that perceived discrimination is a motivator of political participation. According to Dalton, perceived discrimination occurs because neither citizen nor government official are aware of each other's preferences and unable to satisfy the other's wants.

198   Davidoff, Paul. "Advocacy and Pluralism in Planning." JOURNAL OF THE AMERICAN INSTITUTE OF PLANNERS 31 (November 1965): 331-37.

City planning is a means for determining policy. In a democracy appropriate policy is determined through debate. The right course of action is always a matter of choice. Planners should engage in the political process as advocates of the interests of government and groups. Intelligent choice about public policy would be aided if different political, economic, and social interests produced city plans. Plural plans rather than a single agency plan should be presented to the public.

199   DeNuefville, Judith Innes. SOCIAL INDICATORS AND PUBLIC POLICY: INTERACTIVE PROCESSES OF DESIGN AND APPLICATIONS. New York: American Elsevier, 1975. 311 p.

This work addresses the issue of integrating social accounts into the policy process. The author contends that useful social indicators cannot be developed in a policy void.

200   Dolbeare, Kenneth M. "The Impact of Public Policy." POLITICAL SCIENCE ANNUAL  5 (1974): 89-130.

This is an essay on the state-of-the-art of analysis of problems and prospects of public policy. Essay includes an attempt to define public policy, the meaning of impact in policy impact, the kinds of policy impact studies undertaken by political scientists, and a critical evaluation of the problems and prospects of policy-oriented research.

201   Dorfman, Robert, ed. MEASURING THE BENEFITS OF GOVERNMENT EXPENDITURES. Washington, D.C.: Brookings Institution, 1965. 429 p.

This is a collection of papers presented as a Brookings Institution-sponsored conference in 1963. The papers have as a common theme the allocation of public funds on the basis of sensible and consistent criteria of project work and the development of techniques for measuring the benefits and costs of governmental decisions. Topics include government research and development programs, outdoor recreation, preventing high school dropouts, civil aviation expenditures, urban highway investments, and urban renewal programs.

202   Dror, Yehezkel. DESIGN FOR POLICY SCIENCES. New York: American Elsevier, 1971. 156 p.

Dror advocates the use of scientific paradigms for improving policymaking, and examines the history, difficulties, moral validity, and implications of policy sciences, including the weaknesses of the contributions of behavioral and management sciences.

203 _____. "Policy Sciences: Some Global Perspectives." POLICY SCIENCES 5 (March 1974): 83-87.

Pressure of problems seems to constitute a main variable in a policy sciences approach; traditional ways of handling problems have failed, causing a search for new solutions. Policy studies in all countries suffer from an extreme scarcity of persons who are qualified to engage in policy research on complex issues.

204 _____. PUBLIC POLICY MAKING RE-EXAMINED. Scranton, Pa.: Chandler Publishing Co., 1968. 70 p.

Dror argues that a significant gap exists between the way policies are formulated and the available knowledge on how they can best be made. The book includes discussions of present policymaking approaches, evaluation of those approaches, an optimal model of policymaking, and improvements needed in policymaking. The final section discusses muddling through versus shaping the future.

205 _____. VENTURES IN POLICY SCIENCES: CONCEPTS AND APPLICATION. New York: American Elsevier, 1971. 321 p.

Dror describes the manner in which government, business, and other organizations attempt to realize preferred values through policy decisions based on informed knowledge. He analyzes the techniques available for clarifying policy goals, trends, projections, and alternatives.

206 Dye, Thomas R. UNDERSTANDING PUBLIC POLICY. 3d ed. Englewood Cliffs, N.J.: Prentice Hall, 1978. 338 p.

In this widely used textbook, Dye discusses several policy-making models (elite and group theory, incrementalism, systems analysis, etc.), illustrates them with case studies on poverty, civil rights, education, and compares their utility for policy analysis.

207 Dye, Thomas R., and Gray, Virginia. "Determinants of Public Policy." POLICY STUDIES JOURNAL 6 (Autumn 1977): 84-93.

This is a general survey article discussing the determinants of public policy by focusing on types of political systems, types of explanatory models of public policy, types of public policies, and suggestions for future research.

208 Edmunds, Stahrl. THE BASICS OF PRIVATE AND PUBLIC MANAGE-MENT. Lexington, Mass.: Lexington Books, 1978. 315 p.

Edmunds presents the basics of management in terms of human needs and discusses how these needs relate to the management function. He examines how authority is delegated to make the management function work, and how differing organizational structures use different types of management.

209  Ernst, Martin. "The Impact of Management Science on Policy: A Skeptical Viewpoint." In MANAGEMENT AND POLICY SCIENCE IN AMERICAN GOVERNMENT, edited by Michael J. White, Michael Radnor, and David A. Tansik, pp. 171-80. Lexington, Mass.: D.C. Heath, 1975.

There are a number of barriers to management science success in handling large-scale socially oriented problems, including size and the amount of time required to produce a good study. When dealing with highly value-laden decisions where a straightforward optimization process is completely impractical (or even irrelevant), an appropriate approach might be the use of an adversary process.

210  Ferejohn, John A. "Public Policy: Alternative Criteria for Resource Efficiency." In POLITICAL SCIENCE ANNUAL, vol. 6 (1975), edited by Cornelius P. Cotter, pp. 175-253. Indianapolis, Ind.: Bobbs-Merrill, 1976.

Decision makers usually face constraints that prevent them from choosing only projects with positive net results. Some reasonable planning procedures may be devised to work in economic environments where the assumptions of the competitive model are not satisfied.

211  Fisher, Gene A. "Cost Consideration in Policy Analysis." POLICY ANALYSIS 3 (Winter 1977): 107-14.

Issues affecting cost considerations in policy analysis include dollar cost measures, economic costs, and aggregate measures of economic and noneconomic costs. All these approaches have several deficiencies. Not everything can be reduced to dollars.

212  Frankel, Charles, ed. CONTROVERSIES AND DECISIONS: THE SOCIAL SCIENCES AND PUBLIC POLICY. New York: Russell Sage, 1976. 312 p.

Fourteen scholars from a variety of disciplines contributed chapters addressing the varied value problems in policy research, policy evaluation, and the application of scholarship to ongoing policy controversies.

213  Frederickson, H. George, and Wise, Charles R. PUBLIC ADMINISTRATION AND PUBLIC POLICY. Lexington, Mass.: Lexington Books, 1977. 228 p.

Lexington Books and the Policy Studies Organization, publisher of POLICY STUDIES JOURNAL, have entered into an agreement in which Lexington publishes in book form symposia originally appearing in the JOURNAL. This effort presents

sixteen essays on administering and organizing human resources, actors in administering policy, administering public
policy, decision processes, and accountability.

214    Froman, Lewis A., Jr. "Public Policy." INTERNATIONAL ENCY-
CLOPEDIA OF THE SOCIAL SCIENCES 13 (1968): 204-8.

This is a short, introductory level essay on the characteristics of public policy as a subfield of political science. Froman
outlines the different types of policy studies (historical, descriptive, legal, and normative) and discusses some new directions in policy research.

215    Gates, Bruce L. "Better Policy Administration through Management
Science?" In PUBLIC ADMINISTRATION AND PUBLIC POLICY,
edited by H. George Frederickson and Charles R. Wise, pp. 147-58.
Lexington, Mass.: Lexington Books, 1977.

This article explores the past and future role of the management sciences in the administration of public policy. A disparity exists between the technical promise of the management
sciences and the actual results of their application in public
organizations. Accepting this contention as a working premise,
the major question addressed here is why the disparity between
promise and results exist. A secondary question is what can
and what should be done about it.

216    Hash, Edward S., Jr. "Macro-Economics for Macro-Policy." ANNALS
OF THE AMERICAN ACADEMY OF POLITICAL AND SOCIAL SCIENCE
394 (March 1971): 46-56.

In influencing the content and operation of public policy at
the conceptual level, economics has emerged as a super-
discipline among the social sciences. This influence is reflected in the membership of the president's Council of Economic Advisers. The application of professional macro-
economics analysis to macro-policy yields a knowledge-power
relationship that strengthens the leadership and democratic
government.

217    Huitt, Ralph K. "Rationalizing the Policy Sciences." SOCIAL SCIENCE
QUARTERLY 50 (December 1969): 480-85.

This essay is in response to a statement in Daniel Moynihan's
MAXIMUM FEASIBLE MISUNDERSTANDING (1969), that
the role of social science lies in the measurement of social
policy, not in its formulation. He looks at the process by
which public policy is normally made and then discusses contributions made by the social sciences to the making of policy.

218    Jones, Charles O. AN INTRODUCTION TO THE STUDY OF PUBLIC
POLICY. Belmont, Calif.: Wadsworth, 1970. 170 p.

Jones provides a sequential approach to policy analysis, complete with appropriate case studies.

219     Kramer, Fred A. DYNAMICS OF PUBLIC BUREAUCRACY. Cambridge, Mass.: Winthrop Publishers, 1977. 290 p.

> This is an introductory public administration text. It provides discussions of theories of organization, the development of public personnel systems and labor–management relations, and public policymaking. The three concluding chapters focus on different aspects of administrative accountability. They include a discussion of budgetary control, congressional oversight, and administrative responsibility.

220     Lakoff, Sanford. "Knowledge, Power, and Democratic Theory." ANNALS OF THE AMERICAN ACADEMY OF POLITICAL AND SOCIAL SCIENCE 394 (March 1971): 4–12.

> The union of knowledge and power is on the verge of occurring thanks to the advance of science and the indispensability of expert advice in the face of rapid technological change. Social knowledge is a vitally needed complement of natural knowledge. The best way of assuring that knowledge is democracy—democracy suitably modified to meet the needs of a post-industrial era.

221     Lane, Robert E. "The Decline of Politics and Ideology in a Knowledgeable Society." AMERICAN SOCIOLOGICAL REVIEW 31 (October 1966): 649–62.

> Living in a knowledgeable society where people inquire into the nature of their belief systems, seek objective standards of truth, and employ knowledge to evaluate their goals encroaches upon politics. The political domain is shrinking and the knowledge domain is growing. This shift will have an impact upon policy. Knowledge affects policy by making certain situations appear as problems that can be solved, by analyzing problems in their total environments, and by reducing the ideological component in political thinking.

222     Lineberry, Robert L. AMERICAN PUBLIC POLICY: WHAT GOVERNMENT DOES AND WHAT DIFFERENCE IT MAKES. New York: Harper and Row, 1977. 296 p.

> This introductory text attempts to bring an understanding of public policy to the undergraduate student. The book is divided into two main parts: studying public policy and policy issues. The issues are cities, civil liberties, inequality, and the management of scarcity.

223     Loehr, William, and Sandler, Todd, eds. PUBLIC GOODS AND PUBLIC POLICY. Comparative Political Economy and Public Policy Series, vol. 3. Beverly Hills, Calif.: Sage, 1978. 240 p.

> The book has three parts. Part 1 examines the economic and political theories of public goods and externalities. Part 2 contains a series of essays that analyze nonmarket structures including the Olympic games, supranational bodies, and military alliances. Finally, part 3 examines transactions in the international arena involving trade, the assignment of property rights, and taxation.

224 Long, Norton. THE POLITY. Chicago: Rand-McNally, 1962. 247 p.

This is a collection of Long's writings from earlier years divided into four sections: rationality and responsibility in policymaking, politics and the economy, the politics of the metropolis, and the study of local government.

225 Luft, Harold S. "Benefit-Cost Analysis and Public Policy Implementation: From Normative to Positive Analysis." PUBLIC POLICY 24 (Fall 1976): 437-62.

Not only is a positive or predictive analysis necessary to supplement a normative approach to benefit-cost analysis, but a relatively simple conceptual extension of benefit-cost analysis can be usefully applied to the task.

226 MacRae, Duncan, Jr., and Wilde, James A. POLICY ANALYSIS FOR PUBLIC DECISIONS. Belmont, Calif.: Wadsworth, 1979. 325 p.

This is an introductory level text in the field of policy analysis. Its point of departure is that it assumes an important role for citizens in the policymaking process. The book includes eight chapters on policy analysis and six cases designed to illustrate the points being made.

227 Mackett, R.L. "Hierarchical Policy Relationships, Consistency, and Indicators in the Planning Process." SOCIO-ECONOMIC PLANNING SCIENCES 10, no. 4 (1976): 149-55.

The paper describes relationships that exist between variables in the urban planning system. The paper traces the development of planning ideas and how they relate to the planning process; a description of the framework of policy relationships in the form of a spatial hierarchy, with time a fundamental factor in the planning process; and the framework is used to show how consistency in plans can be achieved.

228 May, Judith V., and Wildavsky, Aaron B. THE POLICY CYCLE. Sage Yearbooks in Politics and Public Policy, vol. 5. Beverly Hills, Calif.: Sage, 1978.

Most of the papers in this volume were originally prepared for a series of panels dealing with public policy at the 1977 American Political Science Association meeting.

229 Nadel, Mark V. "The Hidden Dimension of Public Policy: Private Governments and the Policy-Making Process." JOURNAL OF POLITICS 37 (February 1975): 2-34.

Nadel challenges the assumption that public policy is limited to government policy. Nadel suggests that policy ought to be analyzed and then determined who makes it. Using large corporations as an example he presents a three-fold typology of public policy: resource transfer, regulatory, and constituent policies. In all three categories, corporations implement policies that fulfill public policy criteria.

230    Nagel, Stuart S. POLICY STUDIES REVIEW ANNUAL. Vol. 1.
       Beverly Hills, Calif.: Sage, 1977. 704 p.

       This is the first of an annual series of policy-related articles
       gathered from numerous academic specializations. This volume
       divided thirty-seven essays into general and specific policy
       areas. They are subdivided into stages in policy studies
       research, stages in policy formation and implementation,
       policy studies across nations and disciplines, and problems
       with a political science emphasis, with an economic emphasis,
       with a sociology-psychology emphasis, and with a natural
       science or engineering emphasis.

231    Orlans, Harold. "Neutrality and Advocacy in Policy Research." POLICY
       SCIENCES 6 (June 1975): 107-20.

       Orlans charges that a "naive scientism" (value-free) has con-
       strained most federal policy research and research institutes.
       Broader approaches are needed which do not artificially iso-
       late and arbitrarily quantify isolated factors but examine them
       in their social and historical context. The vain search for
       objectivity should be replaced by an admission of the interests
       being served.

232    "The Research Utilization Quandry: A Symposium." POLICY STUDIES
       JOURNAL 4 (Spring 1976): 224-87.

       This essay presents thirteen articles dealing with using re-
       search in the policy process, experiences with research use
       in different political environments, where research is, and
       where it is heading.

233    Rich, Richard C. "Government Structure and the Future of Urban
       Planning and Administration." SOUTHERN REVIEW OF PUBLIC AD-
       MINISTRATION 1 (December 1977): 332-49.

       Rich gives an examination of the ways in which urban planning
       and administrative practices might be more closely linked to
       the political process. He explains how the evaluation of the
       products of planning and administration can be brought closer
       to the people.

234    Ripley, Randall B., ed. PUBLIC POLICIES AND THEIR POLITICS.
       New York: W.W. Norton and Co., 1966. 174 p.

       This volume presents sixteen essays, most of what appeared
       in other publications, address the politics of public policy.
       Included are the analysis of public policies, techniques of
       subsidy, techniques of regulation, and techniques of manipula-
       tion.

235    _____, et al. "Structure, Environment, and Policy Actions: An
       Empirical Exploration." In POLICY MAKING IN THE FEDERAL EXECU-
       TIVE BRANCH, edited by Randall B. Ripley and Grace A. Franklin,
       pp. 117-43. New York: Free Press, 1975.

Four kinds of independent variables--agency maturity, partisan strength in the electorate, economic conditions, and previous policy actions--were related to budgetary policy actions as the dependent variable. The findings show that all of the categories of independent variables have explanatory power. The findings also support the concept of a life cycle of agencies: while agencies are younger, their policy actions (and the latitude for action) are increasing; the relationship reverses as agencies get older and shrinking of policy actions sets in. In middle age, agencies experience stability in both their policy actions and latitude for actions at a high level.

236  Rivlin, Alice M. SYSTEMATIC THINKING FOR SOCIAL ACTION. Washington, D.C.: Brookings Institution, 1971. 150 p.

This study is an examination of decision making in government social action programs. Rivlin looks at the substance, not the process, of decision making. She proposes wider social experimentation and increased accountability.

237  Roos, Leslie L., Jr. "Quasi-Experiments and Environmental Policy." POLICY SCIENCES 6 (September 1975): 249-65.

Even though environmental policy analysis is dominated by engineering approaches, environmental agencies could make greater use of the social sciences in order to develop strategies for site selection, data collection, and treatment. Quasi-experiments, which require fewer controls than true experiments, are an appropriate instrument for the development of such strategies. Illustrations are presented to show the issues involved and the strategies that are appropriate for research on collective goods.

238  Sharkansky, Ira, ed. POLICY ANALYSIS IN POLITICAL SCIENCE. Chicago: Markham, 1970. 476 p.

Although dated in some respects, this book is an introduction to public policy for undergraduate and graduate students. Major topical areas are basic conceptions in policy analysis, the measurement of policy, determinants of public policy, and evaluation of public policy.

239  Sheffer, Gabriel. "Reversibility of Policies and Patterns of Politics." POLICY STUDIES JOURNAL 5 (1977): 535-53.

In this special issue, policy impact is an essential component of both the policy process and politics at large. Governmental outputs define clienteles, create new clienteles, and structure their political responses. Government policies determine whether the public complies or rejects governmental authority. Outputs trigger peaceful or violent political reactions and ultimately contribute to the endless reshaping of the main patterns of politics. This article concludes that only when public reaction can reverse policies are basic democratic principles served.

240   Shull, Steven A.  INTERRELATED CONCEPTS IN POLICY RESEARCH.
      Sage Professional Papers in American Politics, no. 04-036.  Beverly
      Hills, Calif.: Sage, 1977.  76 p.

          This paper seeks to understand the factors affecting policy-
          making and to ascertain the type of policies that are affected
          by those factors.  Policy actions during the period from
          1960 to 1971 are examined for eight federal agencies.  Con-
          cepts considered are internal structure, external environment,
          budgetary policy actions, and functional policy actions.

241   Siegel, Richard L., and Weinberg, Leonard B.  COMPARING PUBLIC
      POLICIES: UNITED STATES, SOVIET UNION, AND EUROPE.
      Homewood, Ill.: Dorsey Press, 1977.  430 p.

          The authors claim three purposes for the book:  to mesh
          public policy and comparative politics; to synthesize and
          fill the gaps in comparative public policy; and give readers
          a sense of the options that confront political decision makers.

242   "Social Science Research and Public Policy."  JOURNAL OF APPLIED
      BEHAVIORAL SCIENCE  11 (January-March 1975):  7-17.

          This entire issue is devoted to the subjects of social science
          and public policy.  Six articles discuss the relation of social
          science to practical affairs, models of applied social science
          research methodology, implementing open housing laws, evalua-
          tion research, power training, and community action agencies.

243   Tugwell, Franklin, ed.  SEARCH FOR ALTERNATIVES: PUBLIC
      POLICY AND THE STUDY OF THE FUTURE.  Cambridge, Mass.:
      Winthrop, 1973.  335 p.

          This collection of essays surveys a field called "policy oriented
          futures research."  Topics include the nature of the future,
          techniques of future studies, social forecasting, values and
          the future, political futures, the post-industrial society, and
          others.  Contributors include Bertrand deJouvenal, O.D.
          Duncan, Irene Taviss, Herman Kahn, Paul Ehrlich, Daniel
          Bell, Bertram Gross, Donald Michael, and Alvin Toffler.

244   Weiss, Janet A.  "Using Social Science for Social Policy."  POLICY
      STUDIES JOURNAL  4 (Spring 1976):  234-38.

          There are three facets to the concept of usefulness in policy
          research:  usefulness is determined by factors inherent in
          the research study itself, usable research satisfies the demands
          of the environment, making it politically possible for govern-
          ment policymakers to pay attention to it; and usable research
          has an impact on broad social understanding, redefining issues,
          or offering new explanations of social phenomena.

245   White, Michael; Radnor, Michael; and Tansik, David A., eds.  MANAGE-
      MENT AND POLICY SCIENCE IN AMERICAN GOVERNMENT.  Lexing-
      ton, Mass.: Lexington Books, 1975.  379 p.

Fourteen articles that attempt to apply the theories and principles of management science to various aspects of the American political process are given. Illustrative examples are systems analysis in the military, manpower programs, evaluation in the Law Enforcement Assistance Administration, input—output models, and others.

246   Wildavsky, Aaron. "If Planning is Everything, Maybe It's Nothing." POLICY SCIENCES 4 (June 1973): 127-53.

In all societies planners have difficulty in explaining who they are and what they are expected to do. If they are supposed to doctor sick societies, how come the patient never gets well? Wildavsky suggests that planning means too many different things to too many different people for a coherent approach to the profession.

247   _____. "The Political Economy of Efficiency: Cost—Benefit Analysis, Systems Analysis, and Program Budgeting." PUBLIC ADMINISTRATION REVIEW 26 (December 1966): 292-310.

The encroachment of economics upon politics is easy to under-stand since being political is bad and being economic is good. Economists claim to know and work to defend their interests in efficiency while political science does not even define its sphere of competence.

248   Woll, Peter. PUBLIC POLICY. Cambridge, Mass.: Winthrop Publishers, 1974. 264 p.

Woll examines the policymaking process, including considering models of the process as well as ways in which Congress, the president, federal courts, and bureaucracy contribute to policy formation. The development of the policy process to the present time is undertaken, and proposals for reform in the wake of Watergate are presented.

# Chapter 2

# DECISION MAKING

249    Alexander, Ernest R. "Choice in a Changing World." POLICY SCI-
ENCES 3 (September 1972): 325-37.

> General decision models are weak because they are either
> divorced from societal assessment or else they assume univer-
> sality of the form of a society. This paper develops a frame-
> work independent of a priori assumptions about the decision
> makers' environment. It suggests that an important factor
> affecting decision makers' style is their perception of change.
> Decision makers in stable or slowly changing environments
> will probably adopt incremental methods while those in
> rapidly changing situations will use more entrepreneurial
> methods.

250    Allison, Graham T. ESSENCE OF DECISION: EXPLAINING THE
CUBAN MISSILE CRISIS. Boston: Little, Brown and Co., 1971.
388 p.

> This analysis of the international event that almost brought
> the world to the brink of nuclear war attempts to explain the
> behavior of the United States and USSR in terms of three
> models. The rational actor model focuses on actions that
> governments choose to make with certain goals in mind; the
> organizational process model indicates that outputs result
> from organizational procedures and features; the governmental
> politics model implies that actions governments perform are a
> result of bargaining.

251    Art, Robert J. THE TFX DECISION: McNAMARA AND THE MILITARY.
Boston: Little, Brown and Co., 1968. 202 p.

> Art provides a case study of the controversy over the decision
> to select a multipurpose aircraft for the military, contrary
> to its wishes. This is a view of decision making within
> bureaucracy.

252    Bolan, Richard S. "Social Planning and Policy Development in Local
Government." In MANAGING HUMAN SERVICES, edited by Wayne F.
Anderson, Bernard J. Frieden, and Michael J. Murphy, pp. 85-127.
Washington, D.C.: International City Management Association, 1977.

Social welfare difficulties facing local government are the need to integrate methodological developments, the lack of agreement on objectives and priorities, increasing problems of coordinating planning, roles and functions in human services planning, and equity and justice in the delivery of human services. Fewer and fewer local governments become involved because localities cannot make decisions independently. Decisions are increasingly being made both from above and below the local governments. Returning planning and decision making to the local level can help to overcome its abstractions and the gaps of understanding and insensitivity that come from a planning process too highly centralized.

253    Bragg, J.E., and Andrews, I.R. "Participative Decision-Making: An Experimental Study in a Hospital." JOURNAL OF APPLIED BEHAVIORAL SCIENCE 9 (November-December 1973): 727-36.

Participatory decision making was introduced into a hospital sub-system where several factors favored its success over a period of eighteen months. Attitudes improved, absences declined, and productivity increased.

254    Buchele, Robert, and Cohen, Howard. EQUITY AND EFFICIENCY IN PUBLIC POLICY. Learning Packages in the Policy Sciences, PS 15. Croton-on-Hudson, N.Y.: Policy Studies Associates, 1978. 28 p.

This learning package discusses the concepts of equity and efficiency, determines the role of incentives and rewards in the distribution of income, and determines the impact of group decision making on the determination of income.

255    Bunn, D.W. "Policy Analytic Implications for a Theory of Prediction and Decision." POLICY SCIENCE 8 (June 1977): 123-34.

This article reviews the development of decision theory. Policy analysis of organizational decision making requires changes in decision theory to deal with group consensus, ill-defined objectives, and disparate informative sources.

256    Burns, Robert E. "Decision Making Processes Governing Federal Expenditures within the Transportation Sector of the United States." TRANSPORTATION 3 (July 1974): 147-64.

Economic efficiency plays virtually no explicit role in the process of allocating federal funds for transportation. Of far more concern to Congress are the issues of regional equity and scandal-free implementation, backed up by the general feeling that federal allocations are promoting commerce and are needed. In urban areas a sense of urgency and need can be generated for costly rail rapid transit systems with federal funds shifting into this area. Another area of federal allocations is the national rail network.

257    Caplan, Nathan. "Factors Associated with Knowledge Use Among Federal Executives." POLICY STUDIES JOURNAL 4 (Spring 1976): 229-34.

The decision-making orientation of the policymaker is characterized by an appreciation of the scientific and the extra-
scientific aspects of a policy issue. The ethical-scientific
values of the policymaker carry a sense of social direction
and responsibility. Policymakers make decisions that are
intuitive and are believable on the grounds of objectivity and
that their action implications are politically feasible.

258   Clark, Terry N. "Citizen Values, Power and Policy Outputs: A
Model of Community Decision-Making." JOURNAL OF COMPARATIVE
ADMINISTRATION 4 (February 1973): 388-429.

Based on data from fifty-one cities, the study showed that
policy outputs are a function of five variables: (1) citizen
values; (2) values weighted by resources to which citizens
have access; (3) community characteristics; (4) leadership
characteristics; and (5) power and decision-making structures.

259   Coppock, Rob. "Decision-Making When Public Opinion Matters." POLICY
SCIENCES 8 (1977): 135-40.

The fact that a bureaucracy exercises control is more important in determining status than either position in the hierarchy
or income. Whenever a decision maker considers a plan of
action, he estimates the degree of support for that plan among
his colleagues, politicians, and the public. The administrator's
decision is always based on the total amount of support expected
to be generated by the policy or program.

260   Etzioni, Amitai. "Mixed Scanning--A Third Approach to Decision-
Making." PUBLIC ADMINISTRATION REVIEW 27 (December 1967):
385-402.

Here is a critique of rational and incremental problem solving.
Etizoni develops an approach analogous to Herbert A. Simon's
"satisficing" concept. "Mixed-Scanning" suggests that there
are power and processes in public policy decision making that
minimize incrementalism's propensity to follow a course established by inertia, yet is not as time and information de-
manding as rational decision making.

261   Fagin, Allen. "The Policy Implications of Predictive Decision-Making:
'Likelihood and Dangerousness' in Civil Commitment Proceedings."
PUBLIC POLICY 24 (Fall 1976): 491-528.

This article examines the civil commitment process for the
mentally ill as a form of predictive decision making under
conditions of uncertainty. The lengthy article warns against
equating mental illness with dangerousness and shows that
the ability to predict dangerous conduct is no greater in the
case of the mentally ill, that preventive confinement is no
more justified in mental illness than in other cases.

262   Friedrich, Carl J. "Political Decision-Making, Public Policy and
Planning." CANADIAN PUBLIC ADMINISTRATION 14 (Spring 1971):
1-15.

In the W. Clark Clifford Memorial Lecture for 1970, Friedrich distinguished among three types of political decisions
linked to different patterns of reaching a decision: individual
decisions, group decisions, and public decisions. He suggests
that in our societies, decision making, policy, and planning
are closely tied and that these processes cannot be considered
in isolation.

263    Geiger, Theodore, and Hansen, Roger D. "The Role of Information
in Decision-Making on Foreign Aid." In THE STUDY OF POLICY
FORMATION, edited by Raymond A. Bauer and Kenneth J. Gergen,
pp. 328-80. New York: Free Press, 1968.

This is an empirical study of foreign aid as a particular issue
area of national decision-making. It seeks to identify and
evaluate the relative importance of the factors that play a
role in the formation of national attitudes regarding this
activity and in the executive and legislative policy operating
decisions. The authors' particular interest is in the role
of information in decision making.

264    Grauhan, Rolf-Richard, and Strubelt, Wendelin. "Political Rationality
Reconsidered: Notes on an Integrated Evaluative Scheme for Policy
Choices." POLICY SCIENCES 2 (Summer 1971): 249-70.

The essay deals with the concept and problem of political
rationality. Following the concept that the presence or absence of rationality manifests itself in choice situations, it
explores the specific characteristics of political choice, the
criteria for rationality, the restrictions for rationality and
analysis inherent in any choice structure, and the differences
between analytical restrictions and the "confining conditions"
for rational political choices provided by the circumstances
of present-day politics.

265    Greenberger, Martin; Crenson, Matthew A.; and Crissey, Brian L.
MODELS IN THE POLICY PROCESS: PUBLIC DECISION MAKING
IN THE COMPUTER ERA. New York: Russell Sage Foundation, 1976.
355 p.

While policy modeling has been impressive, the direct impact
of models on the public decision making process is difficult
to pinpoint. For models to be useful to decision makers, the
relationship between the consumers and producers of models
must be improved. The study must be well timed and the
results must be communicated in terms the policymaker can
comprehend. The modelers must be relatively independent
of the policymakers and must have a reputation for astute
analysis and good sense based on past performance.

266    Heymann, Philip B., and Holtz, Sara. "The Severely Defective Newborn: The Dilemma and the Decision Process." PUBLIC POLICY 23
(Fall 1975): 381-418.

This essay involves the court's judicial policymaking, decision making, and birth defects. It is concerned with the
judicial approach to problem solving and outlines the differences between judicial problem solving and resource allocation decision making. The basic question is by what processes and criteria should the courts decide whether a
severely defective newborn must be kept alive by attending
physicians.

267  Hill, Paul T. A THEORY OF POLITICAL COALITIONS IN SIMPLE
POLICY-MAKING SITUATIONS. Sage Professional Papers in American
Politics, no. 04-008. Beverly Hills, Calif.: Sage, 1973. 46 p.

Social-psychological model is used to develop a theory which
concentrates on explaining some aspects of coalition, informa-
tion--the total resources of the winning coalition, the allocation of rewards among members of the winning coalition, and
the establishment of coalition policies.

268  Holden, Matthew, Jr., and Dresang, Dennis L. WHAT GOVERNMENT
DOES. Sage Yearbooks in Politics and Public Policy, vol. 1. Beverly Hills, Calif.: Sage, 1975. 320 p.

This volume includes essays examining decision making and
policy systems to appraise existing political theory or to
generate new theory; to determine if policies achieve the
desired ends; to study policy impact; and to prescribe what
social choices ought to be.

269  Janis, Irving L. "What Group Dynamics Can Contribute to the Study
of Policy Decisions." In POLICY STUDIES AND THE SOCIAL SCI-
ENCES, edited by Stuart S. Nagel, pp. 125-33. Lexington, Mass.:
D.C. Heath, 1975.

A source of defective judgment that arises in cohesive groups
of decision makers is the "concurrence-seeking tendency,"
which fosters overoptimism, lack of vigilance, and sloganistic
thinking about the weakness and immorality of outgroups. The
more amiability and esprit de corps among the members of a
policymaking in-group, the greater is the danger that independent critical thinking will be replaced by "groupthink,"
which is likely to result in irrational and dehumanizing actions
directed against out-groups. What is needed is a new type
of research in which experienced executives familiar with the
policymaking system from the inside and a variety of specialists familiar with decision-making processes from the outside
collaborate to develop viable improvements.

270  Jones, Bryan D. "Distributional Considerations in Models of Government Service Provision." URBAN AFFAIRS QUARTERLY 12 (March
1977): 291-312.

Three models of the government service provision are examined:
policy output analysis, policy impact analysis, and service
distribution. The first two models rest on a system basis,
which is not useful in the study of the distribution of govern-

mental services. The study of distribution considers empirical factors such as decisions and attitudes of service providers, organizational constraints and arrangements, and legislative mandates. In handling their routine service decisions, local service delivery agencies adopt task performance rules. The rules generally have distributional consequences; that is, groups of citizens who are not members of the service agency are differently affected by the rules.

271 Kolderie, Ted. "New Institutions for Policy-Making: The Twin Cities Area." HABITAT 2, nos. 3-4 (1977): 349-53.

The Twin Cities area of Minnesota demonstrates performance on measures of urban success. Attention is focused on how problems are identified and acted upon. The Twin Cities area has developed institutions for identifying future problems and devising innovative, realistic solutions. Its major accomplishment is the establishment of a planning and decision-making process capable of understanding and dealing with community problems.

272 Lerner, Allan W. THE POLITICS OF DECISION-MAKING: STRATEGY, COOPERATION, AND CONFLICT. Beverly Hills, Calif.: Sage, 1976. 216 p.

Decisions in today's world are generally made with the involvement of outside experts; this is especially true of political decisions. This book is an empirical study of the political effects of advice from extrapolitical experts.

273 Lewin, Arie Y., and Shakun, Melvin F. "Situational Normativism: A Descriptive-Normative Approach to Decision Making and Policy Sciences." POLICY SCIENCES 7 (July 1976): 1-10.

The paper discusses situational normativism by which the components of policy sciences may be put to work on real decision problems. The approach is situational in that each problem must be viewed individually. It involves a synthesis of descriptive and normative approaches. It attempts to combine behavioral knowledge and cost-effectiveness for improved policy-making.

274 Lowi, Theodore E. "Decision Making vs. Policy Making: Toward an Antidote for Technocracy." PUBLIC ADMINISTRATION REVIEW 30 (May-June 1970): 314-25.

This is a book-review essay covering the following works: Mancur Olson, Jr., THE LOGIC OF COLLECTIVE ACTION (1965); Charles E. Lindblom, THE POLICY-MAKING PROCESS (1968); Yehezkel Dror, PUBLIC POLICYMAKING RE-EXAMINED (1968); and Raymond A. Bauer and Kenneth J. Gergen, eds., THE STUDY OF POLICY FORMATION (1968). Like other PAR review essays, this one tends to be a state-of-the-art review of a field as well as book reviews more narrowly defined.

275    Lyden, Fremont J.; Shipman, George A.; and Kroll, Morton, eds. POLICIES, DECISION, AND ORGANIZATION. New York: Appleton-Century-Crofts, 1969.  387 p.

This is a collection of empirical research findings and analytical tools designed to stimulate empirical research on decision making within organizations.  The book is divided into seven parts:  parts 1 through 5 present articles relevant to the organizational life cycle; part 6 is concerned with decision making as a process and with analytical constructs for studying aspects of the process; and part 7 presents two case studies.

276    McBridge, Howard J.  "Benefit-Cost Analysis and Local Government Decision-Making."  GOVERNMENTAL FINANCE  4 (February 1975): 31-34.

Utilizing cost-benefit analysis in local government decision making can mean the difference between an unnecessary extravagance and a beneficial expenditure.

277    McCoy, Clyde B.  "The Impact of an Impact Study:  Contributions of Sociology to Decision-Making in Government."  ENVIRONMENT AND BEHAVIOR  7 (September 1975):  357-72.

A feasibility study on the building of a highway was presented in Lexington, Kentucky.  None of the planning had examined the social aspects of the project, and an environmental impact study was requested.  The mayor indicated that this study had convinced him that approval would be unwise and that he was investigating plans for a sewer project instead.  Finally, the highway plan was dropped.

278    Miller, Dann, and Friesen, Peter H.  "Archetypes of Strategy Formulation."  MANAGEMENT SCIENCE  24 (May 1978):  921-33.

There have been few attempts to understand the strategy-making process by examining the organizational and environmental context in which it occurs.  Rather than adopting contingency theory, the authors decided to look for simultaneous associations among a fairly large number of variables.  The methodology used to isolate archetypes is explained.  Ten archetypes are described.

279    Mintzberg, Henry.  "Patterns in Strategy Formulation."  MANAGEMENT SCIENCE  24 (May 1978):  934-48.

The literature on strategy formulation is largely theoretical and not empirical.  By defining a strategy as "a pattern in a stream of decision," it is possible to research strategy formulation in a broad descriptive context.  A program suggested by this definition is outlined, and two of the completed studies are then reviewed.

280    Moore, Mark.  "A Feasibility Estimate of a Policy Decision to Expand Methadone Maintenance."  PUBLIC POLICY 26 (Spring 1978):  285-304.

Traditional forms of policy analysis ignore political-bureau-
cratic factors that determine if a policy implemented successfully can be adopted. Moore develops a four-step method for
making "feasibility estimates" of specific policy proposals:
(1) identifying major activities and policy chores; (2) gauging
sensitivity of desired outcomes to ways in which activities
are carried out; (3) locating political and bureaucratic factors operating in the local setting that will affect the character of the activities and choices; and (4) making a prediction
above the actual performance of the government in adopting
and implementing the policy proposal.

281     Mushkin, Selma J. "Policy Analysis in the State and Community."
        PUBLIC ADMINISTRATION REVIEW 37 (May–June 1977): 245-53.

        Most states report that they utilize analysis to some degree
        in decision making, particularly in budget evaluation. Some
        analytical studies undertaken at state and local levels have
        examined such diverse areas as public safety, police opera-
        tions, health programs, education, and manpower training.
        Policy analysis as a method of identifying options is becoming
        familiar in the decision-making processes of state and local
        government. It establishes clear statements of intended pur-
        poses and formulated goals. It also helps government to gain
        citizen participation and response.

282     Noll, Roger G. "Information, Decision-Making Procedures, and
        Energy Policy." AMERICAN BEHAVIORAL SCIENTIST 19 (January–
        February 1976): 267-78.

        Concerned with researcher's strategies, the logic of policy
        decisions often calls for an optional solution to a policy prob-
        lem, however, optimization is inappropriate under conditions
        of uncertainty and may help to increase uncertainty. Noll
        suggests that information monopolies be broken, contingency
        plans remain flexible, mixed strategies be used in policy
        formulation, and research on the larger social consequences
        of policy alternatives be undertaken.

283     Ostrom, Elinor. "Institutional Arrangements and the Measurement of
        Policy Consequences: Applications to Evaluating Police Performance."
        URBAN AFFAIRS QUARTERLY 6 (June 1971): 447-76.

        A review of the requirements necessary for good decision
        making in terms of valid and reliable data is given. Ostrom's
        concern is for determining if the measures used to evaluate
        policies and programs do measure what they purport to measure.
        The specific policy area considered is the police function,
        but conclusions can be applied to other areas.

284     Peterson, R.E.; and Seo, K.K. "Public Administration Planning in
        Developing Countries: A Bayesian Decision Theory Approach."
        POLICY SCIENCES 3 (September 1972): 371-78.

        Decision making under uncertainty is seen as a game against
        nature. The policymaker is the player and he has a set of

strategies from which he wants to choose the most effective. After his decision is made, various results (states of nature) are possible. These states are identified and their relationship to the key options available are identified. They show that neglect of the uncertainty aspects of any decision lead to evaluations of reforms and projects which can be seriously upward biased.

285    Pfeffer, Jeffrey, and Salancik, Gerald R. "Organizational Decision Making as a Political Process: The Case of a University Budget." ADMINISTRATIVE SCIENCE QUARTERLY 19 (June 1974): 135-51.

The effect of subunit power on reserve allocation decisions in one university is examined. Measures of departmental power are found to be significantly related to the proportions of the budget received. Subunit power in the organization is also related to the correlation between a subunit's resources and work load overtime.

286    Price, Thomas J. "Behavior Modes: Toward a Theory of Decision-Making." JOURNAL OF POLITICS 37 (May 1975): 417-35.

This is a survey of the decision-making literature concluding that it is unsatisfying because it is divided into a series of partial theoretical statements. A serious deficiency has been the lack of an analytical conceptualization of the ensuing political behavior. Price creates a concept called behavior modes, premised upon goal setting, behavior selection, and specificity of the decision. The result is a statement of possible behavior that is time and actor free, allowing the development of theoretical statements.

287    Sackman, Harold. "Summary Evaluation of Delphi." POLICY ANALYSIS 1 (Fall 1975): 693-718.

Delphi is a method for eliciting expert opinion on a variety of topics through questionnaires. Originally developed by the RAND Corporation, it has come to be used for opinion polling in investigating all sorts of social phenomena. The method stresses anonymity of the panelists, statistical responses, and polling. The methodological principles of this system are examined in the light of current standards approved by the American Psychological Association for social experimentation, test design, and sampling. It is concluded that the conventional version of Delphi is an unreliable technique, which should not be used until its validity has been experimentally established.

288    Schneier, Edward V., ed. POLICY-MAKING IN AMERICAN GOVERNMENT. New York: Basic Books, 1969. 384 p.

The book is an introductory reader which focuses on the process of political decision making rather than on the institutions through which decisions take place. The editor regards policymaking as a continuous process from the time a political problem is first identified until a law has been passed and applied. Twenty-nine articles were chosen to show how this process works in American government.

289  Schultz, Randall L.  "The Use of Simulation for Decision-Making."
BEHAVIORAL SCIENCE  19 (September 1974):  344-50.

When simulation is intended as an aid to decision making,
special problems arise in connection with designing and
using the model.  This paper defines the use of policy simulation, explores factors related to its application, and suggests
implementation for model development.

290  Shapiro, David L., and Shelton, Robert B.  "The Application of an
Agency Decision-Making Model."  PUBLIC CHOICE  32 (Winter 1977):
51-65.

This paper discusses several decision-making models that
operate within public bureaucracies.  The main argument of
the paper is that officials are motivated to increase agency
size and all decisions are formulated with this goal in mind.

291  Sharkansky, Ira.  THE ROUTINES OF POLITICS.  New York:  Van
Nostrand, 1970.  192 p.

Routines are decision procedures used to simplify choices in
selecting a course of action among numerous alternatives.
Sharkansky discusses the how and why of routines and their
impact.  He also explains five routines of policymaking that
influence final decisions.

292  Strauch, Ralph E.  "A Critical Look at Quantitative Methodology."
POLICY ANALYSIS  2 (Winter 1976):  121-44.

Problems arising in policy analysis methods span a spectrum
from reasonably quantifiable to highly "squishy."  Quantitative
methodology has often provided significant insights or even
solutions to squishy problems, but this usually depends on
the skill and insight of the analyst.  Unfortunately, the
theories that support the methodology do not admit a role
for subjective human judgment.

293  _____.  "'Squishy' Problems and Quantitative Methods."  POLICY
SCIENCES  6 (June 1975):  175-84.

Problems come to government policy analysts that cannot be
solved on a purely mathematical basis, problems that tend
to be "squishy"--having no well-defined formulation.  Application of quantitative methods to squishy problems presents
potential hazards; mathematical models are useful as perspectives, but as squishy problems do not have unambiguous logi-
cally defined answers, no real grounds can justify interpreting
an answer produced by a quantitative model or method as the
logical answer to a squishy substantive question.  Quantitative
methods should be used with caution, and unquestioned authority
to apply the results should not be automatically granted.

294  Tuite, Matthew; Chisholm, Roger; and Radnor, Michael, eds.  INTER-
ORGANIZATIONAL DECISION-MAKING.  Chicago:  Aldine Publishing
Co., 1972.  298 p.

Nineteen experts from a variety of disciplines converge to create a book whose goal is to improve cooperation in decision making. Variables are discussed which affect that possibility, including an awareness of individual and collective payoffs, response to boundary personnel, and decision technology.

295 Ugalde, Antonio. "A Decision Model for the Study of Public Bureaucracies." POLICY SCIENCES 4 (March 1973): 75-84.

The paper introduces the idea of "series of decisions." It is defined as the total number of decisions made in the reaching of a goal. Series are divided into two types--programming and implementation. The first are made during the adoption of goals and objectives and the second during their implementation. The distinction between the two types is important because different actors are involved in them.

296 Ukeles, Jacob B. "Policy Analysis: Myth or Reality?" PUBLIC ADMINISTRATION REVIEW 37 (May-June 1977): 223-28.

Policy analysis is a systematic investigation of policy alternatives that represents a problem-solving approach through the collection and interpretation of information and the prediction of consequences of alternative courses of action. Initially, policy analysis was faced with an essentially hostile environment. The function of the analyst seemed already occupied by political staff workers. However, the scope of public policy and complexity of issues generate a need for unbiased information in decision making.

297 Vaupel, James W. "Muddling Through Analytically." In IMPROVING THE QUALITY OF URBAN MANAGEMENT, edited by Willis D. Hawley and David Rogers, pp. 187-209. Beverly Hills, Calif.: Sage, 1974.

The prospects for better individual decision making depend not so much on the refinement of complex analytical techniques as on the extension of analysis to situations where time is short and data are sparse. This paper describes and illustrates some analytical methods useful to busy decision makers.

# Chapter 3

# NATIONAL POLICYMAKING PROCESSES

## NATIONAL POLICYMAKING PROCESS

298    Amara, Roy C. "Toward a Framework for National Goals and Policy Research." POLICY SCIENCES 3 (March 1972): 59-69.

> Amara deals with goal formation and policy planning at the national level. A research framework for the analysis of national policy alternatives is defined. The basic elements of the framework include values, goals, attainments, strategies, societal processes, and societal indicators.

299    Buchanan, James M., and Tullock, Gordon. "The Expanding Public Sector: Wagner Squared." PUBLIC CHOICE 31 (Fall 1977): 147-50.

> This research note suggests that while the growth of government may have assumed a new form, analysis of relevant data shows that government growth may be out of control and not slowing down as others have indicated.

300    Caldwell, Lynton K. "Management of Resources and the Environment: A Problem in Administrative Coordination." INTERNATIONAL REVIEW OF ADMINISTRATIVE SCIENCES 38, no. 2 (1972): 115-27.

> This paper addresses administrative coordination of environmental affairs. It suggests that the ecological and aesthetic elements of environmental policy can provide objective, although not always quantitative criteria against which the effectiveness of coordination can be measured.

301    Caplan, Nathan. "Social Research and National Policy: What Gets Used, by Whom, for What Purpose, and with What Effect?" INTERNATIONAL SOCIAL SCIENCE JOURNAL 28, no.1 (1976): 187-94.

> The use of social science information in important matters of government has been the subject of increasing interest over the past several years. Tested information on the subject is limited. Social science utilization in policymaking is complex and not a subject on which a priori assumptions can be expected to shed much light. Consequently, we know little about what information gets used, by whom, for what purpose, and with what, if any, impact. This paper is designed to reduce some of these uncertainties.

302   Craswell, Richard. "Self-Generating Growth in Public Programs."
      PUBLIC CHOICE 21 (Spring 1975): 91-97.

      One cause of increases in spending is an increase in the
      number of private beneficiaries of the program. A signif-
      icant relationship was shown to exist between the change in
      the number of beneficiaries in one time period and the change
      in spending in the next.

303   Dye, Thomas R. POLICY ANALYSIS: WHAT GOVERNMENTS DO,
      WHY THEY DO IT, AND WHAT DIFFERENCE IT MAKES. Univer-
      sity: University of Alabama Press, 1976. 122 p.

      Public policy is whatever governments choose to do or not to
      do. Policy analysis involves the systematic identification of
      the causes and consequences of public policy, the use of
      scientific standards of inference, and the search for relia-
      bility and generality of knowledge. In studies of the causes
      of public policy, public policies themselves are the dependent
      variables, while in studies of the consequences of public
      policy, public policies themselves are the independent variables.

304   Erskine, Hazel. "The Polls: Governmental Information Policy."
      PUBLIC OPINION QUARTERLY 35 (Winter 1971): 636-51.

      This article reviews some seventy-two published public
      opinion polls from 1941 through 1971 to discover citizens'
      attitudes toward satisfaction with government policy in terms
      of the Pentagon Papers, presidential credibility, and other
      areas.

305   Gregg, Philip M. "Units and Levels of Analysis: A Problem of Policy
      Analysis in Federal Systems." PUBLIUS 4 (Fall 1974): 57-86.

      Policy analysis lacks the necessary tools to explain systema-
      tically the federal arrangements to bring about desirable policy
      changes. This inability is contributing to the piecemeal de-
      struction of the system's regulating capacity and the dismem-
      berment of federal institutions.

306   Hargrove, Erwin C. "Professional Styles in Government: Touchstones
      for the New Policy Scientist." POLICY SCIENCES 2 (June 1971):
      229-47.

      The article reports interviews with urban planners, lawyers,
      economists, and political scientists about their experience in
      government. Propositions are developed about characteristic
      models of thought and problem-solving styles of each pro-
      fession and conclusions drawn about the relative effective-
      ness of each set of professional skills in a policymaking
      process.

307   Harris, Fred R., ed. SOCIAL SCIENCE AND NATIONAL POLICY.
      Chicago: Aldine Publishing Co., 1970. 152 p.

Edited by a former U.S. senator, these essays all originally appeared in TRANS-ACTION magazine in the 1960s. They deal with poverty, the cities, life in Appalachia, and the case for a national social science foundation. Authors include Ken Clark, Senator Daniel P. Moynihan, Lee Rainwater, Herbert J. Gans, Vice-President Mondale and Willard Wirtz.

308    Holmes, William M. "Social Conditions and Policy Change." In POLICY MAKING IN THE FEDERAL EXECUTIVE BRANCH, edited by Randall B. Ripley and Grace A. Franklin, pp. 21-44. New York: Free Press, 1975.

Policy change has been operationalized as change in agency expenditures. Four independent variables were examined and data for twelve federal agencies were collected for the fiscal period 1952 to 1971. The findings show that changes in policy actions are influenced by change in issue-related social conditions, changes in agency maturity, and change in general social conditions, with issue-related social conditions having the most impact.

309    Hoos, Ida R. "Systems Techniques for Managing Society: A Critique." PUBLIC ADMINISTRATION REVIEW 33 (March-April 1973): 157-64.

This is a severe critique of systems management and other sophisticated management techniques that are alleged to produce better public policy. Hoos claims that such efforts deify technique at the expense of substantive knowledge and experience. Her conclusion is that the perfect solution, perfectly executed, is antithetical to a democratic society.

310    House, Peter W., and Williams, Edward R. "Data Inconsistencies and Federal Policy-Making." POLICY ANALYSIS 4 (Spring 1978): 205-26.

The data base for this essay comes from a report by the National Commission on Supplies and Shortages. Forecast data developed for national policymaking contain sufficient variation to impair the consistency of the public policy and regulatory process. The authors propose some steps to increase data consistency.

311    Huitt, Ralph K. "Political Feasibility." In POLITICAL SCIENCE AND PUBLIC POLICY, edited by Austin Ranney, pp. 263-75. Chicago: Markham Publishing Co., 1968.

Huitt establishes some of the conditions of political feasibility which seem to operate in the making of national policy. Analysis is limited to executive and legislative branches and groups associated with them. Analysis is further confined to policymaking in the present, not the evolution of major change.

312    Kaufman, Herbert. RED TAPE: ITS ORIGINS, USES, AND ABUSES. Washington, D.C.: Brookings Institution, 1977. 100 p.

313    Kernaghan, Kenneth. "Responsible Public Bureaucracy: A Rationale and Framework for Analysis." CANADIAN PUBLIC ADMINISTRATION 16 (Winter 1973): 572-603.

   Links between the idea of administrative responsibility and the public interest serve as a basis for describing two hypothetically extreme types of bureaucrat--the objectively responsible and the subjectively responsible official.

314    Lampman, Robert J. "What Does It Do for the Poor?--A New Test for National Policy." PUBLIC INTEREST 34 (Winter 1974): 66-82.

   President Johnson's "War on Poverty" added a new criterion to the measurement of government services; "what does it do for the poor?" This essay argues that many of the alleged failures of the war on poverty were successes when measured against their original goals, but the redefined goals and rising expectations resulted in their being labeled failures. Efficiency and equity issues have replaced the elimination of poverty as a major concern of policy officials.

315    Lane, Robert. "Social Science Research and Public Policy." POLICY STUDIES JOURNAL 1 (Winter 1972): 107-11.

   This article is really a series of random thoughts about public policy and the policy process. The article is a series of taped comments from an extemporaneous talk given by Lane at a National Science Foundation conference in Washington, D.C., 1971. He talked about what happens when government intervenes in the social system, why the influence of social scientists is so limited in government circles, how scientists might make themselves more useful, and the role of the professional associations in advancing the relevance of policy-oriented social science research.

316    LeLoup, Lance T. "Agency Policy Actions: Determinants of Nonincremental Change." In POLICY-MAKING IN THE FEDERAL EXECUTIVE BRANCH, edited by Randall B. Ripley and Grace A. Franklin, pp. 65-90. New York: Free Press, 1975.

   The percent of change in appropriation is determined primarily by percent of change in requests. This indicates the relatively greater importance of the executive branch compared to Congress in affecting change in agencies' budgets. The level of presidential attention and support and changes in agency size were found to be important determinants of change in requests. Change in requests and change in appropriations have little relationship to previous change.

317    Levitan, Sar A., and Taggart, Robert. "The Great Society Did Succeed?" POLITICAL SCIENCE QUARTERLY 91 (Winter 1977): 601-18.

   There is a view widely held that the Great Society failed, yet analysis of the vast array of program data and evaluations show significant accomplishments. Secondary and nonquantifiable goals were frequently ignored, biasing judgments against multipurpose programs.

318 Lowi, Theodore J., and Stone, Alan, eds. NATIONALIZING GOVERN-
MENT: PUBLIC POLICIES IN AMERICA. Beverly Hills, Calif.:
Sage, 1978. 455 p.

This is "a combination of professional analysis and textbook
instruction" in policy studies. The essays are grouped into
four general sections: "The Economic Structure" (do national policies regulate it? reinforce it? undermine it?);
"The Quality of Life" (do national policies accomplish more
than pious hopes and false expectations?); "The Social Fabric"
(can national policies promote the multi-racial society); and
"The International Fabric" (can national policies promote
world peace?).

319 Lynch, Thomas D. POLICY ANALYSIS IN PUBLIC POLICY-MAKING.
Lexington, Mass.: Lexington Books, 1975. 144 p.

This research monograph attempts to show what can be expected of policy analysis as applied to the federal bureaucracy. Lynch studies the planning-programming-budgeting
system (PPBS) as an example of an attempt to "institutionalize
policy analysis" in the urban mass transportation administration (UMTA).

320 Meltsner, Arnold J. "Political Feasibility and Policy Analysis."
PUBLIC ADMINISTRATION REVIEW 32 (November-December 1972):
859-67.

A deficiency of the analysis of public policy issues by governmental agencies is the slighting of political implications. Analysis should lead to policies that can be implemented and the
study of political feasibility is one way of bridging the gap
between the desirable and the possible.

321 Mustafa, Hussain, and Salomone, Anthony. "Administrative Circum-
vention of Public Policy." MIDWEST REVIEW OF PUBLIC ADMINIS-
TRATION 5 (February 1971): 17-26.

The power of bureaucrats to influence policy is not always
exercised to further legislative or constitutional goals. The
authors contend that bureaucrats will do more than just argue their point when they disagree with policy. Thus program implementation actors often deviate from established
goals or procedures.

322 Nagel, Stuart, ed. POLICY STUDIES IN AMERICA AND ELSEWHERE.
Lexington, Mass.: Lexington Books, 1976. 229 p. Bibliog.

This is a collection of essays on various aspects of public
policy. The study raises issues and notes developments.

323 Pynn, Ronald E. "Watergate: Retrospective Policy Implications."
POLICY STUDIES JOURNAL 4 (Autumn 1975): 63-68.

This article addresses the implications of Watergate for the
future study of public policy. Its major areas of concern are:

presidential-congressional relations, civil liberties, presidential establishments, political campaign reform, and increase in public cynicism.

324    Shull, Steven A.    "The Relationship Between Budgetary and Functional Policy Actions."    In POLICY-MAKING IN THE FEDERAL EXECUTIVE BRANCH, edited by Randall B. Ripley and Grace A. Franklin, pp. 64–93. New York:  Free Press, 1975.

Functional actions are measures of what an agency is doing as it implements its programs.  The principal research hypothesis of this study asserts a direct, positive connection between budgetary actions and functional actions.  The findings show that the relationship between budgetary and functional actions was not always positive, nor was it particularly strong.  In general, agencies appeared to have considerable freedom from budgetary constraints as they shaped their functional actions.

325    Sulzner, George T.    "The Policy Process and the Uses of National Governmental Study Commissions."    WESTERN POLITICAL QUARTERLY 24 (September 1971):    438–48.

The governmental study commission has become a common phenomenon in recent years, but it has not received much scholarly attention.  This essay focuses on such study groups and concentrates on the functions it performs in the political process.  Its contributions seem to fall into two categories: (1) problem-solving related functions; and (2) conflict-management functions.

326    Theobold, Robert, ed.    SOCIAL POLICIES FOR AMERICA IN THE SEVENTIES.    Garden City, N.Y.:  Doubleday, 1968.    216 p.

Theobold is concerned with the possible alterations in our economic and social values and systems as we enter a world being fundamentally altered by the impact of science and technology.  Topics include economics, education, job patterns, and income distribution.

327    Warren, Robert.    "Federal-Local Development Planning:  Scale Effects in Representation and Policy Making."    PUBLIC ADMINISTRATION REVIEW    30 (November–December 1970):    584–95.

The article explores the validity of the assumptions used by Congress and the executive branch in setting organizational criteria to be met by nationally subsidized local and regional nonfederal agencies.

328    Weiss, Carol H.    "Research for Policy's Sake; The Enlightenment Function of Social Research."    POLICY ANALYSIS    3 (Fall 1977):    531–46.

Data from three recent studies suggest that the major use of social research is not the application of specific data to specific decisions.  Rather, government decision makers tend to use research indirectly, as a source of ideas, information, and orientation to the world. Although the process is not easily discernible, over time it may have profound effects on policy. Even research that challenges current values and political feasibilities is judged useful by decision makers.

329 Wilson, James Q., and Rachal, Patricia. "Can the Government Regulate Itself?" PUBLIC INTEREST 46 (Winter 1977): 3-14.

It is suggested that federalism and the enlarged range of activities of all governments makes it easier for a public agency to change the behavior of private·organization than that of another public agency.

330 Yessian, Mark R. "Delivering Services in a Rapidly Changing Public Sector." AMERICAN BEHAVIORAL SCIENTIST 21 (July–August 1978): 829-57.

Change is viewed in the broad context of the American governmental bureaucracy. The aims are to illustrate the major underlying changes taking place in that bureaucracy, to highlight the change–resistant qualities of bureaucracy, and to identify some basic approaches that universities might take to help public servants cope with change in more imaginative and effective ways.

## THE PRESIDENT, CONGRESS, AND COURTS

331 Aberbach, Joel D., and Rockman, Bert A. "Clashing Beliefs within the Executive Branch: The Nixon Administration Bureaucracy." AMERICAN POLITICAL SCIENCE REVIEW 70 (June 1976): 456-68.

Agency and party affiliation were important variables in accounting for differences in administrators' views. The White House will continue to reflect short–term political changes and Congress and bureaucracy will be relatively immune to these dynamics. Partisan–based ideological distinctiveness is growing rather than lessening.

332 Arnold, Peri Ethan. "Herbert Hoover and the Continuity of American Public Policy." PUBLIC POLICY 20 (Fall 1972): 525-44.

The continuity of American public policy for the last forty years has failed to bring about a fundamental redistribution of societal benefits. This is so because Herbert Hoover, not FDR, can be seen as the father of modern public policy because of his role as secretary of commerce during the early and middle 1920s.

333 Ashmore, Harry S. "The Policy of Illusion, the Illusion of Policy." CENTER MAGAZINE 3 (May 1970): 2-10.

This is an analysis of presidential foreign policy statements with particular reference to Richard Nixon and his policy statements on American involvement in Vietnam.

334 Bailey, Stephen K., and Mosher, Edith K. ESEA: THE OFFICE OF EDUCATION ADMINISTERS A LAW. Syracuse, N.Y.: Syracuse University Press, 1968. 393 p.

This is a study of public administration as a part of the political process, focusing on the role of U.S. Office of Education in developing and administering the Elementary and Secondary Education Act of 1965. The case study shows the intricacies of the U.S. political system.

335 Beckman, Norman. "Congressional Information Process for National Policy." ANNALS OF THE AMERICAN ACADEMY OF POLITICAL AND SOCIAL SCIENCE 39 (March 1971): 84–99.

Conventional wisdom holds that Congress is too fragmented to identify and act on national priorities. But through constant modification, Congress has managed to maintain its roles of access and creativity without centralization of power or major reorganization. Recent developments reveal strengthened staff support, more active party policymaking, reform of committee procedures and staffing, and expanded information, investigators, and analytical resources.

336 _____. "Use of Staff Agency by the Congress: Experience of the Congressional Research Service under the Legislative Reorganization Act of 1970." In COMPARATIVE LEGISLATIVE REFORMS AND INNOVATIONS, edited by Abdo I. Baaklini and James J. Heaphey, pp. 91–112. Albany: State University of New York Press, 1977.

The Legislative Reorganization Act of 1970 provided for expanded service and designated the major functions of congressional research service as assistance in legislative matters. The CRS was given four new directions under the legislation: provision of policy analysis and research to assist committees in the legislative function, to submit lists of policy areas to each committee at the beginning of each session, to submit lists of terminating programs and activities to the appropriate committees, and to maintain a continuous liaison with all committees.

337 Brady, David W., and Lynn, Naomi B. "Switched-Seat Congressional Districts: Their Effect on Party Voting and Public Policy." AMERICAN JOURNAL OF POLITICAL SCIENCE 17 (August 1973): 528–43.

Freshmen congressmen representing switched-seat districts are an important part of the process by which mass political behavior can sometimes yield significant policy changes. Two Congresses with significant policy changes are the fifty-fifth and eighty-ninth, congressmen from switched-seat districts provided the strongest support from both policy changes and policy position.

338 Carron, Andrew S. "Congress and Energy: A Need for Policy Analysis and More." POLICY ANALYSIS 2 (Spring 1976): 283–97.

In energy legislation Congress is hampered by a lack of committee focus and hence a lack of leadership. Policy analysts are needed to help Congress develop potential energy solutions. Training in analytical techniques, knowledge of the subject area and political independence make the policy analyst particularly well qualified in debates over energy policy.

339     Casper, Jonathan D. "The Supreme Court and National Policy Making." AMERICAN POLITICAL SCIENCE REVIEW 70 (March 1976): 50-63.

The Supreme Court makes significant contributions to national policymaking in a variety of ways. This study challenges conclusions made in a 1957 study by Robert Dahl, which purported to show that the court was not substantially successful in its major objective of protecting the fundamental rights of minorities against majority tyranny. The policymaking process, however, involves more than winners and losers, and often there are no decisive outcomes. Rather, there is a dynamic process in which even losers contribute importantly to eventual outcomes, as in the struggle to develop public welfare policies. The process brings issues to public attention, and the legal system has been an attractive way for those who lack resources to influence public policy.

340     Clausen, Aage R. "State Party Influence on Congressional Policy Decision." MIDWEST JOURNAL OF POLITICAL SCIENCE 16 (February 1972): 77-101.

State party delegations are considered to be a source of voting variation in the U.S. Congress. Few studies have been done to document this assertion. Previous studies are reviewed and the state party variable is conceptually defined. A comparison is drawn between the prediction power of two simulation models and a regression model. The power of all three models depends heavily upon state and regional party effects.

341     "Clients and Analysis: Congress." POLICY ANALYSIS 2 (Spring 1976): 175-324.

Here are seven articles dealing with policy analysis and its uses on Capitol Hill. Specifically, the articles deal with budget reform and policy analysis, the demand for and supply of analysis on the hill, an economist's view of analysis, congressional inability to do analysis, energy, the need for policy analysis, and congressional committees as customers for policy analysis.

342     Davidson, Roger H. "Congressional Committees: The Toughest Customers." POLICY ANALYSIS 2 (Spring 1976): 299-323.

The Congressional Research Service, General Accounting Office, Office of Technology Assessment, and Congressional Budget Office rely heavily on policy analysts, but members of Congress are essentially individual entrepreneurs. The largest potential market for policy analysis is in the committees. It is essential for policy analysts to know some-

thing of the complexities of committee structure and operations if they wish to contribute to legislative policymaking.

343   Davis, Otto A., and Jackson, John E.   "Senate Defeat of the Family
Assistance Plan."  PUBLIC POLICY  22 (Summer 1974):  245-74.

This article examines the failure of the U.S. Senate to pass
the Nixon administration proposed Family Assistance Plan
after the House of Representatives had passed it.  It pos-
tulates that failure was due to the lack of sufficient constituency support from areas that would benefit most from the
plan.

344   Destler, I.M.  PRESIDENTS, BUREAUCRATS AND FOREIGN POLICY:
THE POLITICS OF ORGANIZATIONAL REFORM.  Princeton, N.J.:
Princeton University Press, 1972.  329 p.

This book discusses the problem of organizing government
for foreign policy.  It concerns itself with reducing the
gap between what presidents want to happen and what bureaucrats actually do.

345   Donovan, John C.  THE POLICY MAKERS.  New York:  Pegasus,
1970.  255 p.

This book is a critical reassessment of American policies in
the 1960s and a look to the 1970s.  It covers the role of
technicians within the agencies of the institutionalized presi-
dency, the power of Congress, the military-industrial complex,
the budgetary process, and the American polity.

346   Downs, George W., Jr.  BUREAUCRACY, INNOVATION, AND PUBLIC
POLICY.  Lexington, Mass.: Lexington Books, 1976.  150 p.

This study is based on the premise that an understanding of
"key bureaucratic and task-environmental characteristics"
are essential in predicting policy innovation in the American
states.  The analysis focuses on correctional agencies.  Downs
concludes that socioeconomic factors are probably less important than previously thought in explaining policy innovations,
and that if one is to understand public policy, one must look
to the characteristics and dynamics of public organizations.

347   Dreyfus, Daniel A.  "The Limitations of Policy Research in Congressional Decision-Making."  POLICY STUDIES JOURNAL  4 (Spring 1976):
269-74.

Where decisions involve legislative oversight and policy adjustment, policy research is simply superfluous to the role which
Congress plays.  Major policy decisions frustrate the timely
preparation and introduction of independent policy research
because of the very nature of the congressional decision process.  The Congress should weigh the final positions, remain
sensitive to the tastes and demands of society, and act upon
its collective political instincts.  It will then provide responsive and responsible decisions.

348    Ferejohn, John A., and Fiorina, Morris P. "Purposive Models of
       Legislative Behavior." AMERICAN ECONOMIC REVIEW  65 (May
       1975):  407-14.

       This study highlights recent advancements in filling the theo-
       retical gaps in the study of legislative behavior.  It reviews
       the contribution of game and social choice theorists; of those
       who see legislators as goal-seeking agents who choose from
       an available strategic alternative and the work of those in-
       dividuals bridging the gap between empirical studies and
       game theorists.

349    Fritschler, Lee A.  SMOKING AND POLITICS:  POLICYMAKING AND
       THE FEDERAL BUREAUCRACY.  2d ed.  Englewood Cliffs, N.J.:
       Prentice Hall, 1975.  180 p.

       Beginning from the premise that the bureaucracy is the focal
       point of the policy-making process, the author uses the ciga-
       rette labeling controversy to show policymaking and how
       pressure groups shape its outcome.

350    Froman, Lewis A., Jr.  THE CONGRESSIONAL PROCESS.  Boston:
       Little, Brown, 1967.  221 p.

       Froman explains how congressional procedures can shape
       policy outputs.

351    Frye, Alton.  "Congressional Politics and Policy Analysis:  Bridging
       the Gap."  POLICY ANALYSIS  2 (Spring 1976):  265-81.

       Congress must improve its capacity to define realistic choices
       among competing policy and program proposals.  Participants
       in the revised congressional budget process understand the
       necessity for budgetary analyses to incorporate sound studies
       of scientific, engineering, and other noneconomic elements
       of policy planning.  A private institute for Congress would
       be independent of the executive branch and of the committee
       system and could overcome many of the defects of present
       staffing and research mechanisms.  Its continued existence
       would depend on contractual support from Congress.

352    Gawthrop, Louis C.  BUREAUCRATIC BEHAVIOR IN THE EXECUTIVE
       BRANCH:  AN ANALYSIS OF ORGANIZATIONAL CHANGE.  New
       York:  Free Press, 1969.  288 p.

       This is a discussion of how bureaucratic behavior in the
       executive branch of the federal government is conditioned
       by and responds to the demands of change.  To evaluate or-
       ganizational change, Gawthrop attempts to resolve other ques-
       tions first:  (1) the resolution of internal conflict; (2) deci-
       sion-making processes; and (3) the development of loyalty
       within the ranks.  The overall focus is on the development of
       an analytical model to explain the functioning of bureaucracies
       in their response to internal and external change.

353 Grant, Lawrence V. "Specialization as a Strategy in Legislative Decision-Making." AMERICAN JOURNAL OF POLITICAL SCIENCE 17 (February 1973): 123-47.

Grant evaluates a single theory of specialization based on elementary decision theory. State party delegation appears to be a persuasive source of decision cues. That specialization seems to be an important role expectation for members of the democratic study group.

354 Halperin, Morton H. BUREAUCRATIC POLITICS AND FOREIGN POLICY. Washington, D.C.: Brookings Institution, 1974. 340 p.

This is an analysis of participation and decision-making by foreign policy bureaucrats in American foreign policymaking in the post World War II era.

355 Heidenheimer, Arnold J.; Heclo, Hugh; and Adams, Carolyn Teich. COMPARATIVE PUBLIC POLICY. New York: St. Martin's Press, 1971. 296 p.

A comparison of public policy in the United States, Great Britain, Sweden, France, West Germany, and the Netherlands shows that in income maintenance and education American and European choices on program content are becoming more similar. In the areas of urban planning and housing there are sharp and continued differences.

356 Heveman, Robert H. "Policy Analysis and the Congress: An Economist's View." POLICY ANALYSIS 2 (Spring 1976): 235-50.

The Congressional Budget Act of 1974 can increase the role played by policy analysis in legislative decisions, but there are major obstacles inherent in the structure of Congress and its incentives. By concentrating analytic resources on programs or issues where serious inefficiency or inequity exists, the budget committees and the CBO can enhance understanding of what government does and how it does it.

357 Hinckley, Barbara. "Policy Content, Committee Membership, and Behavior." AMERICAN JOURNAL OF POLITICAL SCIENCE 19 (August 1975): 543-58.

Congressional committee subject matter may substantially affect committee membership and behavior. Two subject matter dimensions are offered: scope and stakes. Results show (1) strong House-Senate intercorrelations of committees dealing with the same subject matter, and (2) in combination, the two subject matter dimensions are capable of organizing and explaining substantial amounts of committee variety.

358 Hy, Ron. "Presidential-Congressional Decision-Making: The Dixon-Yates Controversy." BUREAUCRAT 3 (January 1975): 489-508.

Instead of relying on experimental research, institutional decision makers rely on existing process to solve a problem. The president is central to the decision-making process of the federal government, because he defines many of the problems to be solved and sets the tone of government. The Dixon-Yates controversy of the 1950s is a case study of presidential—congressional decision making. Conclusions from the case provide the following lessons: decision makers must not ignore the implications of any decisions; he/she must keep in touch with subordinates, perceive the problems which affect feedback, work for the optimal expenditure of resources, use technical experts as fully as possible, and not practice excessive secrecy.

359   Jones, Charles O. "Why Congress Can't Do Policy Analysis (or Words to that Effect)." POLICY ANALYSIS 2 (Spring 1976): 251-64.

Congress is not well structured to conduct policy analysis. Congress is an institutional population drawn on by an inestimable number of policy systems because it has the responsibility of legitimating policy.

360   Krasnow, Erwin G., and Lingley, Lawrence D. THE POLITICS OF BROADCAST REGULATION. New York: St. Martin's Press, 1973. 148 p.

This is an analysis of policy formation by the Federal Communications Commission, including a number of case studies of commission action.

361   Lakoff, Sanford A. "Congress and National·Science Policy." POLITICAL SCIENCE QUARTERLY 89 (Fall 1974): 589-612.

As a result of Vietnam and Watergate, Congress has begun to reassert some of its prerogatives in many areas of public policy. This article concerns itself with science policy and suggests that Congress may try to take advantage of the present period of uncertainty to assert more influence in this policy area.

362   Larson, Arthur D. "Representative Bureaucracy and Administrative Responsibility: A Reassessment." MIDWEST REVIEW OF PUBLIC ADMINISTRATION 7 (April 1973): 79-90.

This paper reviews the concept of representative bureaucracy as espoused in the post World War II time, examines some of its deficiencies, assesses its usefulness for enhancing administrative responsibility, and notes other functions served by representatives in the bureaucracy.

363   Light, Alfred R. "The Carter Administration's National Energy Plan: Pressure-Groups and Organizational Politics in Congress." POLICY STUDIES JOURNAL 7 (Autumn 1978): 68-76.

This article examines four political lessons that emerged from Carter's national energy plan: the ironical nature of the energy issue, the cross-pressured nature of interest group positions on the energy issue, the role of organizational politics for the prospects of congressional adoption of comprehensive plans, and presidential dilemmas and imperatives.

364    Meltsner, Arnold. "Bureaucratic Policy Analysis." POLICY ANALYSIS
       1 (Winter 1975):   115-31.

       Bureaucratic policy analysts are a fairly new breed.  This
       article explores their motivations for working in the federal
       government, their notions of success, their relationships
       with agency clients, and their methods and criteria for select-
       ing, defining, and working problems of public policy.

365    _____.  POLICY ANALYSTS IN THE BUREAUCRACY.  Berkeley
       and Los Angeles:  University of California Press, 1976.  310 p.

       Most policy analysts experience a tension between getting
       involved in short-term problems and wanting to think ahead
       about the long-range fundamental issues their agencies face.
       Some analysts are able to spend half their time on important
       long-term basic research activities, but short-term work is
       definitely a prevalent activity.  The bureaucratic context does
       much to liberate the analyst's energy by dividing analytical
       work, expediting, and providing an organization flexible
       enough to respond to policy problems as they emerge.

366    Mields, Hugh, Jr.  "Congress and Urban Growth Policy."  BUREAU-
       CRAT  2 (Spring 1973):  59-68.

       The federal level of government is most likely to produce
       the necessary inputs to the planning process for national
       growth.  Congress can only legislate; it cannot implement
       what it passes.

367    Murphy, James T.  "Political Parties and the Porkbarrel:  Party
       Conflict and Cooperation in House Public Works Committee Decision-
       Making."  AMERICAN POLITICAL SCIENCE REVIEW  68 (March 1974):
       169-89.

       This is a study of the House Public Works Committee that
       examines the relationship between member goals and the de-
       gree of party conflict, identifies conditions of party conflict and
       cooperation, and links it to policies adopted in the House.

368    Neustadt, Richard E.  PRESIDENTIAL POWER.  New York:  John
       Wiley and Sons, 1960.  224 p.

       A study of presidential power and leadership in the policy
       process.  This book has become a classic.  A 1979 paper-
       bound edition is available.

369    Oleszek, Walter J.  CONGRESSIONAL PROCEDURES AND THE POLICY
       PROCESS.  Politics and Public Policy Series.  Washington, D.C.:
       Congressional Quarterly Press, 1978.  256 p.

       This volume examines how the Congress makes laws and how
       its rules and procedures shape public policy.  The book des-
       cribes the procedural route taken by most major legislation.
       The emphasis is on the use of the rules for strategic pur-
       poses, to expedite or delay legislation, to secure passage,
       or to bring about defeat of bills.

370    O'Neill, Hugh V. "Policy Analysis, Technology and the Congress."
       BUREAUCRAT 3 (January 1975): 416-28.

       The Office of Technology Assessment (OTA) has the capability
       of bringing enlightened and rational decision making to Con-
       gress. Technology assessment can provide legislators with
       several alternatives to public policy problems. As of the
       writing of this article, OTA had not achieved its full poten-
       tial. Suggested improvements include maintaining better
       relationships with the Congressional Budget Office, coopera-
       tion with executive agencies, maintenance of an adversary
       relationship with some executive agencies, playing a leader-
       ship role in the advancement of knowledge about TA and de-
       vising five-year plans for the development of professionals
       with a background in TA.

371    Patterson, Samuel C. "Legislative Research and Legislative Reform:
       Evaluating Regime Policy." PUBLIUS 4 (Summer 1974): 109-15.

       The Citizens' Conference on State Legislatures is conducting
       a systematic assessment of variations among the state legis-
       latures in their organization and procedures. The study pro-
       duced rank orders of the American states in the "effective-
       ness" or capability of their legislatures. The fact that the
       report is flawed methodologically, and similarly inadequate
       in many respects reduces its direct scientific contribution to
       nil.

372    Polsby, Nelson W. "Policy Analysis and Congress." PUBLIC POLICY
       18 (Fall 1969): 61-74.

       This article is essentially a defense of the congressional
       system. It seeks to find out what role analytic activity plays
       on Congress's decision-making activities and how can congres-
       sional decision making be made more receptive to the kinds of
       policy analysis that are carried on both inside and outside
       government.

373    Porter, Laurellen. "Congress and Agricultural Policy." POLICY
       STUDIES JOURNAL 6 (Summer 1978): 472-79.

       Reviews the demographic forces that have altered the con-
       stituency base of the House of Representatives, the congres-
       sional reforms of the 1970s, the new congressional budget
       process, and the impact of these changes as they were mani-
       fested in the making of agriculture policy.

374    Portney, Paul R. "Congressional Delays in U.S. Fiscal-Policy-
       Making." JOURNAL OF PUBLIC ECONOMICS 5 (April-May 1976):
       237-47.

       Reports the results of econometric simulations designed to
       measure the effects of congressional delays in implementing
       three major U.S. tax bills of the 1960s. The effects are
       measured by differences between the time paths of three tar-
       get variables in control and immediate implementation solutions.

375  Rieselbach, Leroy.  "Congressional Reform:  Some Policy Implications."
     POLICY STUDIES JOURNAL  4 (Winter 1976):  180–88.

    This paper treats congressional reform in the context of re-
    established congressional involvements in policymaking.  Rather
    than reaching any firm conclusion, it raises a number of
    questions about a vigorous policymaking legislature.

376  _____, ed.  LEGISLATIVE REFORM:  THE POLICY IMPACT.  Lexing-
     ton, Mass.:  Lexington Books, 1978.  253 p.

    This is an empirical investigation of the effects of legislative
    structure, the distribution of influence and power, and deci-
    sion outcomes of recent changes in Congress and state legis-
    latures.

377  Rohde, David W.  "Policy Goals and Opinion Coalitions in the Supreme
     Court."  MIDWEST JOURNAL OF POLITICAL SCIENCE  16 (May 1972):
     208–24.

    Rohde explains a theory of the formation of opinion coalitions
    in the U.S. Supreme Court.  He assumes that justices are
    rational actors motivated by their own preferences about the
    policy issues they consider.  A "threat to the court" con-
    cept is introduced.  Hypotheses are developed with respect
    to coalition formation and, using data from civil liberties
    cases and the Warren Court, all hypotheses are supported.

378  Rourke, Francis E.  BUREAUCRACY, POLITICS, AND PUBLIC POLI-
     CY.  2d ed.  Boston:  Little, Brown and Co., 1976.  208 p.

    The book is concerned with the role of the bureaucracy in the
    policymaking process in American government.  Rourke's
    contention is that it is in the quiet arena of the executive
    agencies that public policy is made by appointed and not elect-
    ed officials.

379  Sapolsky, Harvey M.  THE POLARIS SYSTEM DEVELOPMENT.  Cam-
     bridge, Mass.:  Harvard University Press, 1972.  261 p.

    Sapolsky reviews the development of the Polaris missile proj-
    ects from an organizational, bureaucratic, political, and mana-
    gerial perspective.  His basic goal is to explain the require-
    ments for success in governmental undertakings and the role
    those requirements played in the development of the Polaris
    project.

380  Sayeed, Khalid B.  "Public Policy Analysis in Washington and Ottawa."
     POLICY SCIENCES  4 (March 1973):  85–101.

    Policy analysis in the United States and Canada tends to
    follow the methods of systems analysis and takes into account
    variables relating to substantive matters as well as political
    and administrative constraints that governments face in pur-
    suing different alternatives.

381  Schick, Allen. "Beyond Analysis." PUBLIC ADMINISTRATION RE-
VIEW 37 (May–June 1977): 258–63.

The specific role of analysis in the legislative process has
not been properly determined, but it has made significant contributions to the policymaking process, resulting in better-
informed policymakers and in a greater awareness of the
effects of government programs.

382  _____. "The Supply and Demand for Analysis on Capitol Hill."
POLICY ANALYSIS 2 (Spring 1976): 215–34.

Policy analysts have tended to concentrate on the executive
branch because the opportunities for making an impact on
public policy are more favorable. Congress seems more concerned about the distributive effects of public policies than
about cost–benefit ratios. Members of Congress cannot be
expected to renounce their political aims for efficiency or
to support analysis that conflicts with apparent political
reality. Congress will be more attuned to analysis when
the issues are technical rather than distributional, but
analysis will always have to compete with other inputs.

383  Seidman, Harold. POLITICS, POSITION, AND POWER: THE DY-
NAMICS OF FEDERAL ORGANIZATION. 2d ed. New York: Oxford
University Press, 1975. 354 p.

Seidman presents an inside view of federal administration as
it affects and is affected by the continuing contest among competing forces for power, positions, and political advantage.
The significance of organization structure and administrative
arrangements is emphasized as a means for establishing political control and determining the balance of power among the
executive and legislative branches of government.

384  Snyder, David P. "The Bureaucrat as Scapegoat, and What to Do
About It." BUREAUCRAT 6 (Winter 1977): 112–16.

A serious flaw in our public policymaking system is the absence of an open feed–back mechanism. Today there are
several trends to open the process of government up with
potentially beneficial results: freedom of information act,
congressional reorganization, and other possibilities are men-
tioned.

385  Stanfield, Rochelle L. "The Development of Carter's Urban Policy:
One Small Step for Federalism." PUBLIUS 8 (Winter 1978): 39–53.

This article analyzes the evolution of the Carter administration's
urban policy until its changes in mid–January 1978. According to the author for the first three–fourths of his first year,
Carter forgot the states and has just recently accepted the
idea of tripartite federalism in the effort to solve the problems of the cities.

386  Strom, Gerald S. "Congressional Policy–Making: A Test of a Theory."
JOURNAL OF POLITICS 37 (August 1975): 711–35.

Congressional outputs are divisible and geographically distributed. This applies only to intrapolicy areas in which
federal money is spent and not to spending across several
policy areas. The distributive theory is a reasonably accurate prediction of congressional committee grant fund allocations.

387   Sullivan, Robert R. "The Role of the President in Shaping Lower
Level Policy-Making Processes." POLITY 3 (Winter 1970): 201-21.

The issue is presidential control of policymaking at lower
levels of the federal bureaucracy. Sullivan concludes that
it is not in the president's interests to intrude at this level
because the risk associated with failure is greater than the
benefits associated with success. A successful president
will dominate the policy setting agenda so that acceptable implementation follows at all levels of the organization.

388   Sundquist, James L. "A Comparison of Policy-Making Capacity in the
United States and Five European Countries: The Case of Population
Distribution." POLICY STUDIES JOURNAL 6 (Winter 1977): 194-99.

Because the institutional structure of policymaking is more
complex in the United States than other industrial nations,
because the policy-making circle is broader and more amateur
and less disciplined, because political parties are weaker,
because public participation is more intense, because the
points of potential veto of a policy innovation are more numerous, a higher degree of national consensus and a more intense commitment of national leadership are necessary before
major departures are proposed and adopted.

389   _____. POLITICS AND POLICY: THE EISENHOWER, KENNEDY,
AND JOHNSON YEARS. Washington, D.C.: Brookings Institution,
1968. 560 p.

Case studies of several major areas of domestic policy com-
bined with general explanatory analysis.

390   Thurber, James A. "Congressional Budget Reform and New Demands
for Policy Analysis." POLICY ANALYSIS 2 (Spring 1976): 197-214.

The Budget and Impoundment Control Act of 1974 provides for
a systematic examination of priorities, expenditures, revenues,
and debt. The Congressional Budget Office (CBO) currently
has the best position, structure, legal authority, and leadership to generate useful policy analysis. CBO is developing
five-year projections of budgetary authority and outlays,
revenues and tax expenditures, and deficits and surpluses.

391   _____. "Policy Analysis on Capital Hill: Issues Facing the Four
Analytic Support Agencies of Congress." POLICY STUDIES JOURNAL
6 (Autumn 1977): 101-11.

This article raises six main questions concerning the relationship between Congress and the Office of Technology Assessment, General Accounting Office, Congressional Budget Office, and the Congressional Research Service. The questions raised by the article are: (1) what is the appropriate relationship of the agencies to Congress; (2) is there too much competition and too little cooperation among the agencies; (3) who should each agency serve and with what services; (4) is there a misunderstanding of what each agency is expected to supply Congress; (5) is the analysis that is supplied of high quality, timely, and most importantly, useful; (6) what is the relationship between politicization and responsiveness of the four agencies?

392   Welch, Susan, and Peters, John G. LEGISLATIVE REFORM AND PUBLIC POLICY. New York: Praeger, 1977. 222 p.

This is a collection of original essays arising from a symposium on the impact of legislative reform on public policy at the University of Nebraska in 1976. The fourteen essays are divided into congressional reform and its impact and state legislative reform and its impact.

393   Wilson, James Q. "The Rise of the Bureaucratic State." PUBLIC INTEREST, no.41 (Fall 1975), pp. 77–103.

Wilson traces the emergence of the bureaucratic state in the United States from colonial times to the present. A major concern is the increasing discretion and power given over to agencies by Congress.

## INTEREST GROUPS AND ELECTIONS

394   Abrams, Burton A., and Settle, Russell F. "A Modest Proposal for Election Reform." PUBLIC CHOICE 28 (Winter 1976): 37–54.

Written from a public choice perspective, this paper tries to demonstrate that the goals of less expensive political campaigns and higher voting turnout may be incompatible. It questions the desirability of encouraging greater voter turnouts, and finally recommends institutional change that may help to lower social costs of elections.

395   Bailey, Stephen K. EDUCATION INTEREST GROUPS IN THE NATION'S CAPITAL. Washington, D.C.: American Council on Education, 1975. 87 p.

Bailey provides an overview of the nature and functions of the several hundred Washington, D.C., organizations interested in educational issues. His analysis includes some of the techniques used by interest groups to protect and advance their clients' interests.

396   Bauer, Raymond A.; Pool, Ithiel de Sola; and Dexter, Lewis Anthony. AMERICAN BUSINESS AND PUBLIC POLICY. Chicago: Aldine-Atherton, 1972. 499 p.

The book concerns itself with American politics and international communication and the ethos and actions of business executives when confronted by a political issue in foreign trade legislation. The politics of foreign trade legislation is given full treatment from the Reciprocal Trade Act of 1953 to the Trade Expansion Act of 1962.

397    Beach, Philip F. PUBLIC ACCESS TO POLICY-MAKING IN THE UNITED STATES. Morristown, N.J.: General Learning Press, 1975. 26 p.

Beach's essay examines the possibilities for popular control of government in the United States today. He attempts to show a relationship between what government does and what people expect it to do.

398    Boyd, Richard W. "Popular Control of Public Policy: A Normal Vote Analysis of the 1968 Election." AMERICAN POLITICAL SCIENCE REVIEW 66 (June 1972): 429-49.

Paper presents two arguments: (1) 1968 election shows the importance of issues at critical points in political history; and (2) issues having a similar impact on the election outcome can have very different consequences for popular control of public policy.

399    Browne, William P., and Wiggins, Charles W. "Resolutions and Priorities: Lobbying by the General Farm Organizations." POLICY STUDIES JOURNAL 6 (Summer 1978): 493-99.

The analysis of the lobbying activity of the general farm organizations refutes many of the claims made about the dominance of ideology over material farm interests. Members do provide the outline for organizational lobbying. Yet, in determining priorities, the expectations of pressure on the lobbying staff from the members is a critical factor because they are one source of intragroup tension.

400    Demsetz, Harold. "Industry Structure, Market Rivalry, and Public Policy." JOURNAL OF LAW AND ECONOMICS 16 (April 1973): 1-10.

This paper takes the cultural view of contemporary doctrine in the area of monopolistic structures and presents data suggesting that the continual concern for monopoly is a dangerous base upon which to build a public policy toward business.

401    Dye, Thomas R. "Oligarchic Tendencies in National Policy-Making: The Role of the Private Policy-Planning Organizations." JOURNAL OF POLITICS 40 (May 1978): 309-31.

This article is Dye's presidential address delivered at the Southern Political Science Meeting in 1977. He attempts to refine the elitist model of the policymaking process by suggesting how elites go about the process of deciding about national policy. It focuses on such groups as the Council on Foreign Relations, Committee on Economic Development, and the Brookings Institution. It suggests linkage between corporate and financial worlds and government decision makers, and it suggests ways in which elite consensus is developed and then communicated to government decision makers.

402    Fiorina, Morris P. "Electoral Margins, Constituency Influence, and Policy Moderation: A Critical Assessment." AMERICAN POLITICS QUARTERLY 1 (October 1973): 479-98.

This paper starts from the premise that there is an already large enough "pile" of data on legislative-constituency relationships. Thus, it looks at existing research, cuts out what seems solid and what seems shaky and draws some conclusions. The author contends that very serious leaps in logic characterize several existing studies and it is these inferential leaps which cause much of the confusion.

403    Ginsberg, Benjamin. "Elections and Public Policy." AMERICAN POLITICAL SCIENCE REVIEW 70 (March 1976): 41-49.

This paper establishes criteria for citizens policy choices that do not depend on opinion surveys. Data drawn from national party platforms, U.S. statutes, and aggregate voting data are compared to determine the extent to which majority choices are translated into national policy over time. Whether or not voters are aware of the implications of their actions, over time popular majorities appear to govern.

404    Guth, James L. "Consumer Organizations and Federal Dairy Policy." POLICY STUDIES JOURNAL 6 (Summer 1978): 499-503.

Since 1933 milk prices in the United States have been heavily influenced by two interrelated federal programs: price supports for manufactured products and federal marketing orders for fluid milk. Policy has usually been determined within a classic subgovernment. Recently, however, there has been some intrusion of consumer and other interests into the process, but the conclusion of the essay is that the old time subgovernment is far from dead.

405    Hibbs, D., Jr. "Political Parties and Macroeconomic Policy." AMERICAN POLITICAL SCIENCE REVIEW 71 (December 1977): 1467-87.

This article argues that the objective economic interests as well as subjective preferences of lower income and occupational status groups are best served by a relatively low unemployment, high inflation configuration, whereas the opposite configuration better serves the high income, high status groups. Governments pursue macroeconomic policies broadly in accordance with the objective economic interests, subjective preferences of their class, defined core political constituences.

406    Kirkpatrick, Evron M. "Toward a More Responsible Two-Party System: Political Science, Policy Science, or Pseudo-Science." AMERICAN POLITICAL SCIENCE REVIEW 65 (December 1971): 965-90.

This essay examines the 1950 Report of the APSA Committee on Political Parties, "Toward a More Responsible Two-Party System." From a policy science perspective, the errors in the report decrease its policy science utility, especially in terms of the failure to clarify the role of political scientist as policy scientist.

407 Kuklinski, James H. "Representativeness and Elections: A Policy Analysis." AMERICAN POLITICAL SCIENCE REVIEW 72 (March 1978): 165-77.

The author examines representatives in terms of policy dimensions. The level of policy agreement varies across policy domains. Linkage is weak on government administration and taxation questions and reasonably high on "contemporary liberalism." The frequency of elections conditions representatives' loyalty to the preferences of the represented.

408 Lewis, Eugene. AMERICAN POLITICS IN A BUREAUCRATIC AGE: CITIZENS, CONSTITUENTS, CLIENTS, AND VICTIMS. Cambridge, Mass.: Winthrop Publishers, 1977. 182 p.

This book is an introduction to the role and impact of public bureaucracies in policymaking and politics in the United States. Lewis argues that citizenship is best understood today in terms of the individual relationship to public bureaucracies. He concludes that American politics are best characterized as a kind of bureaucratic pluralism. The concluding chapter evaluates the overall role of bureaucracy in American politics, focusing on the conflict between bureaucracy and democracy.

409 Meier, Kenneth John. "Client Representation in USDA Bureaucracies: Causes and Consequences." POLICY STUDIES JOURNAL 6 (Summer 1978): 484-88.

This research empirically examines interest group support for USDA bureaus. After devising a procedure to measure interest group support, the reasons why support varies from bureau to bureau and the benefits of that support are assessed.

410 Merelman, Richard M. "The Development of Policy Thinking in Adolescence." AMERICAN POLITICAL SCIENCE REVIEW 65 (December 1971): 1033-47.

Merelman identifies four modes of thought used in the cognition of policy problems. These are moral, cause-effect, sociocentric, and imaginative. Nine variants of these are de-- scribed among a small sample of adolescents. It concludes with some speculation about the structure of socialization theory as it relates to the development of fundamental forms of political thinking.

411 Monroe, Alan D. "Public Opinion as a Factor in Public Policy Formation." POLICY STUDIES JOURNAL 6 (Summer 1978): 542-48.

The research reported here deals with relationship between
public opinion and national policy outcomes over a period of
sixteen years, dealing with all issues for which national opinion survey data are available. After collecting the information
the author compares what the public wanted government to do
with what government actually did.

412    Morgan, David R.   "Political Linkage and Public Policy:  Attitudinal
       Congruence between Citizens and Officials."   WESTERN POLITICAL
       QUARTERLY   26 (June 1973):  209-23.

       Traditional democratic political theory postulates a model of
       electoral accountability of representatives as trustees of the
       people.  More recent research suggests that accountability
       occurs due to fear of the ballot box.  Data based on San
       Francisco indicates that local level offices operate on the
       basis of their own images of the community's needs and have
       little fear of the ballot box.  This research addresses the
       San Francisco situation and suggests that nonprofessional
       local governing bodies may be adhering closely to the policy
       views of the larger community.

413    Ornstein, Norman J., and Elder, Shirley.  INTEREST GROUPS,
       LOBBYING AND POLICYMAKING.  Politics and Public Policy Series.
       Washington, D.C.:  Congressional Quarterly Press, 1978.  245 p.

       This book examines why and how Washington lobbies attempt
       to influence government policy and legislative action.  It
       analyzes the types of lobbies, the role they play, their re-
       sources, tactics, and regulation.  The case studies illus-
       trate the common-site picketing bill, clean air legislation,
       and the B-1 bomber.

414    Page, Benjamin I., and Brody, Richard.  "Policy Voting and the Elec-
       toral Process:  The Vietnam War Issue."  AMERICAN POLITICAL
       SCIENCE REVIEW  67 (December 1973):  979-95.

       The infrequency of issue voting in American presidential elec-
       tions is usually attributed to a lack of policy rationality among
       voters.  Examining Vietnam as an issue in the 1968 election
       reveals that other factors may be at work.  This article exa-
       mines several alternate explanations for the seeming lack of
       issue orientation among voters and draws some general con-
       clusions about the nature of electoral competition in two-
       party systems.

415    Porter, David O.  "Responsiveness to Citizen-Consumers in a Federal
       System."  PUBLIUS  5 (Fall 1975):  51-77.

       Porter is concerned with the nonresponsiveness of producer-
       agencies to expressions of dissatisfaction from citizen-consumer-
       clients.  He has a preference for vouchers in some public
       service programs allowing consumers preferences to impact
       on inattentive public agencies.

416    Riecken, Henry W.  "The Federal Government and Social Science
       Policy."  ANNALS OF THE AMERICAN ACADEMY OF POLITICAL AND
       SOCIAL SCIENCE  394 (March 1971):  100–113.

       While there is no official government social science policy,
       there are three nongovernmental organizations that play
       special roles in social science policy (Social Science Re-
       search Council, National Research Council, and the Russell
       Sage Foundation through study committees and advisory
       groups they provide emphases and development of uses of
       social science.  These groups have made a number of rec-
       ommendations with respect to social science policy.  Basi-
       cally the principal emphasis is to bring social science into
       close conjunction with the practical affairs of the society.

417    Roberts, Marc J.  "An Evolutionary and Institutional View of the Be-
       havior of Public and Private Companies."  AMERICAN ECONOMIC
       REVIEW  65 (May 1975):  415–27.

       Reports on an extensive study designed to explain the varia-
       tions with and among three public and three private electric
       utilities in their impact on environmental quality.  It also
       shows the value of a disaggregated model of the behavior of
       an organization based on the intended rational choices of
       its individual members.  Internal features of the organization
       are potentially important explanations.

418    Rubin, Paul H.  "On the Form of Special Interest Legislation."
       PUBLIC CHOICE  21 (Spring 1975):  79–90.

       Economists had believed that government intervention in eco-
       nomic processes was aimed at correcting flaws in the com-
       petitive process; now such intervention is aimed at benefitting
       some special interest group.  The form that government sub-
       sidies take is at issue.  The goal of an interest group is to
       maximize its share of the benefits.  Short-lived benefits would
       be favored by politicians or parties which had safer tenure.

419    Sullivan, John L., and O'Connor, Robert E.  "Electoral Choice and
       Popular Control of Public Policy:  The Case of the 1966 House Elec-
       tions."  AMERICAN POLITICAL SCIENCE REVIEW  66 (December
       1972):  1256–68.

       This essay examines two conditions of the linkage process
       between public opinion and public policy to explain why the
       linkage appears to be so weak.  The conditions are that op-
       posing candidates for the same position must differ in their
       issue-related attitudes; and the winner's policy positions after
       the election must be consistent with preelection perceptions.

420    Truman, David B.  THE GOVERNMENTAL PROCESS.  New York:
       Alfred A. Knopf, 1951.  544 p.

       This is a classic study of the role of interest groups in the
       American political process.  Reviewers have called it indis-
       pensable for an understanding of group theory.

421  Tubbesing, Carl D. "Predicting the Present: Realigning Elections and Redistributive Policies." POLITY 7 (Summer 1975): 478-503.

> Policy analysis and party realignment theory come together in the development of a view regarding realigning elections and the likely shape of our politics, policies, and parties. In place of periodic realignment, the author sees a series of intense elections with substantial switches.

422  Waterman, Nan. "A Creative Partnership of Government and Citizens." NATIONAL CIVIC REVIEW 67 (February 1978): 71-75.

> Citizens have become increasingly responsible in their efforts to influence public policy; government has become more responsive to their suggestions. Involvement by citizens in the governmental process aids decision making in bringing changes which are mutually desirable. Creative citizen participation involves citizens at appropriate levels, such as allowing them to determine goals and priorities which have impact on their futures.

# Chapter 4

# STATE AND LOCAL POLICY PROCESSES

423    Ball, Carolyn L.; Beyle, Thad L.; and Williams, Oliver. "Science, State Government, and Federalism: A Case Study." PUBLIUS 3 (Spring 1973): 109-36.

A study of the North Carolina Board of Science and Technology, its goals, objectives, biases, and successes in supporting research and development activities in the state, is given. The authors conclude that despite the scientific nature of the policy area, the decisions of the board are primarily political, involving the patronage process.

424    Barnett, Richard R., and Topham, Neville. "Evaluating the Distribution of Local Outputs in a Decentralized Structure of Government." POLICY AND POLITICS 6 (September 1977): 51-70.

A structure of government that is decentralized reflects the fact that individuals in society have national and local interests. Although local governments act on behalf of the local citizenry, their actions have spillover effects beyond the local level.

425    Brooks, James. "State Lotteries: Profits and Problems." STATE GOVERNMENT 48 (Winter 1975): 23-31.

Criticisms of state lotteries include unhappiness with the revenues produced and the costs of producing them. While advocates and opponents debate the merits of lotteries, psychological factors affecting their attractiveness must also be considered if the desired amounts of revenue are to be realized.

426    Brosz, Allyn, and Morgan, David R. IMPROVING MUNICIPAL PRODUCTIVITY. Norman: University of Oklahoma, Bureau of Government Research, 1977. 58 p.

This is a self-help guide for local government officers interested in improving productivity levels but lacking the necessary technical help.

427    Caldwell, Kenneth S. "Efficiency and Effectiveness Measurement in State and Local Government." GOVERNMENTAL FINANCE 2 (November 1973): 19-26.

In June 1972, the U.S. General Accounting Office issued
standards and guidelines for the audit of governmental programs and activities. While the guidelines state that GAO
is interested in efficiency and effectiveness, they do not indicate how a local unit is to meet the standards.

428    Cho, Yong Myo, and Frederickson, H. George. DETERMINANTS OF
PUBLIC POLICY IN THE AMERICAN STATES: A MODEL FOR SYN-
THESIS. Sage Professional Papers in Administrative and Policy Studies.
Beverly Hills, Calif.: Sage, 1973. 55 p.

This study tries to identify patterns of relationships between
socioeconomic and political variables and state policy outcomes.
The authors find that tax and expenditure outcomes are better
explained by economic and social factors, while changes in
tax and spending levels are explained by political factors.

429    Clarke, Susan E. "Determinants of State Growth Management Policies."
POLICY STUDIES JOURNAL 7 (Summer 1979): 753–62.

States adopt growth management policies because of the magni-
tude, urgency, and character of pressures in this area.
Clarke finds that states with growth policies that differ from
traditional patterns are more likely to adopt such policies
than are more traditional states.

430    Coke, James G., and Brown, Steven R. "Public Attitudes about Land
Use Policy and Their Impact on State Policy-Makers." PUBLIUS 6
(Winter 1976): 97–134.

Results from an Ohio study, confirmed in six additional states,
show public opinion toward state land use regulation to be
aggregated around two major attitudes: environmental versus
local interests. Policymakers are basically in agreement with
the environmental position but are constrained by intra-agency
rivalries and apprehension about public opinion.

431    Connery, Robert H., and Benjamin, Gerald, eds. "Governing New
York State: The Rockefeller Years." PROCEEDINGS OF THE ACA-
DEMY OF POLITICAL SCIENCE 31 (May 1974): entire issue.

Eleven essays of varying length on the policy issues important
during Rockefeller's years as governor. Included are essays
on finance, higher education, social welfare, public employee
labor relations, health care, housing, prison reform, transportation, education, narcotics addition, and environmental
protection.

432    Cowing, Thomas G., and Holtman, A.G. THE ECONOMICS OF LOCAL
PUBLIC SERVICE CONSOLIDATION. Lexington, Mass.: Lexington
Books, 1976. 166 p.

The authors examine the economic theory that deals with the
efficient provision of local public services. After a theoretical
framework is developed, case studies, a summary of the
economic analysis, and the policy implications are presented.

433 Crenson, Matthew. "Organizational Factors in Citizen Participation." JOURNAL OF POLITICS 36 (May 1974): 356-78.

>This is a comparative study of community organizations in one city that examines the relationships between the internal characteristics of such groups and their relative inability to generate political demands on behalf of their constituency. Intraorganizational conflict was found to be an important obstacle to the production of demands.

434 Danziger, James N., and Dutton, William H. "Technological Innovation in Local Government: The Case of Computers." POLICY AND POLITICS 6 (September 1977): 27-49.

>A theoretical framework for the analysis of technological innovation within a political setting is provided. Four types of factors help to explain innovative decisions: (1) aspects of the technology's environment that make it worthwhile; (2) the presence of factors facilitating the use of the technology; (3) interests and values served by the technology; and (4) the distribution of control over decisions regarding the innovation.

435 Dawson, Richard, and Robinson, James. "Inter-Party Competition, Economic Variables, and Welfare Policies in the American States." JOURNAL OF POLITICS 25 (February 1963): 265-89.

>This paper seeks to discover the relationship among interparty competition, certain economic factors, and the extent of public welfare policies. The general concern is to investigate the relationship between political processes and policies adopted by the states.

436 Dye, Thomas R. "Executive Powers and Public Policy in the States." WESTERN POLITICAL QUARTERLY 22 (December 1969): 926-39.

>The article explores linkages between structural characteristics of the states and the content of public decisions. Consistent with his other work in this area, Dye finds that economic development levels are more influential determinants of policy outcomes than are political structures.

437 _____. "Malapportionment and Public Policy in the States." JOURNAL OF POLITICS 27, no.3 (1965): 586-601.

>A general assumption among political scientists is that malapportionment can be expected to have an impact on state policies. However, Dye concludes that policies of malapportioned legislatures are not significantly different from the policy choices of well-apportioned legislatures.

438 _____. POLITICS, ECONOMICS, AND THE PUBLIC: POLICY OUTCOMES IN THE AMERICAN STATES. Chicago: Rand McNally and Co., 1966. 374 p.

Dye seeks to account for policy differences in the states in education, welfare, taxation, and the regulation of public morals using urbanization, industrialization, wealth, and the level of adult education as variables. He concludes that political characteristics have little independent effect upon policy while economic developments shape political systems and outcomes.

439    Fairbanks, David. "Politics, Economics, and the Public Morality: Why Some States Are More 'Moral' Than Others." POLICY STUDIES JOURNAL  7 (Summer 1979): 714-21.

Interstate differences in morality policies are better explained by religious culture than by economic development measures. Political factors act as intervening variables and affect the types of morality policies a state pursues.

440    Finz, Samuel A. "Productivity Analysis: Its Use in Local Government." GOVERNMENTAL FINANCE  2 (November 1973): 29-33.

Successful implementation of a productivity measurement program can fill a gap that might otherwise have been filled by a planning-programming-budgeting system.

441    Frederickson, H. George, and Cho, Yong Hyo. "Legislative Apportionment and Fiscal Policy in the American States." WESTERN POLITICAL QUARTERLY  27 (March 1974): 5-37.

The authors enter the debate as to whether or not types of legislative apportionment are an indicator of policy behavior or fiscal behavior. They find that legislative apportionment affects the distribution process but not the actual size of a state's budget.

442    Game, Kingsley W. "Controlling Air Pollution: Why Some States Try Harder." POLICY STUDIES JOURNAL  7 (Summer 1979): 728-38.

The main influences on state spending for air pollution control were the ability to delegate effort to lower government levels, the level of bureaucratization in the state, energy plenty, and crowding. These factors were more important than were actual levels of pollution.

443    Gary, Lawrence E. "Policy Dimensions in the Aid to Families with Dependent Children Programs: A Comparative State Analysis." JOURNAL OF POLITICS  35 (November 1973): 886-923.

When comparing policy decision outside the budgetary process, political variables play an important role in predicting the outcome of welfare policy decisions.

444    Gibson, Lay James. "Local Impact Analysis: An Arizona Case Study." ARIZONA REVIEW  24 (January 1975): 1-10.

Economic base analysis and input—output analysis provide an indication of the employment or income that will be generated within a community by new investment. Input-output analysis provides more detail than economic base analysis and is able to determine sectoral multipliers.

445 Gray, Virginia. "Expenditures and Innovation as Dimensions of 'Progressivism': A Note on the American States." AMERICAN JOUR-NAL OF POLITICAL SCIENCE 18 (November 1974): 693-99.

Data from 1938 to 1969 show that expenditures for education are independent of welfare spending and innovation in one area seems independent of innovation in the other.

446 _____. "Innovation in the States: A Diffusion Study." AMERICAN POLITICAL SCIENCE REVIEW 67 (December 1973): 1174-85.

Innovations were studied in education, welfare, and civil rights. Diffusion patterns differ by issue area and by the level of federal involvement. While political and economic explanations do help to determine which states are first in adopting new policies, innovativeness is issue and time specific.

447 _____. "Models of Comparative State Politics: A Comparison of Cross-Sectional and Time Series Analysis." AMERICAN JOURNAL OF POLITICAL SCIENCE 20 (May 1976): 235-56.

"Competitive threat" and "economic resources" models are developed to determine if cross—sectional analysis of inter-state policy variations are adequate to explain the dynamics of the policy process.

448 Griffin, Kenyon N., and Shelton, Robert B. "Coal Severance Tax in the Rocky Mountain States." POLICY STUDIES JOURNAL 7 (Autumn 1978): 29-40.

The essay examines the coal severance tax policies of the six coal exporting states in the Rocky Mountain area and analyzes the context of each state's ability to export the tax burden to out-of-state consumers.

449 Grupp, Fred W., and Richards, Alan R. "Variations in Elite Percep-tions of American States as Referents for Public Policy-Making." AMERICAN POLITICAL SCIENCE REVIEW 49 (September 1975): 850-58.

State executives are more likely to take policy cues from effective state agencies than from "less worthy" ones, or from emulating other executives.

450 Harrar, William S., and Bawden, D. Lee. "The Use of Experimenta-tion in Policy Formulation and Analysis." URBAN AFFAIRS QUARTER-LY 7 (June 1972): 419-30.

Based on the New Jersey negative income tax experiment, an effort to extend the formal use of experimentation to the testing of the designs of national programs, this paper discusses the prospects for large-scale experimentation in social public policy.

451  Hatry, Harry P. "Applications of Productivity Measurment in Local Government." GOVERNMENTAL FINANCE 2 (November 1973): 6-11.

There are at least four areas where productivity measurements are useful to local governments: cost reduction, managerial control, program and policy formulation, and the development of employee incentives.

452  _____. "State of PPBS in State and Local Governments in the United States." POLICY SCIENCES 2 (June 1971): 177-89.

Most of the concern with implementing PPBS at the state and local levels has been with the structural aspects of the idea. The major obstacle of implementation to date has been the lack of quality analytical staffs in state and local government.

453  Hedlund, Ronald D., and Hamm, Keith E. "Institutional Innovation and Performance Effectiveness in Public Policy Making." In LEGISLATIVE REFORM, THE POLICY IMPACT, edited by Leroy N. Rieselbach, pp. 117-32. Lexington, Mass.: Lexington Books, 1978.

The authors look at the effect of institutional innovation on policymaking performance in the Wisconsin State Assembly from 1971 through 1974. Institutional innovations affected productivity and expeditiousness and the substance of public policy.

454  Heiss, William F. "The Politics of Local Government Policy Evaluation, Some Observations." URBAN ANALYSIS 5 (May 1978): 37-45.

This article explores some of the politics of evaluation at the local government level and suggests that policy and program evaluation may be constrained by problems unique to this level of government.

455  Hofferbert, Richard I. "Ecological Development and Policy Change in the American States." MIDWEST JOURNAL OF POLITICAL SCIENCE 10 (November 1966): 464-83.

The American states are becoming increasingly similar to one another along ecological lines. Narrowing the gap between them serves to reduce the pressures in certain basic policy areas for those states which have trailed in the provision of expected basic services.

456  _____. "Elite Influence in State Policy Formation: A Model for Comparative Inquiry." POLITY 2 (Spring 1970): 316-44.

A model using concepts from the urban power studies is developed to explain the complexities of the policy process. Utilizing the model might be difficult, yet we stand to gain much by studying the states comparatively.

457 _____. "The Relationship between Public Policy and Some Structural and Environmental Variables in the American States." AMERICAN POLITICAL SCIENCE REVIEW 60 (March 1966): 73–82.

Differences in policy are more readily explained in terms of differences in socioeconomic environments of the states than by an examination of political structure variables.

458 Hopkins, Anne H. "Opinion Publics and Support for Public Policy in the American States." AMERICAN JOURNAL OF POLITICAL SCIENCE 18 (February 1974): 167–78.

Hopkins examines the linkage between public opinion and public policy in the American states. Nine policy areas at two points in time, and the opinions of four publics, are included in the analysis.

459 Hutcheson, John D., Jr., and Taylor, George A. "Religious Variables, Political System Characteristics, and Policy Outputs in the American States." AMERICAN JOURNAL OF POLITICAL SCIENCE 17 (May 1973): 414–21.

This study takes issue with the finding that economic characteristics are the only important antecedents of state public policy outputs. It concludes that political system, cultural, and social characteristics may be just as important.

460 Jennings, Edward T., Jr. "Civil Turmoil and the Growth of State Welfare Rolls: A Comparative State Policy Analysis." POLICY STUDIES JOURNAL 7 (Summer 1979): 739–45.

This article assesses the effects of urban riots, the creation of community action agencies, and unemployment levels upon relief rolls in the American states. The level of urban rioting was linked to increased recipient rates, but spending for community action was not.

461 Karnig, Albert K., and Siegelman, Lee. "State Legislative Reform and Public Policy, Another Look." WESTERN POLITICAL QUARTERLY 28 (September 1975): 548–52.

Are reformed legislatures more innovative, and do they spend at higher levels than their unreformed counterparts? Controlling for political culture and socioeconomic development effects, state legislative reform makes little independent contribution in accounting for public policy differences.

462 Kirk, Frank A. "State Policy Issues in New Towns and Large-Scale Developments." PUBLIC ADMINISTRATION REVIEW 35 (May–June 1975): 246–49.

The governance system of new towns is typically fragmented
and competitive. Local governments are professionally under-
staffed and indecisive. State government policymaking tends
to be functionally specialized and short term.

463  Kirkpatrick, Samuel A. "Multidimensional Aspects of Local Political
Systems: A Conceptual Approach to Public Policy." WESTERN POLI-
TICAL QUARTERLY 23 (December 1970): 808-28.

This is an attempt to categorize theory building about local
political systems. A conceptual scheme is developed that
asks questions about the local system in the context of the
ends of that system.

464  Kirkpatrick, Samuel A.; Morgan, David R.; and Lyons, William.
"Municipal Training Needs and Personnel Practices: Implications for
Program Planning and Policy Making." MIDWEST REVIEW OF PUBLIC
ADMINISTRATION 8 (January 1974): 3-16.

This is a report on Oklahoma's efforts to improve the quality
of public service delivery. The article addresses the use
of the Intergovernmental Personnel Act (1970) funds with respect to training needs.

465  Klass, Gary M. "The Determination of Policy and Politics in the
American States, 1948-1974." POLICY STUDIES JOURNAL 7
(Summer 1979): 745-52.

Short-term changes in policy performance have a greater
effect on partisan control than partisan control has on policy
performance. Changes in partisan control are of consequence
in defining short-term change in budget priorities.

466  Koehler, Cortus T. "Policy Development and Legislative Oversight
in Council-Manager Cities: An Information and Communications Analysis." PUBLIC ADMINISTRATION REVIEW 33 (September-October
1973): 433-42.

Using aspects of cybernetic analysis, this study focuses on
the legislative oversight process in council-manager cities.
While the tools for legislative oversight are readily available,
the public elects too few council persons with the desire to
use the tools.

467  Kraemer, Kenneth. POLICY ANALYSIS IN LOCAL GOVERNMENT.
Municipal Management Series. Washington, D.C.: International City
Management Association, 1973. 165 p.

This volume is devoted to the concepts and principles, tools
and techniques, and strengths and weaknesses of policy analysis in local government.

468  Landy, Marc K. THE POLITICS OF ENVIRONMENTAL REFORM:
CONTROLLING KENTUCKY STRIP MINING. Baltimore: Johns Hopkins
Press, 1976. 400 p.

This is a study of the development and administration of strip mining regulations in Kentucky from 1946 to 1972. Specific policy concerns are integrated with general political developments. He demonstrates the wide range of impacts that a seemingly narrow technical case study can provide.

469    Lazarus, Irma. "Nurturing the Life of the Spirit: A Report on State Art Councils." STATE GOVERNMENT 48 (Winter 1975): 18-22.

Arts institutions have been playing an increasingly significant role as instruments for social change and economic health in their communities. Some states are taking an aggressive stance in supporting the arts via much innovative programming.

470    Lee, Robert D., Jr., and Staffeldt, Raymond J. "Executive and Legislative Use of Policy Analysis in the State Budgetary Process: Survey Results." POLICY ANALYSIS 3 (Summer 1977): 395-405.

Policy analysis by state budget officers have increased since 1970. Budget officers now conduct effectiveness analysis and productivity analysis. The executive branch has a considerable lead over the legislature in using and applying analysis for policymaking.

471    Lyden, Fremont J., and Miller, Ernest G. "Policy Perspectives of the Northwest City Manager, 1966-1974: Continuity or Change?" ADMINISTRATION AND SOCIETY 8 (February 1977): 469-80.

While a larger percentage of city managers interviewed in 1974 were willing to initiate policy in general policy and budgetary matters then in 1966, many managers felt that neutrality was desirable when community support was evenly divided on an issue.

472    Mahajan, Vijay, and Haynes, Kingsley E. "Modeling the Diffusion of Public Policy Innovations Among the U.S. States." SOCIO-ECONOMIC PLANNING SCIENCES 11, no. 5 (1977): 259-63.

This article describes and validates a model that explains public policy innovation diffusions among the U.S. states. The model identifies when new policies are likely to be infused into a state and how long it is likely to take.

473    Mead, Lawrence M. "Institutional Analysis for State and Local Government." PUBLIC ADMINISTRATION REVIEW 39 (January-February 1979): 26-30.

Institutional analysis is a way of studying the administrative and political factors that affect the implementation of government programs. The need for this type of work may be the greatest at state and local governmental levels where fiscal constraints have left bureaucratic reorganization as the best hope for improving program performance.

474    Mollenkopf, John, and Pynoos, Jon. "Property, Politics, and Local Housing Policy." POLITICS AND SOCIETY 2 (Summer 1972): 407-32.

The authors look at economic and political power and their effects on the housing of Cambridge, Massachusetts, residents. With 6 percent of the households controlling 70 percent of the housing units, policies have been adopted favoring large property owning interests.

475   Morehouse, Sarah McCally. "The State Political Party and the Policy-Making Process." AMERICAN POLITICAL SCIENCE REVIEW 67 (March 1973): 55-72.

Variations in the structure of political parties can account for variations in the types of policy produced. The article reports on conditions under which legislators of the governor's party supported his legislative requests in sixteen legislative sessions.

476   Morgan, David R., and Kirkpatrick, Samuel A. "Policy Variations, Political Recruitment, and Suburban Social Rank, A Comparative Analysis." SOCIOLOGICAL QUARTERLY 11 (Fall 1970): 452-62.

The authors are concerned with the social characteristics of suburban political officials, attitude variations among officials, and differences in land-use patterns in the suburbs of Oklahoma City, Philadelphia, and St. Louis. Variations in social rank are found to be associated with differences in policy orientations and outcomes.

477   "National Municipal Management Policy." PUBLIC MANAGEMENT 55 (September 1973): 4-35.

This article reports on the activities of five International City Management Association municipal management committees. The reports are concerned with growth management, human resource management, quality local government, regionalism, and federal block grant programs.

478   Riley, Dennis D. "Party Competition and State Policy Making: The Need for a Reexamination." WESTERN POLITICAL QUARTERLY 24 (September 1971): 514-26.

The methodology used to establish the finding that party competition has little effect on policy outcome is faulty and needs to be reexamined. The measures of party competition have serious weaknesses, and the policy output measures used are inappropriate to test the relationship between competitiveness and policymaking.

479   Romans, Neil T. "The Role of State Supreme Courts in Judicial Policy Making: Escobedo, Miranda, and the Use of Judicial Impact Analysis." WESTERN POLITICAL QUARTERLY 27 (March 1974): 38-59.

Romans focuses on the reactions of state supreme courts to the Miranda and Escobedo decisions. It provides empirical data on the impact of these decisions on state courts, the level of support for implementing these decisions, and the liberalism or conservatism of state courts.

480    Rose, Douglas D.  "National and Local Forces in State Politics:  The Implications of Multi-Level Policy Analysis."  AMERICAN POLITICAL SCIENCE REVIEW  67 (December 1973):  1162-73.

The use of single-level analysis in studying U.S. politics severely distorts the results.  The extent of the distortion suggests that relations among the states and between the states and federal governments are the prime determinants of state policy.

481    Savas, E.S. "Policy Analysis for Local Government:  Public vs. Private Refuse Collection."  POLICY ANALYSIS  3 (Winter 1977):  49-74.

This study identifies the prevalence and comparative efficiency of different organizational arrangements used to provide refuse collection services in U.S. metropolitan areas.  Private firms under contract to the city are significantly more efficient than is collection by municipal agencies.

482    Schmandt, Henry.  "Municipal Decentralization:  An Overview."  In URBAN ADMINISTRATION, MANAGEMENT, POLITICS, AND CHANGE, edited by Alan E. Dent and Ralph A. Rossum, pp. 287-315.  Port Washington, N.Y.:  Kennikat Press, 1976.

This essay is primarily concerned with decentralization of urban governmental functions.  Schmandt concludes that the form decentralization will take depends on such factors as population size, territorial boundaries, community needs, and financial ability.

483    Schneider, Mark, and Swinton, David.  "Policy Analysis in State and Local Government."  PUBLIC ADMINISTRATION REVIEW  39 (January-February 1979):  12-16.

A specific focus on state and local government in developing policy analysis methods is important.  The political and social environments of state and local governments are different enough from the federal level to warrant separate consideration and development.

484    Schnore, Leo, and Alford, Robert.  "Forms of Government and Socio-economic Characteristics of Suburbs."  ADMINISTRATIVE SCIENCE QUARTERLY  8 (June 1963):  1-17.

Three hundred U.S. suburbs are classified according to commission, council-manager, and mayor-council forms of government.  It is suggested that socioeconomic characteristics may partly determine political structure.

485    Scism, Thomas E.  "Public Opinion and Public Policy Decisions in Small Cities:  A Case Study."  SOCIAL SCIENCE QUARTERLY  52 (June 1971):  204-10.

The article attempts to determine what links exist between government decisions and public opinion at the local level.  No specific individual or group was able to persuade the council to avoid a decision.  Rather each councilman's assessment of the public mood determined his vote on a water flouridation issue.

486     Sharkansky, Ira. "Government Expenditures and Public Services in the American States." AMERICAN POLITICAL SCIENCE REVIEW 61 (December 1967): 1066-77.

      Tests the assumption that the amount of money spent in a jurisdiction indicates the nature of the services provided. It defines state relationships between measures of spending and measures of public services as it examines these relationships over time to discover if increases in spending are likely to bring about increases in the quality or quantity of public services.

487     Sharkansky, Ira, and Hofferbert, Richard I. "Dimensions of State Politics, Economics, and Public Policy." AMERICAN POLITICAL SCIENCE REVIEW 63 (September 1969): 867-79.

      Different social and economic characteristics have different relevance for public policies, and their relevance varies among substantive areas of public policy. Central features of state politics are important for some policies, even when socioeconomic variations are controlled.

488     Shepard, W. Bruce. "Participation in Local Policy Making: The Case of Referenda." SOCIAL SCIENCE QUARTERLY 56 (June 1975): 55-70.

      Using data from 470 referenda elections at the local level in the United States, Shepard rejects the alienated voter model. The data support conclusions based on participation rate differences for different socioeconomic strata and on rational computations with regard to voting utility.

489     Sherman, Joel D. "Financing Local Schools: The Impact of Desegregation." POLICY STUDIES JOURNAL 7 (Summer 1979): 701-7.

      School desegregation was accompanied by increased disparities in tax rates and local revenues between white and black school districts. During the desegregation period, the racial composition of the school districts and school board fiscal dependence became the major determinants of school districts' tax efforts.

490     Silverman, Eli B., and Gatti, Francis C., Jr. "PPB on the State Level: The Case of Pennsylvania." BUREAUCRAT 4 (July 1975): 117-46.

      While PPB has disappeared at the federal level, it appears to be alive and well at state and local levels. This paper assesses the extent to which Pennsylvania has operationalized its PPB goals.

491     Stonecash, Jeff. "Local Policy Analysis and Autonomy: On Intergovernmental Relations and Theory Specification." COMPARATIVE URBAN RESEARCH 5, no.2 (1978): 5-23.

This paper is concerned with basic theoretical conceptualization of external impacts on local public policy. It discusses
the comparative problem imposed by external constraints and
their impact on local policymaking processes.

492    Stowe, Eric, and Rehfuss, John. "Federal New Towns Policy:
'Muddling Through' at the Local Level." PUBLIC ADMINISTRATION
REVIEW 35 (May–June 1975): 222–28.

While Title VII of the Urban Growth and New Community
Act of 1970 seeks to motivate private investment in new
community development, one of the side effects is the increased demand for public services that the community places
on governmental units in its area.

493    Taube, Gerald, and Levin, Jack. "Public Housing as Neighborhood:
The Effect of Local and Non-Local Participation." SOCIAL SCIENCE
QUARTERLY 52 (December 1971): 534–42.

Interviews with 525 public housing tenants show that both
local and nonlocal social participation enhances positive attitudes and behavior orientations toward public housing as
neighborhood.

494    Von Stroh, Gordon E. "Decentralization of Local Affairs: Making
Government More Responsive." NATIONAL CIVIC REVIEW 67 (October
1978): 402–6.

Governmental responsiveness requires citizen involvement in
decision making. Neighborhood decentralization is intended
to provide greater resources to citizens and to recognize
differing local needs in the delivery of services.

495    Walker, Jack L. "The Diffusion of Innovation among the American
States." AMERICAN POLITICAL SCIENCE REVIEW 63 (September
1969): 880–99.

This is an exercise in theory building to develop propositions
to be used as guides to the study of the diffusion of innovation.
The article explains the adoption of innovation using the literature of decision making, reference group theory, and the diffusion of innovations.

496    Whisler, Marilyn W. "Growth Management Strategies: Population Policy
Implementation by Local Governments." POLICY STUDIES JOURNAL
6 (Winter 1977): 208–17.

Formulation of population distribution alternatives has occurred
because of dissatisfaction with traditional regulatory techniques.
Local governments are adopting a more individualized regulation of development and are encouraging the provision of public
amenities in connection with construction activity.

497    White, Michelle. "Self-Interest in the Suburbs: The Trend Toward
No-Growth Zoning." POLICY ANALYSIS 4 (Spring 1978): 185–203.

Under the no-growth banner, suburban communities have been passing zoning ordinances that restrict the building of new housing. This practice is contrasted with the older practice of exclusionary zoning, discusses some incentives that might account for the change, and suggests policy measures to reverse the no-growth trend.

498    Wholey, Joseph S. "Using Performance Measures in Long-Range Planning and Policy Formulation." BUREAUCRAT 5 (April 1976): 65-86.

Wholey describes the efforts of Arlington, Virginia, to agree on long-range objectives and to realize what kinds of public and private actions are required to meet goals.

499    Wolfinger, Raymond W. "Non-Decisions and the Study of Local Politics." AMERICAN POLITICAL SCIENCE REVIEW 65 (September 1971): 1063-1104.

The impracticality of research on nondecisions is not a setback for political science because most of the component ideas are being studied without reference to nondecision ideas. Judged by its utility for empirical research, the idea of nondecisions appears to be superfluous.

500    Wright, Ward J. "Building the Capacities of Municipal Governments." PUBLIC ADMINISTRATION REVIEW 35 (December 1975): 748-54.

The processes used in making and managing policy in municipal affairs are about the same today as they were twenty years ago. In order to provide an incentive for trying new ways of doing things, the federal government should concentrate on reducing the risks for local officials who choose to undertake new approaches to policymaking.

501    Yarmolinsky, Adam. "How Good Was the Answer? How Good Was The Question?" In CONTROVERSIES AND DECISIONS: THE SOCIAL SCIENCE AND PUBLIC POLICY, edited by Charles Frankel, pp. 259-72. New York: Russell Sage Foundation, 1976.

Social science research is a potentially helpful tool for policymakers, but policymakers must be more open to what the university has to offer and scholars must become more aware of the constraints within which policymakers operate.

# Chapter 5

# URBAN POLICY

502 Ashley, Thomas L. "A New Urban Growth Strategy for the United States." URBAN AND SOCIAL CHANGE REVIEW 4 (Spring 1971): 50-53.

> Representative Ashley (D-Ohio), who played a major role in writing the urban growth and new communities development title of the Housing and Urban Development Act of 1970, calls for the establishment of a national urban growth policy. His emphasis is on greater regional planning and development as opposed to national planning.

503 Averch, Harvey, and Levine, Robert A. "Two Models of the Urban Crisis: An Analytical Essay on Banfield and Forrester." POLICY SCIENCES 2 (June 1971): 143-58.

> This essay examines the arguments and evidence used in two recent models of the urban crisis--Edward C. Banfield's THE UNHEAVENLY CITY (1970) and Jay W. Forrester's URBAN DYNAMICS (1969). Both imply that not much can be done to alleviate urban problems and that positive programs may make them worse. The authors of this critique contend that the evidence is inadequate to support the implication. They advocate that promising current programs be refined on the basis of evidence and experience and that policymakers continue to search for efficient new programs through social experiments.

504 Bachrach, Peter. "A Power Analysis: The Shaping of Anti-Poverty Policy in Baltimore." PUBLIC POLICY 18 (Winter 1970): 155-86.

> The article analyzes two periods of struggle between ghetto residents and white leaders. In 1966-67, the system effectively precluded serious resolution of ghetto issues; in 1968-69, access to decision making was more open. Two reasons are given: (1) unification and militancy of black community; (2) federally funded programs gave blacks sources of power.

505 Baer, William C. "On the Death of Cities." PUBLIC INTEREST, no. 45 (Fall 1976), pp. 3-19.

Neighborhood death in U.S. cities is becoming a reality. It can be delayed by numerous intercessions but it will come. Baer's purpose is to open the issue to discussion. He suggests that resources be allocated with some regard to cost-effectiveness, but that enough slack exist to hold out the hope of aid to those whose cases could not meet a cost-benefit analysis.

506    Baines, Tyrone R. "Categorical Grants and the Local Community:  The Delivery of Relocation Services." PUBLIUS 5 (Fall 1975):  101-22.

This article is concerned with the macro-approach of grant consolidation as a means of correcting some inadequacies of categorical grants. From the perspective of clients of four relocation assistance programs, Baines finds that important facilitative roles are played by third-party groups, such as civic-motivated and profit-motivated groups.

507    Banfield, Edward C.  "A Critical View of the Urban Crisis." ANNALS OF THE AMERICAN ACADEMY OF POLITICAL AND SOCIAL SCIENCE 405 (January 1973):  7-14.

Typical accounts of urban crisis are not satisfactory. Changes in the state of the public mind are main causes of the "crises." Set in motion by ideas of philosophers, their ideas involve authority, self, rational, egotism, hedonism, egalitarianism, consumerism. Thus, crisis will not be ended by government programs.

508    Barro, Stephen M.  THE URBAN IMPACT OF FEDERAL POLICIES: THEIR DIRECT AND INDIRECT EFFECTS ON THE LOCAL PUBLIC SECTOR. Rand Paper P-5793. Santa Monica, Calif.:  Rand Corporation, 1977.  39 p.

A study is being undertaken to survey what is known about the impacts on the urban economy of a broad array of federal programs and policies. The study has two closely related purposes. The first is to construct a conceptual framework for analyzing effects of federal actions on the cities. The second purpose is to determine from selective reviews of the relevant literature (1) what is known about each of the major linkages in the network, and (2) where there are significant gaps in existing information about policy effects. The present paper outlines the conceptual approach, demonstrates how the framework can be used to examine the effects of federal policies on specific urban outcomes, and sketches some potential applications of the approach to the development of federal urban policy.

509    Beaton, W. Patrick, and Cox, James L.  "Toward an Accidental National Urbanization Policy." JOURNAL OF THE AMERICAN INSTITUTE OF PLANNERS  43 (January 1977):  54-61.

Federal domestic policy has been a major contributor to national redistribution of population and commerce through various programs. Recent programs support a new settlement pattern of extensive rural development through the allocation of nonmetropolitan grant money. This support underwrites

the changing trend of population growth from metropolitan
to nonmetropolitan counties. Many of these allocations tend
to favor unincorporated areas of rural counties which often
lack legal controls and land use management. Valuable rural
lands are subject to exploitation instead of being controlled
as a scarce resource.

510 Beckman, Norman. "National Urban Growth Policy: 1974 Congressional and Executive Action." JOURNAL OF THE AMERICAN IN-
STITUTE OF PLANNERS 41 (July 1975): 234-49.

A summary of federal action in the areas of mass transportation, highways, health planning, elementary and secondary
education, social services, and others.

511 Bergsman, Joel, and Wiener, Howard L., eds. URBAN PROBLEMS
AND POLICY CHOICES. New York: Praeger Publishers, 1975.
346 p.

This volume is an outgrowth of a symposium on urban growth
and development sponsored by the Washington Operations Research Council and the Urban Institute in Washington, D.C.,
April 1973. The seventeen papers include urban research
and policymaking; the delivery of public services; social and
political urban process models; the impact of public policies
on urban markets; urban land use and transportation; and
environmental goals and urban development.

512 Bingham, Richard D. "The Diffusion of Innovation among Local Governments." URBAN AFFAIRS QUARTERLY 13 (December 1977): 223-32.

Bingham's conclusion to his study is that innovation is issue
specific. In general, there are no innovative or noninnova-
tive cities.

513 _____. "Innovations in Urban Governments: A Preliminary Model."
In THE NEW URBAN POLITICS, edited by Louis H. Masotti and
Robert L. Lineberry, pp. 135-46. Cambridge, Mass.: Ballinger, 1976.

There is an inherent risk to political innovation, a risk not
found in later policies built on the experience of the innovators.
Bureaucratic innovation is a change in process, organization,
or product leading to the actual public service output of local
government. Innovation adoptions are predictable phenomena,
at least as long as incentives are presented to decision makers.
Political innovations are influenced directly by the community
environment, while bureaucratic innovations are not. The
complex interrelationships between public policy, intergovernmental relations and assistance, and output feedback appear
to determine bureaucratic innovation, with the community environment influencing adoptions only indirectly.

514 Bloomberg, Warner, Jr., and Schmandt, Henry J., eds. POWER,
POVERTY, AND URBAN POLICY. Urban Affairs Annual Reviews,
vol. 2. Beverly Hills, Calif.: Sage, 1968. 604 p.

Topics include: affluence and poverty; urban institutions and the deprived; poverty and power; and knowledge, poverty, and power.

515    Boyce, David E. "Toward a Framework for Defining and Applying Urban Indicators in Planning." URBAN AFFAIRS QUARTERLY 6 (December 1970): 145-72.

Two questions surrounding urban indicators and applications to urban planners are: (1) what indicators are important; (2) how can they be applied in preparing and evaluating plans. This paper presents some findings and analyses concerning a general framework relating urban indicators to forecasts, studies, and criteria.

516    Brewer, Garry. POLITICIANS, BUREAUCRATS AND THE CONSULTANT: A CRITIQUE OF URBAN PROBLEM SOLVING. New York: Basic Books, 1973. 291 p.

A study of the pitfalls and potential in the use of sophisticated methods of problem solving, especially as applied by consultants. The author interviewed persons concerned with the design of urban renewal programs in Pittsburgh and San Francisco and examined the computer simulation models on which the designs were based. He explains why the results were disastrous, with a strong emphasis on the theoretical basis for what happened.

517    Brewer, Garry D., and Hall, Owen P. "Policy Analysis by Computer Simulation: The Need for Appraisal." PUBLIC POLICY 21 (Summer 1973): 343-66.

If existing trends in the computer simulation of social policy continue, they will have harmful effects for the method of problem-solving processes in broader social contexts. Clear and concise standards to assess simulations must be developed. The authors develop several questions, sketch out a model, and apply it to Jay Forrester's URBAN DYNAMICS (1969).

518    Brown, F. Gerald, and Murphy, Thomas P., eds. EMERGING PATTERNS IN URBAN ADMINISTRATION. Lexington, Mass.: Lexington Books, 1970. 196 p.

The essays and discussions in this book are built around two basic issues: the need to develop an effective synthesis of theory relevant to urban administration, and the need to deal with the continuing gap between the state-of-the-art academically and the state-of-the-art as practiced by working professionals. The theme of the book is how we can get things done in our cities.

519    Bryan, Frank M. "Does the Town Meeting Offer an Option for Urban America?" NATIONAL CIVIC REVIEW 64 (December 1978): 523-27.

The town meeting has resurfaced as a popular idea in order to allow for greater citizen access to government. This essay questions their applicability as a policy-setting device for urban and rural America.

520 Bryant, Stephen. "The Dimensions of Reformism in Urban Policy Analysis." URBAN AFFAIRS QUARTERLY 12 (September 1976): 117-24.

Urban policy research results have been inconclusive about determining the effect which the form of government has on reform. Data on the type of governmental structure for all U.S. cities over twenty-five thousand in population were collected and subjected to a series of tests using Guttman scaling and factor analysis to examine the dimensions of reformism. Two distinctive characteristics of reformism are revealed: the allocation of executive power in the reform system and matters that concern the council exclusively. The independent effects of each dimension on policy formulation and outputs must be studied, rather than treating reformism as a unitary variable.

521 Browne, Edmund, Jr., and Rehfuss, John. "Policy Evaluation, Citizen Participation, and Revenue Sharing in Aurora, Illinois." PUBLIC ADMINISTRATION REVIEW 35 (March-April 1975): 150-57.

Any major innovation in American intergovernmental relations will have as many unanticipated as expected consequences. This article examines the unanticipated consequences of revenue sharing on the city of Aurora, Illinois. Specifically, two consequences are studied: the application of policy analysis at the local level, and the development of new and/or additional forms of citizen participation.

522 Campbell, Alan K., and Sacks, Seymour. METROPOLITAN AMERICA: FISCAL PATTERNS AND GOVERNMENTAL SYSTEMS. New York: Free Press, 1967. 239 p.

This study concentrates on the fiscal aspects of metropolitan problems. It is a comparative analysis of the differences in fiscal performance among cities and between cities and their suburbs. Variations in intergovernmental relationships are studied for their relevance to differences in fiscal performance. Finally, the policy implications of the findings are discussed.

523 Caraley, Demetrious. CITY GOVERNMENTS AND URBAN PROBLEMS: A NEW INTRODUCTION TO URBAN PROBLEMS. Englewood Cliffs, N.J.: Prentice-Hall, 1977. 448 p.

City government decision making is political because it takes place in a context of conflict among various coalitions of individuals and groups and because the eventual decision is determined by the relative amount of influence that can be exerted by the opposing participants. The increasing involvement of the states and the federal government in the operations of large city government is not an example of the usurpation of the latter's power; city governments are still important loci of independent decision making. If the present level of inadequate performance of city governments continues, the most likely future for large cities will be a drift into underserviced, crime-ridden, bankruptcy-skirting slum ghettoes. But if key obstacles can be overcome--epistemological, fiscal, and particularly political--cities can move toward healthy multiracial futures.

524    Chibuk, John H. "Should New Communities Serve Government Policy or Should Government Policy Serve New Communities?" CONTACT 8 (August 1976): 57–66.

New communities are generally framed within such government policy contexts as a national or regional urban policy, a national or regional economic policy, or a national defense policy. The contemporary new community vehicle can be applied to other government policy contexts, such as housing, land use, or environmental policies. New communities should serve as vehicles for government policies, and government policies should otherwise serve as vehicles for new communities. This position offers increased opportunity for integrating and coordinating the diverse government policies, for private sector participation, and a greater flexibility in responding to societal issues.

525    Cho, Yong Hyo. "A Multiple Regression Model for the Measurement of the Public Policy Impact on Big City Crime." POLICY SCIENCES 3 (December 1972): 435–55.

Using multiple regression techniques, the paper determines if various public policies have significant effect in reducing serious crimes and in decreasing the upward trend of serious crime rates in the fifty large cities. Policies are conceptually divided into control policies, comprising those directly concerned with law enforcement and justice administration, and service policies, which are general well-being oriented.

526    "Citizen Preferences and Urban Policy: Models, Measures, Uses." POLICY AND POLITICS 4 (June 1976): 13–141.

Eight articles dealing with models of collective decision making, voting rules when coalitions are not present, preference revelation and policy decisions, the democratic response of urban governments, citizen preferences, budgets and citizen preferences, measures of citizen evaluation of local government services, and citizen surveys for local governments.

527    Clark, Terry Nichols. "On Decentralization." POLITY 2 (Summer 1970): 508–14.

A book review essay on the advantages of decentralizing the city's functions into smaller, neighborhood-built organizational structures. He concludes his review by noting that the decentralization of certain functions may resolve some pressing urban problems, but we will never understand the consequence of these efforts unless there is more systematic social scientific analysis of them.

528    _____. "Policy Research and Urban Public Policy." POLICY ANALYSIS 4 (Winter 1978): 67–90.

According to Clark, many policy analysis discussions assume that a client is also the policymaker who can implement the results of an analysis. The assumption of this article is that such a belief is erroneous, at least for most domestic social programs. Policy decisions tend to be decentralized and involve numerous actors.

529  Cole, Richard L. CITIZEN PARTICIPATION AND THE URBAN POLICY PROCESS. Lexington, Mass.: Lexington Books, 1974. 192 p.

Cole examines the variety of citizen participation programs which have been initiated by municipalities and the federal government over the past decade. The author explores the impact of these programs on individual participants and on the political system as a whole.

530  _____. "The Urban Policy Process: A Note on Structural and Regional Influences." SOCIAL SCIENCE QUARTERLY 52 (December 1971): 646–55.

Based on a survey of all U.S. cities over fifty thousand, Cole suggests that, although regional influences account for more of the total intercity variance of policy than the degree of reformed administrative structure, neither is an adequate predictor.

531  Corder, Carol. PLANNED CITIES: NEW TOWNS IN BRITAIN AND AMERICA. Beverly Hills, Calif.: Sage, 1977. 224 p.

This is an examination of new towns as policy tools which national governments can use to deal with such problems as urban congestion, rural depopulation, and regionally unbalanced development. The author views new towns programs as a way of moving government from passive, problem-oriented policies to deal with urbanization and economic development.

532  David, Stephen M., and Peterson, Paul E., eds. URBAN POLITICS AND PUBLIC POLICY: THE CITY IN CRISIS. New York: Praeger Publishers, 1973. 337 p.

This is a reader on urban, especially metropolitan politics. The first part deals with fragmentation and its consequences, especially the limitations on citizen participation. A second part contains two to three essays each on housing, transportation, education, and the police. A final section deals with changing political systems in the context of coalition politics and protest.

533  Davis, Ross D. "Urban Policy and Urban Systems." HABITAT 2, nos. 3–4 (1977): 311–19.

Desirable structures of urban policy must be identified, and a basis established for efficient budgetary decisions. Separate city government activities should relate to each other and overall policy objectives. Urban policy is concerned with setting up a workable system which controls the functioning of those elements. Useful policy should direct, rationalize, and explain all parts of city government in the context of the total system.

534    Day, George S., and Weitz, Barton A.   "Comparative Urban Social
       Indicators:  Problems and Prospects."  POLICY SCIENCES  8
       (December 1977):  423-36.

       The increasing availability of urban social indicators offers
       the possibility of an overall quality of life measure which
       can be used to compare cities.  This article considers the
       problems of combining several single indicators into an over-
       all comparative measure.  The best results were obtained
       when cities were grouped according to the similarities of
       their profiles on the indicators.

535    Dickey, John W.; Glancy, David M.; and Jennelle, Ernest M.   TECH-
       NOLOGY ASSESSMENT:  ITS APPLICATION TO MANAGEMENT PRO-
       GRAMS OF URBAN GOVERNMENTS.  Lexington, Mass.: Lexington
       Books, 1973.  194 p.

       Until recently, technology assessment (TA) has been more a
       concept than a methodology.  This pilot study of TA in local
       government decision making uses methods developed for the
       MITRE Corporation.  It concludes that TA is sound enough
       to be effectively adapted to numerous local government uses.

536    Downs, Anthony.  "Citizen Participation in Community Development:
       Why Some Changes are Needed."  NATIONAL CIVIC REVIEW  64
       (May 1975):  237-48.

       Every community seeking funds under the Housing and Commu-
       nity Development Act of 1974 has created some citizen par-
       ticipation arrangements as required by the law.  These will
       prove to be inadequate for attracting large amounts of pri-
       vate capital and other nonfederal resources to supplement
       the meager federal funds.  To alleviate these problems,
       mayors, city managers, and city council members must modi-
       fy citizen participation arrangements.  Several communities
       were surveyed, and some suggestions received were:  to
       better acquaint citizen participants with the basic nature of
       their community, with key ongoing trends and with types of
       actions they can take; to form a strong political consensus
       behind one recommended program; and to develop a practical
       understanding of how to cope with the federal bureaucracy
       and how to engage in truly comprehensive community develop-
       ment planning.

537    Dye, Thomas R., and Garcia, John A.  "The Political Economy of
       Growth Policies in Cities."  POLICY STUDIES JOURNAL  6 (Winter
       1977):  175-84.

       The article presents evidence of the dollar cost of curtailing
       growth to municipal governments and urban populations.  In
       addition, the authors contend that growth limitation policies
       do not necessarily produce economies in municipal taxing
       and spending.  Per capita expenditures are only minimally
       related to size and growing cities have lower per capita
       costs than cities that are stable or declining in size.

538  Elazar, Daniel, ed. "Serving the Public in a Metropolitan Society. A Symposium." PUBLIUS 6 (Spring 1976): 1–67.

>   Seven essays covering: different kinds of citizenships in a metropolitan society, restructuring federal housing programs, federalism and the delivery of governmental services, social services as a professional fiefdom, and a real federalism and public opinion.

539  Eldredge, H. Wentworth, ed. TAMING MEGALOPOLIS. 2 vols. New York: Anchor Books, 1967. 1,166 p.

>   More than sixty writers contributed to these volumes which analyze the present and look at the future. Volume 1, "What Is and What Could Be," describes the current urban situation as of 1967 and seeks to determine valid planning goals. Volume 2, "How to Manage an Urbanized World," presents the problems of urban areas through the year 2000.

540  Ershkowitz, Miriam. "Environmental Politics in the Metropolis." BUREAUCRAT 4 (July 1975): 147–62.

>   This is a case study of air resource management designed to show the difficulties faced by local government in regulating large local corporations, such as utilities that supply vital services and employ many local workers. It focuses on the relationship between the Consolidated Edison Company and the New York City political system.

541  Eulau, Heinz, and Eyestone, Robert. "Policy Maps of City Councils and Policy Outcomes: A Developmental Analysis." AMERICAN POLITICAL SCIENCE REVIEW 62 (March 1968): 124–43.

>   Cities within the same metropolitan region are developing distinct and unique public life–styles. The article suggests that in addition to historic differences, differences in public life–styles may be the result of consciously pursued public policy. Data confirmed that policy development is greatly affected by predictions, preferences, orientations, and expectations of the policymakers themselves.

542  Eyestone, Robert. THE THREADS OF PUBLIC POLICY: STUDY IN POLICY LEADERSHIP. Indianapolis, Ind.: Bobbs–Merrill, 1971. 197 p.

>   A study of the city council member, how he/she reacts to the pressures and limitations of the role and an analysis of the city council as a whole. Based on data gathered in eighty–seven towns and cities, this volume focuses on the problem of urban growth and planning from the perspective of the policy leaders.

543  Fainstein, Susan E., and Fainstein, Norman I. "City Planning and Political Values." URBAN AFFAIRS QUARTERLY 6 (March 1971): 341–62.

The authors develop a typology of planning methods on the basis of who determines the plan's goals and who determines its means. Analogies between kinds of planning and political theories serve two purposes: they show the implications of each type of planning in terms of political benefits and they help to explain why certain types of planning have been favored by different societies.

544 _____. "Local Control as Social Reform: Planning for Big Cities in the Seventies." JOURNAL OF THE AMERICAN INSTITUTE OF PLANNERS 42 (July 1976): 275-85.

Decentralization of administrative programs is favored by all racial groups as well as administrators. Implementation of decentralization is made difficult because of contradictions between class and locational interests. Urban decentralization remains one path to moderate but viable political reform.

545 Fantini, Mario, and Gittell, Marilyn. DECENTRALIZATION: ACHIEVING REFORM. New York: Praeger Publishers, 1973. 23 p.

This is a study of the recent movement toward the decentralization of urban governments. Using the experience of big city school system decentralization, the authors outline some of the means by which political institutions can be reformed to meet the changing needs of society.

546 Fisk, Donald M., and Winnie, Richard E. "Output Measurement in Urban Government: Current Status and Likely Prospects." SOCIAL SCIENCE QUARTERLY 54 (March 1974): 725-40.

Output measurement is not new to local government. As far back as the 1920s, efforts were being made to improve data on the consequences of local government services. This paper summarizes the present state of knowledge of output measurement in urban government as well as the use being made of it, and briefly discusses prospects for its use and further development in the immediate future.

547 Forrester, Jay W. URBAN DYNAMICS. Cambridge: MIT Press, 1970. 285 p.

Forrester says that the cause of the degeneration of the cities is the inequalities in our tax and legal systems. The underlying processes which affect the lifelines and the longevity of the city were isolated for examination in a new model developed by the author. His theory considers forces and their interplay which activate patterns of change and affect the urban environment benefically and adversely.

548 Fowler, E.P., and White, David. "Big City Downtown: The Non-Impact of Zoning." POLICY STUDIES JOURNAL 7 (Summer 1979): 690-700.

Do land prices determine zoning policy, or vice versa? The case of one big city downtown suggests that it depends on the political climate. Different political climates not only change the determinants of zoning decisions but also the nature of their relationships with those "determinants" and the relative importance of zoning itself.

549    Frederickson, H. George, ed. "Curriculum Essays on Citizens, Politics, and Administration in Urban Neighborhoods." PUBLIC ADMINISTRATION REVIEW 32 (October 1972): 565–738.

Twelve experts contribute original "curriculum essays" on problems, policies, and directions in urban neighborhoods. In addition to the subject areas—municipal decentralization, citizen participation, government theories, management, race, education, social services, health services—each essay is accompanied by a lengthy bibliography.

550    Froman, Lewis A., Jr. "Analysis of Public Policies in Cities." JOURNAL OF POLITICS 28 (February 1967): 94–108.

This paper summarizes much of the literature relating environmental variables with policy outcomes in local government. It also provides some additional data to illustrate the proposition that different policies have associated with them different kinds of explanatory variables. Finally, a theory is proposed to subsume the current findings.

551    Gans, Herbert J. "Planning for Declining and Poor Cities." JOURNAL OF THE AMERICAN INSTITUTE OF PLANNERS 41 (September 1975): 305–7.

This is a short analysis of the Cleveland Policy Planning Report that Gans suggests may signify a radical change in American planning thought and practice. Gans highlights what he feels are six significant aspects of the report.

552    Ganz, Alexander, and O'Brien, Thomas. "The City: Sandbox, Reservation or Dynamo?" PUBLIC POLICY 21 (Winter 1973): 107–24.

The article presents new information on the roles of large cities as places to work and live. Its intention is to provide new insights on the impact of the services revolution on the economy of large cities; to assess shortcomings in federal and state policy, to bring into sharper focus the nature of the problems and needs of the cities; and to offer a new measure of the importance of our larger cities in American life.

553    _____. "The City: Sandbox, Reservation or Dynamo? A Rejoiner." PUBLIC POLICY 22 (Spring 1974): 243–99.

The final installment of the debate between Ganz, O'Brien, and James. Here they argue that greater attention must be paid to shaping policies to meet challenges posed by increased residential demand in cities.

554    Garn, Harvey A., and Springer, Michael. "Formulating Urban Growth Policies: Dynamic Interactions among People, Places and Clubs." PUBLIUS 5 (Fall 1975): 25–49.

An essay on metropolitan growth policies that attempts to come to grips with urban growth policies at the level of basic theory.

The authors develop a formal and explicit scheme that permits them to interrelate individual preferences and actions, group behavior, and governmental roles. Their prime purpose is strategic in that they want to improve the postures and perspectives by which analysts approach urban growth issues.

555   Gittell, Marilyn. PARTICIPANTS AND PARTICIPATION: A STUDY OF SCHOOL POLICY IN NEW YORK CITY. New York: Center for Urban Education, 1967. 136 p.

This is a study of the power structure and decision-making system within New York City's school system. The general conclusion is that control of the school system rests in the hands of the professional bureaucracy, with students, teachers, and parents shut out. Attention is paid to how decisions are made with the general conclusion that more decentralization is needed.

556   _____, ed. EDUCATING AN URBAN POPULATION. Beverly Hills, Calif.: Sage, 1967. 320 p.

The author claims that "the failure of urban systems to meet the demands of a changing technology and a changing population, results from an inability to readily adjust institutions and public policy." This collection of sixteen articles aims at analysis of the responsiveness of urban educational systems. The book discusses 1960s' pressures on the urban school system, research findings in different areas of policy-making, and alternative solutions.

557   Gittell, Marilyn, and Hollander, T. Edward. SIX URBAN SCHOOL DISTRICTS: A COMPARATIVE STUDY OF INSTITUTIONAL RESPONSE. New York: Praeger Publishers, 1968. 329 p.

This study creates a model of school systems in which innovation is the output of a system with administrative and fiscal input. The authors examine change as it relates to the social, political, and economic forces which shape school policy in Baltimore, Chicago, Detroit, New York, Philadelphia, and St. Louis.

558   Goodman, Jay S., ed. PERSPECTIVES ON URBAN POLITICS. Boston: Allyn and Bacon, 1970. 558 p.

This is a collection of readings on urban politics, presenting a combination of topical writings and scholarly articles arranged in a micro, people problems, and macrostudies perspective.

559   Gorvine, Albert, and Margulies, Samuel L. "The Urban Crisis: An Alternative Perspective." URBAN AFFAIRS QUARTERLY 6 (March 1971): 263-76.

This article examines the elements within the urban political system that help contribute to the urban crisis and presents some implications of the analysis.

560 "Governmental Structure, Urban Environment, and Educational Policy."
MIDWEST JOURNAL OF POLITICAL SCIENCE 11, no.3 (1967): 353–80.

>  Data from sixty-seven large cities is used to assess the impact of the structure of city school systems on educational outcomes, and to compare the effect of structural and environmental variables upon educational outcomes. In general, environmental variables were more closely prosecuted with educational policies than were structural variables.

561 Grier, George. "Metropolitan Population Dynamics: Implications for Urban Growth Policy." BUREAUCRAT 2 (Spring 1973): 9–16.

>  Three major trends seem likely to dominate urban population patterns in the 1970s. They are the baby bust, the marriage bust, and black suburbanization. These trends offer potentials for more rational growth patterns than those that have predominated during the past few decades.

562 Hart, D.A. "Ordering Change and Changing Orders: A Study of Urban Policy Development." POLICY AND POLITICS 2 (September 1973): 27–41.

>  There are at least three different general ways of approaching planning: the cohesive, the factored, and the diffused. Most plans and the planning process itself are in fact a combination of these approaches. Some conclusions may be drawn: the plan as a land-use map for the city with its connotations of infallibility and inviolateness cannot be sustained; the policy chain which results from the interaction of these modes shapes the planning process; one of planning's major tasks is to reflect change.

563 Havighurst, Robert J. "Educational Policy for the Large Cities." SOCIAL PROBLEMS 24 (December 1976): 271–81.

>  All big cities show below-average scores on tests of school achievement. Attention and action should focus on the family, school, and city. In recent years, the child-parent center procedure has been developed in a number of big city school systems to help children in low-income areas. Another major step in dealing with the problem is to make the central parts of big metropolitan areas more attractive to middle-income people of all ethnic groups. The third area of policy and practice leading toward basic and permanent improvement lies within the school system.

564 Hawkins, Brett W. PUBLICS AND URBAN POLICIES. Indianapolis, Ind.: Bobbs-Merrill, 1971. 127 p.

>  Forces that shape public policy decisions on national, state, and local levels are the concerns of this exploration of environmental conditions, governmental arrangements and external operations. Linkages involving community makeup, political structures and external conditions organize the book.

565  Hawley, Willis D., Lipsky, Michael, et al. THEORETICAL PERSPEC-
     TIVES ON URBAN POLITICS. Englewood Cliffs, N.J.: Prentice
     Hall, 1976. 299 p.

     This is a collection of original essays attempting to provide
     new perspectives to the study of urban politics, policy, and
     governance.

566  Hawley, Willis J., and Rogers, David. IMPROVING THE QUALITY
     OF URBAN MANAGEMENT. Beverly Hills, Calif.: Sage, 1974. 640 p.

     The authors provide an overview of approaches for improving
     delivery of urban services. Specific recommendations are
     proposed for using information systems to increase effective-
     ness and for involving the private sector in the delivery of
     services. Decentralization and government restructuring are
     also assessed to determine their influence on reducing unre-
     sponsiveness and the bureaucratic character of certain urban
     public institutions.

567  Hennessey, Timothy M., and Feen, Richard H. "Social Science as
     Social Philosophy: Edward C. Banfield and the 'New Realism' in
     Urban Politics." AMERICAN BEHAVIORAL SCIENTIST 17 (November-
     December 1973): 171-204.

     All articles in this issue are devoted to varieties of political
     conservatism in the United States and abroad. This essay
     is a critique of the conservative explanation of social behavior
     and defense of public policy in Banfield's THE UNHEAVENLY
     CITY (1970).

568  Hudson, Barclay M.; Wachs, Martin; and Schofer, Joseph L. "Local
     Impact Evaluation in the Design of Large-Scale Urban Systems." JOUR-
     NAL OF THE AMERICAN INSTITUTE OF PLANNERS 40 (July 1974):
     255-65.

     When public service systems are designed in accordance with
     a highly aggregated definition of the public interest, their
     impacts often clash with community welfare from a local per-
     spective. In this article, public utilities and conflicts are
     viewed as an inherent and central issue of designing and
     evaluating public services in urban areas. The discussion
     focuses on the evaluation strategies that might best cope with
     the conflicts; including cost-benefit analysis, computer inter-
     action techniques, and "dialectical scanning."

569  Hughes, James W. URBAN INDICATORS, METROPOLITAN EVOLUTION,
     AND PUBLIC POLICY. New Brunswick, N.J.: Center for Urban
     Policy Research, Rutgers University, 1973. 233 p.

     Through the use of a factor-analytic model summarizing the
     residential social patterns of cities, a scheme of urban social
     indicators is developed. Its utility is demonstrated by examining
     the convergence of the principle North American urban centers
     toward similar forms of residential differentiation. Public
     policy implications are reviewed.

570   James, Franklin J., Jr. "The City: Sandbox, Reservation, or Dy-
      namo? A Reply." PUBLIC POLICY 22 (Winter 1974): 39-52.

      This paper replies to Ganz and O'Brien (no. 553) by
      claiming that city industrial growth is not entirely attribu-
      table to the industrial transformation of their economies but
      to a larger extent resulted from the demand pressures created
      by the Vietnam military build-up. They also claim that federal
      grants-in-aid do not discriminate against large cities. The
      Ganz and O'Brien picture is too simple and is not a useful
      policy guide nor helpful in improving or understanding the
      functioning of urban areas.

571   Jones, E. Terrence. "Mass Media and the Urban Policy Process."
      POLICY STUDIES JOURNAL 3 (Summer 1975): 359-63.

      It is increasingly important to examine the role played by
      the metropolitan mass media in the kind of information about
      policy outcomes that is fed back into the initial stages of
      the next round of urban policymaking. The metropolitan mass
      media serve as rough evaluators of outcomes and conditions.

572   Kaiser, Harvey H. THE BUILDING OF CITIES, DEVELOPMENT AND
      CONFLICT. Ithaca, N.Y.: Cornell University Press, 1978. 219 p.

      Kaiser is concerned with the impact of land use policies,
      and especially the development of new towns on the social,
      economic, and political interests of the citizens affected.
      His focus is on conditions which lead to opposition or support
      for land use policies.

573   Kasarda, John D. "The Impact of Suburban Population Growth on
      Central City Service Functions." AMERICAN JOURNAL OF SOCIOL-
      OGY 77 (May 1972): 1111-24.

      Kasarda investigates the relationship between suburban popula-
      tion growth and service functions performed in central cities.
      Suburban population has a large impact on central city retail
      trade, wholesale trade, business and repair services, and
      public services provided by central city government.

      Impact of suburban population on central city services is
      strong and remains so even when such controls as central
      city size and age, annexation, per capita income of central
      city residents, and nonwhite percent of central city popula-
      tion are introduced.

574   Kaufman, Clifford. "Political Urbanism: Urban Spatial Organization,
      Policy, and Politics." URBAN AFFAIRS QUARTERLY 9 (June 1974):
      421-36.

      Kaufman makes an attempt to define and interrelate urbanism
      and urban policy. Dimensions of urbanism are used as a basis
      to classify forms of urban conflict and policy and to help de-
      fine basic urban resources related to the level and distribu-
      tion of welfare among urban actors.

575    Kirlin, John J., and Erie, Steven P. "The Study of City Governance
       and Public Policy: A Critical Appraisal." PUBLIC ADMINISTRATION
       REVIEW  32 (March–April 1972):  173–84.

       The essay reviews existing studies of local governments and
       suggests new research directions which the authors feel are
       necessary if the study of urban governance is to contribute
       to public policymaking.  They suggest that concern must be
       directed away from concern with the character of local govern-
       ment personnel and processes and toward the results of
       governmental activity for citizens.

576    Kitchen, Harry M.  "Some Organizational Implications of Providing
       an Urban Service:  The Case of Water." CANADIAN PUBLIC ADMINIS-
       TRATION  18 (Summer 1975):  297–308.

       This study shows how organizational structure significantly
       affects the costs of service provision.  Data are drawn from
       providing water to cities and towns in Canada.

577    Krumholz, Norman, and Cogger, Janice M.  "Social Science Research
       and Public Policy:  Bridging the Gap." SOCIOLOGICAL SYMPOSIUM
       21 (Winter 1978):  34–45.

       In 1968 federal funding was used to establish a number of
       urban observatories in American cities.  The observatories
       enlisted the aid of university researchers and social scien-
       tists in helping local government to understand their problems
       and how they might be resolved.  The problem encountered
       with each of these studies is that none of them had any visible
       effect on public policy.  The observatories were regarded as
       simply a means to funnel federal funds to universities.

578    Krumholz, Norman; Cogger, Janice M.; and Linner, John H.  "The
       Cleveland Policy Planning Report." JOURNAL OF THE AMERICAN
       INSTITUTE OF PLANNERS  4 (September 1975):  298–304.

       This is a summary of the Cleveland Policy Planning Report
       which started as an orthodox family planning effort and wound
       up becoming a catalog of recommendations for solving or ame-
       liorating some of the more pressing problems of Cleveland
       and its people.  It is also a description of how an activist
       staff is attempting to shape local policy in pursuit of specific
       objectives.

579    Kuo, Wen H.  "Mayoral Influence in Urban Policy Making." AMERICAN
       JOURNAL OF SOCIOLOGY  79 (November 1973):  620–38.

       Political behavior of big–city mayors in community policy-
       making was examined to explore its impact on decision making.
       City government plays an important role in initiating community
       programs, particularly when the city provides a strong or-
       ganization for the mayor.

580    Landry, Lawrence D.  "City Councils as Policy Makers:  Myths That
       Destroy Effectiveness." NATIONAL CIVIC REVIEW  66 (December
       1977):  553–57.

City councils have five things to do to be effective in making policy (set broad goals and objectives, develop implementation strategies, take the evaluation and oversight role seriously, cooperate in a system of citizen participation and feedback, and exert leadership in community affairs), but because of attitudes brought to the job, council members have difficulty doing these things. A more careful definition of the role of legislature in the policy process is needed.

581    LeMay, Michael. "Expenditure and Nonexpenditure Measures of State Urban Policy Output: A Research Note." AMERICAN POLITICS QUARTERLY 1 (October 1973): 511-28.

This research report discusses a study that examines political decisions outside the budgetary process in order to better evaluate the relative importance of structural and political factors as well as the social and economic determinants of public policy. A research question addressed is whether or not nonexpenditure indicators of output improve the correlation of political-structural variables with policy outputs.

582    Levine, Charles H., ed. MANAGING HUMAN RESOURCES: A CHALLENGE TO URBAN GOVERNMENTS. Beverly Hills, Calif.: Sage, 1977. 320 p.

This collection reflects the variety that has developed in the study of municipal public employee systems since 1960. The authors generally show the central significance of urban bureaucracies in the formation and implementation of public policy. Chapters are divided into five sections corresponding to those areas of public employee politics that have undergone the most changes in the post-World War II era: bureaucratic roles, affirmative action, collective bargaining, human resource development techniques, and national public employee programming.

583    Levy, Francis S.; Meltsner, Arnold J.; and Wildavsky, Aaron. URBAN OUTCOMES. Oakland Project Series. Berkeley and Los Angeles: University of California Press, 1974. 278 p.

It focuses on the outcomes of public policies in the areas of schools, streets, and libraries. The authors' concerns are how Oakland and its administrative agencies decide to distribute goods and services to the citizens of Oakland, why goods and services are distributed as they are, and what difference it makes in the lives of the city's citizens.

584    Liebert, Roland J. "Municipal Functions, Structure and Expenditures: A Reanalysis of Recent Research." SOCIAL SCIENCE QUARTERLY 54 (March 1974): 765-83.

Previous research has generally overlooked one of the most significant sources of variation in the structure and output of local government--the extent to which urban governmental functions are assigned to city hall rather to some other government. He finds that this level of functional inclusiveness not only explains most of the variance in expenditure levels, but

also accounts for much of the measurable differences in the
bureaucratization, reformism, and elite centralization of
municipal government.

585 Lineberry, Robert L. EQUALITY AND URBAN POLICY: THE DIS-
TRIBUTION OF MUNICIPAL PUBLIC SERVICES. Sage Library of
Social Research, vol. 39. Beverly Hills, Calif.: Sage, 1977. 205 p.

Five hypotheses are offered to explain the distribution of
urban services. Three of these can be categorized as the
"underclass" explanation. A fourth hypothesis is that the
distribution of urban services is a function of ecological aspects of a neighborhood. The fifth hypothesis is that urban
services are distributed according to bureaucratic decision
rules made to simplify complex allocation of administrative
time and resources.

586 _____. "On the Politics and Economics of Urban Services." URBAN
AFFAIRS QUARTERLY 12 (March 1977): 267-72.

The provision of public services may not be responsive to
citizen demands because institutionalized bureaucracies dominate this provision. Questions of equity pertain to who gets
what and are approached differently from community to community and from service to service; these questions are closely
related to decisions about appropriate size of jurisdiction.

587 Lineberry, Robert L., and Fowler, Edmund P. "Reformism and Public
Policy in American Cities." AMERICAN POLITICAL SCIENCE RE-
VIEW 61 (September 1967): 706-16.

The essay treats two policy outputs--taxation and expenditure
levels of cities--as dependent variables. These are related
to socioeconomic characteristics of cities and to structural
characteristics of their governments. The central research
issue is to examine the impact of political structures, reformed and unreformed, on policymaking in American cities.

588 Lineberry, Robert L., and Masotti, Louis H., eds. URBAN PROBLEMS
AND PUBLIC POLICY. Lexington, Mass.: Lexington Books, 1975.
209 p.

Lexington Books and the Policy Studies Organization have
reached an agreement whereby some POLICY STUDIES
JOURNAL symposia will be reproduced in book form. This
is one of those efforts. In June 1975 the journal devoted
an issue to urban policy. Eight of the original eleven essays
are reproduced in the book and seven lengthier pieces were
commissioned especially for the book. Topics include: models
in urban planning, organizing the poor, police and urban
crime, mass media and urban policy, Catholics and policy
outputs, and managing public sector labor relations.

589 Lineberry, Robert L., and Welch, Robert E., Jr. "Who Gets What:
Measuring the Distribution of Urban Public Services." SOCIAL SCI-
ENCE QUARTERLY 54 (March 1974): 700-712.

The prevailing fiscal-level focus of comparative urban policy research can only lead those interested in the effects of social and political factors on public policy down a blind alley. Policy researchers should redirect their attention toward a policy dimension more likely to be affected by these factors: the distribution of policy costs, benefits, and sanctions. This article argues the importance of distributional questions, especially those related to the distribution of urban public services. Based on San Antonio, Texas, data, the authors show some of the problems encountered in trying to measure the distribution of services to a neighborhood.

590    Lipsky, Michael. PROTEST IN CITY POLITICS: RENT, STRIKES, HOUSING AND THE POWER OF THE POOR. Chicago: Rand McNally, 1970. 214 p.

The New York City rent strike of 1963-65 provides the data base for this book. Lipsky argues that powerless groups lack the minimum resources necessary to initiate or sustain protest activity. Thus, for the poor and powerless, rent strikes were an unsuccessful weapon for gaining political power.

591    _____. "Street-Level Bureaucracy and the Analysis of Urban Reform." URBAN AFFAIRS QUARTERLY 6 (June 1971): 391-410.

This essay focuses on the contradictory perceptions of non-voluntary clients of urban bureaucracies and the bureaucrats who staff those agencies. Lipsky reveals that the charges of racism made by the clients and the countercharge that clients do not understand the complex nature of service provision are both valid.

592    Liu, Ben-Chieh. "Economic and Non-Economic Quality of Life: Empirical Indicators and Policy Implications for Large Standard Metropolitan Areas." AMERICAN JOURNAL OF ECONOMICS AND SOCIOLOGY 36 (July 1977): 225-40.

The primary objective of this study is to assess quantitatively the urban economic and noneconomic quality of life in U.S. metropolitan areas with populations greater than 500,000 in 1970. The trade-offs between economic growth and changes in noneconomic conditions among the urban areas were studied, and policy implications were deduced and recommended.

593    Long, Norton E. "Making Urban Policy Useful and Corrigible." URBAN AFFAIRS QUARTERLY 10 (June 1975): 379-97.

If the city were conceptualized as a kind of producer and consumer cooperative run for the benefit of its inhabitants, it would more readily appear that its books must balance and that it must be able to pay its way or become dependent on outside sources. It would also be clear that neither the states nor the nation can afford any large number of local losers. Conceptualizing the city this way makes it possible to discuss what principles of justice should be applied to the way the political economy allocates the values it produces among its members.

594    _____.  "A Marshall Plan for Cities?"  PUBLIC INTEREST, no.46 (Winter 1977), pp. 48–58.

> The idea of a Marshall Plan for cities has frequently been advocated.  The federal government must help cities develop adequate plans for improving local economies and should assist in the training and supply of competent staffs.  Seriously addressing the problems of cities requires a politics of civic and moral reconstruction that far transcends central business district renewal, mass transit, low-interest loans, or the shifting of the burden of welfare to the shoulders of the national government.

595    Lowe, Jeanne R.  CITIES IN A RACE WITH TIME:  PROGRESS AND POVERTY IN RENEWING AMERICA'S CITIES.  New York:  Vintage Books, 1967.  608 p.

> "As we pay the costly consequences of our careless past, it would profit us to inquire first, where did we go wrong and why."  This statement sets the scene for a series of case studies of attempts to rebuild our cities, preceded by a presentation of how they arrived at their present condition.  Lowe argues that local action must be shaped by local need, with help from the outside to realize local goals.  Lacking community goals and standards, as well as a national policy, cities have reacted only to crisis and continue to repeat the errors of the past, frequently confusing means for ends.

596    Lowenstein, Louis K., and McGrath, Dorn C.  "The Planning Imperative in America's Future."  ANNALS OF THE AMERICAN ACADEMY OF POLITICAL AND SOCIAL SCIENCE  405 (January 1973):  15–24.

> Urban policy has not been as established and articulated as foreign policy.  With most urban aid legislation inadequately funded, urban planning must deal with pollution, declining resources, and population issues so that appropriate policy choices can be made.

597    Lowry, Ira S.  "Reforming Rent Control in New York City:  The Role of Research in Policy-Making."  POLICY SCIENCES  3 (March 1972): 47–58.

> The article describes the role of the New York City Rand Institute and other research groups in the rent control reforms enacted by New York City in June 1970.  It also offers some lesson for those contemplating similar work for other public agencies.

598    Lucy, William H.  "Metropolitan Dynamics:  A Cross-National Framework for Analyzing Public Policy Effects in Metropolitan Areas."  URBAN AFFAIRS QUARTERLY  11 (December 1975):  155–85.

> The essence of metropolitan dynamics is that mobility and territorial protection strategies will be used to increase security.  The pattern of structures, values, and policies in society will determine the extent to which these strategies result in inequalities and separation between public needs and public resources.  The capabilities of local governments

will be determined by the relationships between inequalities and separation of needs and resources.

599   Lucy, William H.; Gilbert, Dennis; and Birkhead, Guthrie S. "Equity in Local Service Distribution." PUBLIC ADMINISTRATION REVIEW 36 (November 1977): 687-97.

> The article develops a general set of tests for local adminis-trators to use in public service delivery. Four categories of service are distinguished and a methodology for the anal-ysis of service distribution is proposed. The authors con-clude that if analysis of equity becomes part of decision makers operating routines, a sounder basis for decisions about service distribution will exist.

600   Lupsha, Peter A. "Constraints on Urban Leadership, or Why Cities Cannot be Creatively Governed." In IMPROVING THE QUALITY OF URBAN MANAGEMENT, edited by Willis D. Hawley and David Rogers, pp. 607-23. Beverly Hills, Calif.: Sage, 1974.

> We have erred in our myth-making when we expect mayors, managers, and other elected city officials to lead, for the constraints and ratio of reinforcement are such that leader-ship is nearly impossible, and management and incremental reaction become the only possibilities. The demands for innovative, dynamic leadership often confront headon the typical demands passing over a mayor's desk. Each requires a different style of leadership and a different set of leader-ship tactics and cues. While creative, anticipatory policy leadership is one of the most needed resources in urban poli-tics today, reactive politics and crisis policy will in all likelihood continue to be our main avenue to creative change.

601   Lyons, William. "Reform and Response in American Cities: Structure and Policy Reconsidered." SOCIAL SCIENCE QUARTERLY 59 (June 1978): 118-32.

> Cities with reformed political structures are more likely to respond to pressures to reduce spending, while cities with unreformed political structures are more likely to respond to pressure to increase spending. Political structure continues to have an impact on policy.

602   _____. "Urban Structures and Policy: Reassessing Additive Assump-tions of Reform." POLITICAL METHODOLOGY 4, no.2 (1977): 213-26.

> According to the author's research on the policy impacts of reformed government structures, they have failed to place policy impact in the proper perspective. Either each reform has been assumed to have equal value and weight, and thus one reform is added to another giving a net effect; or each reform is treated independently of every other reform. Lyons finds that there is no evidence that reforms can be added.

603   McGregor, Eugene B. "Issues and Problems in Applying Quantitative Analysis to Public Sector Human Resources Management." In MANAG-ING HUMAN RESOURCES: A CHALLENGE TO URBAN GOVERNMENTS,

edited by Charles H. Levine, pp. 225-52. Urban Affairs Annual Reviews, vol. 13. Beverly Hills, Calif.: Sage, 1977.

Human resource management is a necessary part of urban management. Several quantitative modes of analysis can be applied to evaluating public sector urban systems. Quantitative analysis is the system most adaptable to the changing realities of urban service delivery.

604 Marando, Vincent L. "A Metropolitan Lower Income Housing Allocation Policy." AMERICAN BEHAVIORAL SCIENTIST 19 (September-October 1975): 75-103.

This paper deals with social policy regulation, for instance, regulation that deals with the social side effects of poor economic decisions. In the public housing market, the effort is to regulate racial discrimination and Marando discovers that such regulation is informal or semiformal at best.

605 Michael, Donald N. "Urban Policy in the Rationalized Society." JOURNAL OF THE AMERICAN INSTITUTE OF PLANNERS 31 (November 1969): 283-88.

For the next twenty years, much of the customary environment of the planning process will be in flux. The urban policy professions will be pushed into a new shape by new problems, priorities, and methods. There must be a rationalization of problem solving.

606 Miller, Zane. "Urban History, Urban Crises, and Public Policy." URBANISM PAST AND PRESENT 1 (Winter 1975-1976): 1-6.

New methodologies in social, medical, scientific, technological, oral, and psychohistory have introduced urban-oriented scholars to the jargon, techniques, conceptual frameworks, and analytic focus of both the social and behavioral sciences. That process is producing a generation of methodologically sophisticated historians. Urban specialists must be able to avoid jargon and complex mathematical expression in presenting their research findings to the public.

607 Millett, Ricardo A. EXAMINATION OF WIDESPREAD CITIZEN PARTICIPATION IN THE MODEL CITIES PROGRAM AND THE DEMANDS OF ETHNIC MINORITIES FOR A GREATER DECISION MAKING ROLE IN AMERICAN CITIES. San Francisco: R and E Research Associates, 1977. 151 p.

Generally, the kind or level of resident participation which evolved in the model cities program was subject to the will and competence both of the city on the one hand and of the residents in the community on the other. But, in fact, the have-nots of the slums of American cities are at a distinct disadvantage with regard to institutionalized norms of competence. Perhaps the most obvious outcome of the Model Cities Program is its failure to promote, encourage, stimulate, or lead urban institutions to meet the needs of ethnic minority groups. Where municipal governments and official policy makers sought to impose a traditional definition and to limit the participation concept, ethnic minorities have sought to define participation in terms of collective self-determination.

608    Mladenka, Kenneth R. "Citizen Demand and Bureaucratic Response: Direct Dialing Democracy in a Major American City." URBAN AFFAIRS QUARTERLY 12 (March 1977): 273-90.

To what extent do citizens influence the response of local governments and the bureaucrats who work for those governments? Based on data from Houston, Texas, this study finds that citizens are generally unsuccessful in obtaining benefits from government contact for two reasons: few contacts are made, and many of those that are made are ignored by the government.

609    _____. "Organizational Rules, Service Equality, and Distributional Decisions in Urban Politics." SOCIAL SCIENCE QUARTERLY 59 (June 1978): 192-201.

A popular theme in recent urban research is that of "equity in the delivery of public services." It is popular to assume that minority and low-income areas are systematically deprived of their fair share of urban services. This article, based on data from several Virginia cities, indicates that organizational rules and administrative routine explain distributional decisions. Consequences for minority and low-income neighborhoods are the same.

610    Mladenka, Kenneth R., and Hill, K.Q. "The Distribution of Benefits in an Urban Environment." URBAN AFFAIRS QUARTERLY 13 (September 1977): 73-94.

The neighborhood distribution of park and library services in Houston is analyzed. Inequalities in distribution based on race and income are dispersed rather than cumulative. Distributional decisions are made on the basis of bureaucratic rules and are little affected by explicit racial and socioeconomic criteria. However, the service rules may have distributional consequences.

611    Moynihan, Daniel P. TOWARD A NATIONAL URBAN POLICY. New York: Basic Books, 1970. 348 p.

In his introduction, Moynihan writes: ". . . for the men charged with the governance of our cities, great and small, politics has become a matter of highest priority." Twenty-four urban experts explore different facets of urban policy from housing to transportation and from crime to education.

612    Mudd, John. "Beyond Community Control: A Neighborhood Strategy for City Government." PUBLIUS 6 (Fall 1976): 113-35.

The thrust of the decentralization movement of the past ten years has been almost exclusively directed toward increased citizen participation, or political decentralization. This focus

has led to the demand for local control of the public schools
and ultimately to various proposals for full-scale neighborhood government. Political and administrative decentralization are closely tied and either, if implemented in isolation,
will tend to be ineffective.

613    Murphy, Thomas P., and Warren, Charles R., eds. ORGANIZING
PUBLIC SERVICES TO METROPOLITAN AMERICA. Lexington, Mass.:
Lexington Books, 1974. 245 p.

This is a collection of thirteen essays in handbook form discussing different ways to deliver public services in a metropolitan area. Among the topics included: political feasibility
of local government reorganization, centralizing reorganizations,
allocation of urban government functions, impact of centralization on access and equity, several pieces on decentralization,
and the metropolitan future.

614    Nicoson, William. "The United States: The Battle for Title VII."
In NEW PERSPECTIVES ON COMMUNITY DEVELOPMENT, edited by
Mahlon Apgar, pp. 38-58. London and New York: McGraw-Hill, 1976.

The objectives of the 1970 Urban Growth and New Community
Development Act (Title VII) were to promote the orderly development of planned new communities, strengthen the capacity
of state and local government, increase the capabilities of the
home-building industry, and aid the economic potential of older
central cities. A set of carefully tailored programs offered
financial and technical assistance to public and private land
developers who complied with federal standards. The absence of national growth policy was dramatized by recurring
debates over the location of new communities, and HUD was
accused of offering a program before it had a policy. By
1974, the recession had thrown a number of the approved projects into serious financial crisis, and in January 1975 HUD
suspended application processing for quaranty assistance,
the only surviving Title VI program.

615    Nordlinger, Eric A., and Hardy, Jim. "Urban Decentralization: An
Evaluation of Four Models." PUBLIC POLICY 20 (Summer 1972):
359-96.

Decentralization supporters argue that city services will improve, political alienation will decrease, and government will
be more responsive to the people than under current centralized
approaches. The authors review bureaucratic, advisory, governmental, and little city hall decentralization models and assess
their respective strengths and weaknesses according to the
goals of the proponents.

616    Nuttall, Ronald L., and Bolan, Richard S. URBAN PLANNING AND
POLITICS. Lexington, Mass.: Lexington Books, 1975. 211 p.

The book presents a comprehensive theory of community decision making which draws on the approaches of such urban
writers as Edward Banfield, Robert Dahl, Alan Altshuler,
Francine Rabinowitz, and Kenneth Clarke.

617    Oates, W.E.; Howrey, E.P.; and Baumol, W.J.    "The Analysis of
       Public Policy in Dynamic Urban Models."    JOURNAL OF POLITICAL
       ECONOMY    79 (January–February 1971):    142–53.

       In a process of cumulative city deterioration, dynamic models
       incorporating policy variables may be critical in determining
       which measures are likely to produce the desired change.
       This paper presents several dynamic models and explores
       their implications for policies to achieve various goals.

618    O'Dell, Doyne D.    "The Structure of Metropolitan Political Systems:
       A Conceptual Model."    WESTERN POLITICAL QUARTERLY    26
       (March 1973):    64–82.

       Metropolitan political systems are classified according to
       structural–functional analysis which assumes that political
       structures have an effect on the performance of political
       functions.

619    Orr, Larry L.    INCOME, EMPLOYMENT, AND URBAN RESIDENTIAL
       LOCATION.    New York:    Academic Press, 1975.    140 p.

       A model of the spatial distribution of employment and residence
       by income class in an urban area was developed in order to
       test certain hypotheses.    The results generally support the
       hypothesis that the residential location of low–income house-
       holds is more sensitive to employment opportunities and housing
       costs than that of higher income households, while some
       support was lent to the hypothesis that the residential location
       of high–income families is sensitive to municipal finance varia-
       bles, such as service quality and tax rates.    Doubt was cast
       upon the third premise––that restrictive density zoning ordi-
       nances in suburban communities operate to exclude low–income
       families.

620    Ostrom, Elinor.    "Exclusion Choice and Divisibility:    Factors Affecting
       the Measurement of Urban Agency Output and Impact."    SOCIAL SCI-
       ENCE QUARTERLY    54 (March 1974):    691–99.

       This article introduces a symposium devoted to measuring
       urban agency output and performance.    It reviews four major
       papers and two comments and considers three attributes of
       urban agency output:    exclusion, choice, and divisibility.

621    _____.    "Metropolitan Reform:    Propositions Derived from Two Tradi-
       tions."    SOCIAL SCIENCE QUARTERLY    53 (December 1972):    474–93.

       This is an essay based on a review of the political reform
       literature.    Ostrom discusses the underlying theoretical struc-
       ture of the metropolitan reform tradition and an alternative
       theoretical structure from political economy literature.

622    _____, ed.    THE DELIVERY OF URBAN SERVICES:    OUTCOMES
       OF CHANGE.    Sage Urban Affairs Annual Reviews, vol. 10.    Beverly
       Hills, Calif.:    Sage, 1976.    320 p.

This effort seeks to determine if social scientists know anything of value to help local public officials and citizens in
organizing the delivery of urban services more effectively.
Each of the eleven chapters deal with a different public service
area: housing, juvenile corrections, fiscal-equalization,
education, water resources, special districts, ballot reform,
solid waste collection, fire protection, police provision of
physicians' services.

623  Papageorgiou, G.J. "Political Aspects of Social Justice and Physical
     Planning in an Abstract City." GEOGRAPHICAL ANALYSIS 10
     (October 1978): 373-85.

     Short-run (or direct) policy impacts in cities cause other
     policies, especially in democracies where such direct policy
     has strong political impact. The author analyzes the marginal
     utility and benefits of public expenditure. He then explores
     the inconsistency between short-run criteria and incidences
     of urban policy; inconsistency is dependent upon the structure
     of individual preferences.

624  Petersen, Nancy Mitchell. "Federal Policy: Reflections on Dayton."
     NATION'S CITIES 14 (March 1976): 26-27.

     More than a hundred cities are beginning to conserve their
     urban areas through improved growth management and planning,
     changed housing codes and enforcement regulations, restored
     historic areas, and better public service programs. The
     national government has a long history of not assessing the
     impact of federal policy on cities, but some federal policy-
     makers are supporting ideas and programs that are similar
     to urban conservation.

625  Pressman, Jeffrey L. "Preconditions of Mayoral Leadership." AMERI-
     CAN POLITICAL SCIENCE REVIEW 66 (June 1972): 511-24.

     Mayoral leadership is a crucial element in a city's ability
     to deal with its problems. This study suggests that success-
     ful mayoral leadership and resource pyramiding may be limited
     by governmental structure, the personality of the mayor, and
     the nature of the political system.

626  Prottas, Jeffrey Manditch. "The Power of the Street-Level Bureaucrat
     in Public Service Bureaucracies." URBAN AFFAIRS QUARTERLY
     13 (March 1978): 285-312.

     The article develops a theoretical explanation for the difficulty
     public organizations have in controlling the daily behavior of
     street level bureaucrats. Prottas develops the concept "bound-
     ary actor" and suggests that the power base of the SLB is
     his unique role as mediator between the bureaucracy and its
     representation on the street.

627  Ranney, David C. PLANNING AND POLITICS IN THE METROPOLIS.
     Columbus, Ohio: Charles E. Merrill Publishing Co., 1969. 179 p.

This book analyzes the concern for planning by governments in metropolitan areas. It is intended to provide the reader with a basic understanding of the planning function. Among the general topics covered are: the planner's heritage of physical design, utopias and reform; planning organization in local governments; intergovernmental relations and local planning; metropolitanism and the planning function; the politics of planning; and the determinants of political involvement in planning.

628    Rapp, Brian; and Patitucci, Frank. "Improving the Performance of City Government: A Third Alternative." PUBLIUS 6 (Fall 1976): 63-91.

A third alternative is available to local government officials faced with soaring costs and increased demands for more and better services aside from raising taxes or cutting back services; for example, increasing the capacity of local officials to use available resources more efficiently and effectively. Strengthening the management process can improve the performances of any institution, public or private, for it will be produced with available resources than would otherwise be the case.

629    Reinning, Henry, Jr., ed. "Governing Megacentropolis." PUBLIC ADMINISTRATION REVIEW 30 (September-October 1970): 473-520.

This series of articles grew out of a 1969 Los Angeles City Charter Commission Study and, as the symposium editor says, ". . . a sense of frustration." It is frustration in the sense that Los Angeles is not a city in a governance sense, and no ideal regional government has yet been designed in this nation. The six articles are simply titled "The People," "The Problem," "The Constraints," "The Politics," "The Leader," and "The Goals."

630    Roeseler, W.G. "Supercity--Last Phase: Toward New National Goals of Urbanization." MIDWEST REVIEW OF PUBLIC ADMINISTRATION 11 (March 1977): 79-82.

Large American cities exhibit a combination of total size and intensity of human settlement which is consistently counter-productive when compared with more satisfying conditions elsewhere. Tax incentives may be used to encourage a massive resettlement program. Any person living in designated areas of overcrowding will be given a tax reduction if that person settles in another area seen as capable of rational urban development.

631    Rogers, David. CAN BUSINESS MANAGEMENT SAVE THE CITIES? THE CASE OF NEW YORK. New York: Free Press, 1978. 276 p.

This is an evaluation of a policy of corporate and governmental cooperation in urban revitalization, the Economic Development Council of New York. Rogers analyzes the efforts of the EDC to reverse the socioeconomic decline of New York through the application of private sector management techniques to public agencies (especially the schools and courts), and finds serious failings. In conclusion, he suggests where similar policies might work and notes the continued salience of politics to city management.

632 _____. THE MANAGEMENT OF BIG CITIES. Beverly Hills, Calif.: Sage, 1971. 192 p.

This is a comparative study of the power structures in New York City, Philadelphia, and Cleveland. Rogers examines the obstacles to reform and to innovative government arising from the lack of adaptability of bureaucracies. In order for large cities to solve their problems, there must be change in the structure of the organizations that comprise government.

633 Rondinelli, Dennis A. "Urban Planning As Policy Analysis: Management of Urban Change." JOURNAL OF THE AMERICAN INSTITUTE OF PLANNERS 39 (January 1973): 13-22.

Current approaches to a methodology of urban planning are inadequate for effective urban policy analysis. Policy planning is a complex process that is linked to urban change. Research is needed into the structure of urban policy formulation and implementation, intervention strategies, processes of interaction, and techniques of change-program management.

634 Rosenbloom, Richard S., and Russell, John R. NEW TOOLS FOR URBAN MANAGEMENT. Cambridge, Mass.: Harvard University Press, 1971. 298 p.

Four case studies make up this work. The first compares the kinds of tools necessary for solving unemployment problems in Dayton, Ohio, model cities neighborhood with the application of system analysis to locating a fire station in another city. The second case studies the application of systems analysis to New York state's budget bureau; the third shows the application of systems analysis in New Jersey's Housing Finance Agency; and the last relates innovations in planning and building Columbia, Maryland.

635 Rosenthal, Donald B. "Power, Politics, and Public Policy in American Urban Research." POLITY 5 (Summer 1973): 531-46.

This is a review essay of ten books concerned with various dimensions of urban policy and politics. The thrust of recent writings as demonstrated in these works is that public policy decisions are political, not scientific, and thus choices made by political actors are extremely important to the process.

636 Rowe, Lloyd A. "The Coming Crisis of the Urban Administrator." MIDWEST REVIEW OF PUBLIC ADMINISTRATION 5 (August 1971): 105-9.

It is time to reevaluate the role of the local professional administrator in the urban political process. It is necessary that the modern administration play a larger role than merely that of "neutral expert."

637  Sacco, John F., and Parle, William M. "Policy Preferences among Urban Mayors: A Comparative Analysis." URBAN AFFAIRS QUARTER-LY 13 (September 1977): 49-72.

The purpose of this paper is to determine which of a selected number of factors in the urban environment are important in influencing the priorities and goals mayors espouse for their cities. Four goal areas--community attractiveness, economic development, aid to the disadvantaged, and government effi-ciency--were selected for analysis. The results suggest that no one political or social factor in the urban environ-ment dominates across all four goal areas, but rather that there tends to be a different politics at work in each goal area.

638  Savas, Emmanuel S. "An Empirical Study of Competition in Municipal Service Delivery." PUBLIC ADMINISTRATION REVIEW 37 (November-December 1977): 717-24.

Most urban services exist within a monopolistic organizational framework; for example, there is one school system, one fire department, one police department. In the area of refuse collection, however, it is possible to compare the relative effectiveness and efficiency of competition versus monopoly. Based on the experience of Minneapolis, Minnesota, this study concludes that the delivery of a public service can be improved by introducing competition.

639  _____. "New Directions for Urban Analysis." INTERFACES 6 (November 1975): 1-9.

Quantitative analysis has been applied to many urban service systems; however, its application to the strategic or policy level to solve urban problems has been less successful. Some of the difficulties are similar to those found in other applica-tion areas, while others are common to public sector problems or peculiar to local government.

640  Schnore, Leo F., and Fagin, Henry. URBAN RESEARCH AND POLICY PLANNING. Sage Urban Affairs Annual Reviews, vol. 1. Beverly Hills, Calif.: Sage, 1967. 638 p.

The twenty papers are grouped according to research priori-ties in urban affairs, and then by area of study, such as social psychology and political science. The planning papers deal with expanding the horizon of planning: technology, human environment, policy and action, and the world and nation.

641  Solomon, Arthur P. "Five Land Use Reforms Suggested to Resolve Problems of Urban Growth." JOURNAL OF HOUSING 34 (June 1977): 276-81.

Land use in the United States is primarily viewed in commercial terms, rather than as a precious resource. To use land for profitable means exclusively may not be in the best interest of society. Currently, there is little incentive to use land consistently with larger social objectives. A land-use system responsive to both public planning and private use must be devised.

642    Sonenblum, Sidney; Kirlin, John J.; and Ries, John C. HOW CITIES PROVIDE SERVICES: AN EVALUATION OF ALTERNATIVE DELIVERY STRUCTURES. Cambridge, Mass.: Ballinger Publishing Co., 1977. 272 p.

This volume reports on the findings of a research study and presents a model of the processes used by city officials in deciding whether and how to change existing structures or adopt new structures for providing municipal services. The study is a comparison of municipal service contracting with other ways cities provide services in Los Angeles County and throughout California.

643    Sternlieb, George, and Hughes, James W. "Neighborhood Dynamics and Government Policy." AMERICAN REAL ESTATE AND URBAN ECONOMICS ASSOCIATION JOURNAL 2 (Fall 1974): 7-23.

The forces for neighborhood deterioration are separable into those of internal origin and those external to the neighborhood itself. The most ordered conceptions of neighborhood evolution focus upon five distinct, identifiable stages in the decline process. A broad system of neighborhood and urban indicators should be utilized as a basic sorting mechanism for programs which are going either into areas in which success has a high probability or into those which have a high danger content.

644    Stipak, Brian. "Citizen Satisfaction with Urban Services: Potential Misuses as a Performance Indicator." PUBLIC ADMINISTRATION REVIEW 39 (January-February 1979): 46-52.

Policy analysts should use caution in using survey data on citizen satisfaction with local services to measure governmental performance. Response to survey items may not reflect the actual service that government provides. Statistical and conceptual problems may often invalidate using such data to evaluate local services.

645    Strange, John H., ed. "Citizens Action in Model Cities and CAP Program: Case Studies and Evaluation." PUBLIC ADMINISTRATION REVIEW 32 (September 1972): 377-470.

Prepared as part of the National Academy of Public Administration's study of "Crisis, Conflict, and Creativity" in model cities and community action programs, these eight essays served on background and discussion papers for two HUD-sponsored conferences in 1970. They deal with a city hall view of citizen participation, a Philadelphia example, participation versus cooperation, federally financed citizen involvement programs, and several other topics.

646    Swanson, Cheryl. "The Influence of Organization and Environment on Arrest Policies in Major U.S. Cities." POLICY STUDIES JOURNAL 7, no.3 (1978): 390–97.

This study examines factors that influence discretionary decisions in police departments in large U.S. cities using variation in arrest patterns as the dependent variable. Police organizations are viewed as both closed and open systems. Findings show support for viewing police departments as open systems so that in addition to levels of crime activity, citizens' preferences and values have an important influence on law enforcement decisions.

647    Swant, Frank. "Linking Theory and Method in Urban Policy Analysis: Problems of Test Interpretation." POLITICAL METHODOLOGY 4, no. 3 (1977): 333–46.

Statistical techniques have not helped to determine whether political or sociological variables are more important in explaining public policy. This paper explains why it is wrong to test the strength of different variables by using partial correlation and why single equation regression analysis may lead to overestimating the strength of socioeconomic variables.

648    Szanton, Peter L. "Analysis and Urban Government: Experience of the New York City–Rand Institute." POLICY SCIENCES 3 (1972): 153–61.

Szanton reviews the experiment between New York City and Rand of subjecting city problems to independent evaluation. The background of the experiment is described along with the efforts made to institutionalize it. In addition, the nature and effect of analyses and the lessons learned by participants are described.

649    "Technology for the City." PUBLIC MANAGEMENT 55 (August 1973): 2–23.

Here are thirteen short pieces devoted to the application of technology to urban problems. Included are police, fire, training, computers, technology applications, and the future of technology.

650    Teune, Henry. "Macro Theoretical Approaches to Public Policy Analysis: The Fiscal Crisis of American Cities." ANNALS OF THE AMERICAN ACADEMY OF POLITICAL AND SOCIAL SCIENCE 434 (November 1977): 174–85.

Most empirical research on the consequences of public policy follows a micro, historical, and incremental approach. The validity of predictions is limited. A macro, theoretical, and structural approach is presented as an alternative. Such a reorganization will not only provide understanding of the context of policy predictions, but also opportunities for testing them historically and comparatively. The approach is illustrated with three macro structural theories of the urban fiscal crisis of the United States: the conflict between the demand for wel-

fare and capital for economic growth; the decline of the city
as a political force in the national politics of economic distribution; and the changing technological base of cities and
their economic viability.

651    Tropman, John E., and Lind, Roger.  "Urban Policy Perspectives in
the U.S.A.:  An Extension of the Yarmolinksy Option."  POLICY SCI-
ENCES  4 (June 1973):  223-27.

Adam Yarmolinsky has suggested that the federal government
guarantee the equity that homeowners have developed in their
property.  Tropman and Lind expand on that idea to develop
a more complete urban policy package.  They claim that the
value of a house depends to a great deal on the perceived
quality of educational access available to the household.

652    "Urban Policy:  A Symposium."  POLICY STUDIES JOURNAL  3
(Summer 1975):  320-69.

This is a collection of eleven articles on urban policy divided
into urbanization, metropolitanism, and policy; the politics
of policy change; and changing parameters of the policy-making
system.

653    Walker, David.  "The Prospects for Administrative Decentralization
in Our Cities."  PUBLIUS  6 (Fall 1976):  137-39.

In order for decentralizing efforts to succeed, they must sur-
mount five hurdles:  the civil service systems, the high degree
of professionalization in many city bureaucracies, the public
sector unions, the absence of a strong territorial basis for
political organization, and finally, a fiscal factor.

654    Walker, Warren E.  PERFORMING POLICY ANALYSIS FOR MUNICIPAL
AGENCIES:  LESSONS FROM NEW YORK CITY-RAND INSTITUTE'S
FIRE PROJECT.  New York:  Rand Institute, 1975.  22 p.

Numerous changes were made in fire department operations
as a result of Rand's suggestions.  It is not clear if the
ultimate objective, the ability to transfer the mathematical
models and methods to a city, can be realized without outside technical assistance.

655    Warren, Robert, and Weschler, Louis.  "Governing Urban Space:  Multi-
Boundary Politics."  POLICY STUDIES JOURNAL  3 (Spring 1975):
240-47.

Cities are affected by events and transactions well beyond
their corporate boundaries, and they produce external effects
for other communities.  Some argue that cities are becoming
less able to control affairs within their own boundaries.  We
have few concepts and no agreed-upon language which might
allow us to deal systematically with these and other issues.
The categorization and differentiation of boundaries provide
a basis for mapping the external space upon which a city
is dependent for resources and for considering possible sub-
stitutions as the availability of external resources is changed.

656    Warren, Roland L.   "The Sociology of Knowledge and the Problems
       of the Inner Cities."   SOCIAL SCIENCE QUARTERLY   52 (December
       1971):   469-91.

       This is a study of community decision organizations in nine
       cities in which Warren attempts to trace some of the inter-
       connections between knowledge and the social structure.   Two
       alternative paradigms for diagnosing poverty are discussed:
       one stressing deficient individuals, the other dysfunctions of
       the social system.

657    Welch, Susan, and Karnig, Albert K.   "The Impact of Black Elected
       Officials on Urban Social Expenditures."   POLICY STUDIES JOURNAL
       7 (Summer 1979):   707-14.

       The presence of a black mayor promotes greater increases
       in social welfare spending than in cities with no black mayor.
       However, black representation on the city council makes little
       difference in social welfare spending.

658    Wikstrom, Nelson.   "The Mayor as a Policy Leader in the Council-
       Manager Form of Government:   A View from the Field."   PUBLIC
       ADMINISTRATION REVIEW   39 (May-June 1979):   270-76.

       Textbook descriptions of the role of the mayor in the council-
       manager form of government describe his role as symbolic
       and rather restricted.   This paper argues that in fact he plays
       a strong policy-determining role.   The implications include
       the emergence of teamwork governance, merging of policy-
       making and administration, and the democratization of the
       council-manager plan.

659    Wilson, James Q., ed.   CITY POLITICS AND PUBLIC POLICY.   New
       York:   John Wiley and Sons, 1968.   300 p.

       A volume of empirical studies deals with city public policies
       in the areas of community development, finance, education,
       law enforcement, health and welfare.   More than half of the
       studies come from a panel at the 1966 American Political
       Science Association meeting held in New York City.

660    _____.   THE METROPOLITAN ENIGMA:   INQUIRIES INTO THE
       NATURE AND DIMENSIONS OF AMERICA'S URBAN CRISIS.   Cam-
       bridge, Mass.:   Harvard University Press, 1968.   300 p.

       Wilson attempts to analyze the various problems which are sub-
       sumed in the phrase "urban crisis."   He contends that not all
       problems in the cities are uniquely urban.   The essays in this
       book are an effort to clear away the generalities and explore
       the complexities of urban problems.   Topics include employ-
       ment and industrial mobility, transportation, financing urban
       government, pollution, race, housing, poverty, crime, and
       urban design and planning.

661    Wilson, James Q., and Wilde, Harold R.   "The Urban Mood."   COM-
       MENTARY   48 (October 1969):   52-61.

This article concerns itself with the importance of "backlash" in the election of mayors and what difference public opinion makes in the choice of public officials and the formation of public policy.

662    Wolfinger, Raymond, and Field, James. "Political Ethos and the Structure of City Government." AMERICAN POLITICAL SCIENCE REVIEW 60 (June 1966): 303-26.

The public and private-regarding ethos theory of government assumes that much of what people think about government can be subsumed under one of these categories. This article examines the association between these ethics and the demographic characteristics said to be their foundation. Based on the data presented, the ethos theory needs considerable modification to take into account ethnic, regional and other variables.

663    Wood, Robert C. "A Matter of National Urgency." NATIONAL CIVIC REVIEW 66 (January 1977): 15-18.

It is clear that in the absence of a national urban policy, our cities are now carrying much more than their fair share of the national burden. If we restore the appropriate lines of responsibility for our common efforts, then we can think more clearly about the outlines of a feasible national policy for our urban regions.

664    Yates, Douglas T., Jr. "Making Decentralization Work: The View from City Hall." POLICY SCIENCES 5 (September 1974): 363-73.

The success of decentralization experiments depends upon central government. Programs and approaches that look promising to city hall fail at the street level because they are seen as insensitive to the needs of residents and consumers of the service. Successful decentralization depends on a learning process between citizens and public employees to develop strategies for working together on neighborhood problems.

665    _____. "Neighborhood Government." POLICY SCIENCES 3 (July 1972): 209-17.

Advocacy of neighborhood government should be based on a careful assessment of dangers and deficiencies as well as merits. There are many obstacles to increasing neighborhood power. Serious participation is likely to occur only when neighborhood governments offer visible rewards and seek to solve tangible problems.

666    Yin, Robert K.; Hearn, Robert W.; and Shapiro, Paula M. "Administrative Decentralization of Municipal Services: Assessing the New York City Experience." POLICY SCIENCES 5 (March 1974): 54-70.

This study evaluates New York City's Office of Neighborhood
Government experiment with administrative decentralization.
The study concludes that major shifts in responsibility from
city hall to the district level occurred only in one management function, interagency communication.  The authors doubt
that administrative decentralization is a feasible alternative
for reorganizing municipal services to increase responsiveness
to neighborhoods.

667    Yin, Robert K., and Yates, Douglas T., Jr.  STREET-LEVEL GOVERN-
MENTS: ASSESSING DECENTRALIZATION AND URBAN SERVICES.
Lexington, Mass.:  D.C. Heath, 1975.  276 p.

STREET-LEVEL GOVERNMENT accounts for the success of
efforts to decentralize urban services.  Yin and Yates argue
the inapplicability of short term, rigorously scientific evaluation techniques to ongoing decentralizing efforts.  They agree
with the reformist critique that decentralization has not given
clients substantial authority, with participants who claim that
gains were not worth the individual effort, and with the majority culture that, overall, decentralization didn't improve the
services.

668    Young, Dennis R.  "Institutional Change and the Delivery of Urban
Public Services."  POLICY SCIENCES  2 (December 1971):  425-38.

The problems associated with the efficient and equitable distribution of public services can be traced in part to the in-
abilities of government and other public institutions to be responsive to the needs of their clientele.  The paper looks at
urban service delivery in a system perspective and identifies
error signals a system needs to generate corrective mechanisms
it may use, and then discusses performance evaluation, decentralization, and market competition as modes of institutional
reform.

# Chapter 6

# INTERGOVERNMENTAL ASPECTS OF PUBLIC POLICY

669    Adams, Bruce, and Sherman, Betsy. "Sunset Implementation:   A
       Positive Partnership to Make Government Work." PUBLIC ADMINISTRA-
       TION REVIEW   38 (January–February 1978):   78–81.

       This study presents a review of the specifics of sunset legis-
       lation, its workings, and advantages and disadvantages.   The
       authors conclude that sunset legislation should not be seen as
       a cure-all for governmental ills but as an idea with promise.

670    Ahlbrandt, Roger S., Jr.   "Governmentally Assisted Housing:   Institu-
       tions and Incentives."   In THE DELIVERY OF URBAN SERVICES:
       OUTCOMES OF CHANGE, edited by Elinor Ostrom, pp. 15–47.   Urban
       Affairs Annual Reviews.   Beverly Hills, Calif.: Sage, 1976.

       Federal housing policy has emphasized private-sector involve-
       ment.   The role of local governments should be in halting
       neighborhood decline.

671    Bernstein, Samuel J.; Mellon, W.G.; and Handelman, Sigmund. "Re-
       gional Stabilization: A Model for Policy Decision." POLICY SCIENCES
       4 (September 1973):   309–25.

       The paper develops a simulation model of the effects of alter-
       native policy choices and their resulting impacts.   Issues
       dealt with include budgeting, federal grants, and city sales
       taxes.

672    Brintnall, Michael A.   "Federal Influence and Urban Policy Entrepre-
       neurship in the Local Prosecution of Economic Crime."   POLICY
       STUDIES JOURNAL   7 (Spring 1979):   577–92.

       In the early 1970s local prosecutors began programs aimed
       at white collar crime and consumer fraud.   It addresses the
       sources, character, and consequences of local policy initia-
       tives and the character of federal influence.

673    Carter, Marshall.   "Law Enforcement and Federalism:   Bordering on
       Trouble."   POLICY STUDIES JOURNAL   7 (Special Issue) (1978):
       413–18.

       The complexity of U.S. federalism is most apparent in the
       area of law enforcement with over forty thousand separate
       law enforcement agencies.

The complexity is even more apparent in the United States-
Mexico border area because of the extensiveness of enforcement and the presence of another federal system's police
agencies.

674 Clark, Terry Nichols. "Community Social Indicators: From Analytical
Models to Policy Applications." URBAN AFFAIRS QUARTERLY 9
(September 1973): 3-36.

Two types of social indicators may be identified according
to their use: descriptive and analytical. To develop more
reliable indicators the federal government should encourage
more standardization in the collecting and reporting of data.

675 _____. "Community Structure, Decision-Making, Budget Expenditures,
and Urban Renewal in Fifty-One American Communities." AMERICAN
SOCIOLOGICAL REVIEW 33 (August 1968): 576-93.

A body of propositions relating community structural characteristics to decision-making patterns and to budget and urban
renewal expenditures was tested. Larger, more economically
diversified communities with governmental structures favoring
citizen participation had more decentralized decision making.

676 Clayton, Ross; Conklin, Patrick; and Shapek, Raymond, eds. "Policy
Management Assistance: A Developing Dialogue." PUBLIC ADMINIS-
TRATION REVIEW 35 (December 1975): 693-818.

This is a special issue devoted to a symposium on policy
management assistance. The twenty-one essays are divided
into six major subject headings; all deal with the public
management capabilities of local officials.

677 Daly, George, and Brady, David W. "Federal Regulation of Economic
Activity: Failures and Reforms." In ECONOMIC REGULATORY POLI-
CIES, edited by James Anderson, pp. 171-86. Lexington, Mass.:
Lexington Books, 1976.

The paper outlines rationales and methods of regulation and
shows the reasoning behind different kinds of regulation reform. It analyzes the future of economic regulatory reform,
summarizes economic and political rationales for regulation
and outlines the major methods of regulation.

678 Danielson, Michael N.; Hershey, Alan M.; and Bayne, John M. ONE
NATION, SO MANY GOVERNMENTS. Lexington, Mass.: Lexington
Books, 1977. 160 p.

The book examines urbanization, economic growth and other
large-scale shifts in the United States. It focuses on the
impact of specific changes that have occurred over the past
decade.

679 Derthick, Martha. "Defeat at Fort Lincoln." PUBLIC INTEREST,
no. 20, (Summer 1970): pp. 3-39.

Derthick gives a detailed analysis of what happened when
political leaders and planners set out to demonstrate how
much they could do in an American city. The idea was to
build housing for the poor on federally owned land in U.S.
cities. It is a case study of the interests and actors involved in the Fort Lincoln project in Washington, D.C.

680 _____. THE INFLUENCE OF FEDERAL GRANTS: PUBLIC ASSIS-
TANCE IN MASSACHUSETTS. Cambridge, Mass.: Harvard University Press, 1970. 295 p.

The essay analyzes the administration of a public assistance
program in Massachusetts from 1930 through 1967. It shows
what federal administrators sought to achieve, their techniques
and strategies, and the effect their actions had on state and
local governments. The book examines the federal process
at work in the interaction of governments.

681 Dommel, Paul R. "Distributive Politics and Urban Policy." POLICY
STUDIES JOURNAL 3, no. 4 (1975): 370-75.

At a time when pressure is mounting to control the growth
of federal aid and spending is growing, increasing amounts
of federal aid are available under the influence of the "something for everyone" philosophy of distributive politics.

682 Doron, Gideon. "Administrative Regulation of an Industry: The Cigarette
Case." PUBLIC ADMINISTRATION REVIEW 39 (March-April 1979):
163-70.

While regulation might be initiated to serve the public interest,
its consequences may be in tune with the interests of the
regulated industry. The decision to prohibit cigarette advertising on the broadcast media might be viewed as an industry victory from several perspectives.

683 "Economic Regulation Policy, A Symposium." POLICY STUDIES JOUR-
NAL 4 (Autumn 1975): 7-62.

Nine articles on economic regulatory policy divided into economic stability, agriculture, consumer protection, and govern-
ment-business relationships.

684 Elazar, Daniel J. "Toward Federal-State Partnerships in Science and
Technology." STATE GOVERNMENT 48 (Spring 1975): 131-35.

In science and technology, states should undertake new functions in cooperation with federal agencies in policymaking and
implementation, diffusion of knowledge, innovation, regulatory
activities, and resource allocation.

685 Emanuel, Aaron. "Regional Policy: The Issue Facing Governments."
OECD OBSERVER 67 (December 1973): 11-13.

Regional and intraregional development is influenced by population, occupational distribution, GNP, technological change,
and inflationary trends.

686     Farkas, Suzanne. "The Federal Role in Urban Decentralization."
AMERICAN BEHAVIORAL SCIENTIST 15 (September-October 1971):
15-35.

> The impact of federal funding and guidelines has contributed
> to the demand for the decentralization of municipal services.
> Urban decentralization has been viewed as a matter of re-
> structuring or reforming local government.

687     Flajser, Steven H. "Revenue Sharing Voucher Program (RSVP)."
POLICY SCIENCES 5 (September 1974): 309-15.

> At a time when there is a challenge to provide more and
> better-informed citizen participation in decision making, there
> is also a demand for increased efficiency in the delivery of
> governmental services. These challenges can be met via
> the RSVP program. It involves giving revenue sharing money
> to citizens in the form of vouchers and allowing them to "buy"
> local government services.

688     Fox, Douglas M. "Intergovernmental Relations." In THE POLITICS
OF CITY AND STATE BUREAUCRACY, edited by Douglas M. Fox,
pp. 72-85. Pacific Palisades, Calif.: Goodyear Publishing Co.,
1974.

> While many states have home-rule provisions in their constitu-
> tions, a state agency can still force a local government to
> accede to state law. Federal grants have altered the nature
> of subnational policy implementation by enlarging state and
> local civil services, by limiting local implementation authority,
> and by the imposition of single-state agency requirements.

689     Gold, Byron D. "The Role of the Federal Government in the Provision
of Social Services to Older Americans." ANNALS OF THE AMERICAN
ACADEMY OF POLITICAL AND SOCIAL SCIENCE 415 (September
1974): 55-69.

> A role of the federal government in trying to improve the
> conditions of the elderly is the financing of social services
> provision. Until a more appropriate response mechanism is
> found (such as the private sector market), government will
> continue to provide such services and in increasing amounts.

690     Goldman, Lawrence. "Federal Policy and the UDC." PLANNER 61
(May 1975): 176-79.

> The New York State Urban Development Corporation (UDC)
> is designed to develop and finance housing for low, moderate,
> and middle-income families; to assist in industrial and com-
> mercial development; and to provide educational, cultural,
> and other civic facilities. Its most serious problem is the
> lack of resources to lower rents in its housing.

691     _____. "Is There a Future for the UDC?" PLANNER 61 (May 1975):
197.

In February 1975, the New York State Urban Development
Corporation (UDC) defaulted on $135 million worth of out-
standing debts.  If sufficient funds are not found the housing
poor stand to lose the most from the disappearance of the
UDC.  The author views the situation as one in which a
changing value structure and the desire to innovate are
giving way to the necessity to survive.

692    Gordon, Robert M., and Hanke, Steven H.  "Federal Milk Marketing
       Orders:  A Policy in Need of Analysis."  POLICY ANALYSIS  4
       (Winter 1978):  23-32.

       The economic effects of federal milk marketing orders have
       not been evaluated to date.  The authors use data from New
       Jersey to show that the costs to consumers from such orders
       can be estimated with moderate effort and expense.  They
       suggest that Congress should pursue a full-scale analysis
       of the costs and benefits of federal milk marketing orders.

693    Gross, Neal.  "Theoretical and Policy Implications of Case Study
       Findings about Federal Efforts to Improve Public Schools."  ANNALS
       OF THE AMERICAN ACADEMY OF POLITICAL AND SOCIAL SCIENCE
       434 (November 1977):  71-87.

       Impediments to educational change were identified in six case
       studies of efforts to institute major innovations in school sys-
       tems.  The major theoretical scheme to account for change--
       overcoming resistance to change--is too simplistic as a tool
       of analysis because it ignores internal and external conditions
       than can have an impact on the fate of innovations.

694    Haar, Charles M., ed.  THE PRESIDENT'S TASK FORCE ON SUBUR-
       BAN PROBLEMS.  Cambridge, Mass.:  Ballinger Books, 1974. 212 p.

       A Lyndon Johnson task force on suburban problems found that
       the suburbs of the United States are in a state of a quiet and
       slowly building crisis which is part of the larger urban crisis.
       They propose several institutional and policy responses to turn
       crisis into an opportunity for renewal and reform.

695    Hale, George, and Palley, Marion Lief.  "The Impact of Federal Funds
       on the State Budgetary Process."  NATIONAL CIVIC REVIEW  67
       (November 1978):  461-64.

       State and local decision making has been altered by increases
       in federal aid.  A consequence is thought to be the creation
       of alliances between professional administrators at the several
       levels of government.  It is also suggested that the presence
       of federal grants reduces the ability of local elected officials
       to control their agencies.

696    Harrison, Russell.  "Federal Categorical Grants and the Stimulation
       of State-Local Expenditures."  PUBLIUS 5 (Fall 1975):  123-36.

After concluding that most research on the question of whether categorical grants stimulate additional spending by recipient agencies has been plagued by systematic biases, Harrison offers revised estimates of the stimulus effects of federal aid on state and local expenditures. He concludes that the stimulus effect is greatly overstated.

697    Jones, Charles O., and Thomas, Robert D. PUBLIC POLICY MAKING IN A FEDERAL SYSTEM. Sage Yearbooks in Politics and Public Policy, vol. 3. Beverly Hills, Calif.: Sage, 1976. 288 p.

The authors examine the relationships between the federal government and state and local agencies, focusing on the evaluation and implementation of various programs. Specific programs included are revenue sharing, environmental protection, model cities, and health delivery systems.

698    Lambright, W. Henry. "Government, Industry and the Research Partnership: The Case of Patent Policy." PUBLIC ADMINISTRATION REVIEW 28 (May–June 1968): 214–21.

Patent policy is one of the most troubling areas of government industry partnership. Government agencies have a variety of approaches to the control of the technology developed through the partnership, and there are a variety of consequences in terms of property rights and commercial value.

699    Lazin, Frederick Aaron. "The Failure of Federal Enforcement of Civil Rights Regulations in Public Housing, 1963–1971: The Co–Optation of a Federal Agency By Its Local Constituency." POLICY SCIENCES 4 (September 1973): 263–73.

This paper discusses the federal role in light of racially discriminatory practices in public housing. It is a case study of federal efforts to deal with the inadequate housing of low–income people in Chicago.

700    Light, Alfred R. "Intergovernmental Sources of Innovation in State Administration." AMERICAN POLITICS QUARTERLY 6 (April 1978): 147–66.

Based on a 1974 survey of state government officials, this article seeks to determine the sources of innovations and ideas for new programs and policy areas.

701    Lurie, Jonathan. "The Commodities Exchanges and Federal Regulation, 1922–1974: The Decline of Self–Government." POLICY STUDIES JOURNAL 6 (Summer 1978): 488–93.

While the Grain Futures Act of 1922 is the basis for all subsequent federal commodities exchange regulation, Congress has enacted several revisions in the legislation. The article seeks to determine how the revisions have affected the exchanges and what insights are provided on the interplay between private enterprise, open markets, and external regulation.

702  Manvel, Allen D.  "The Fiscal Impact of Revenue Sharing."  ANNALS
     OF THE AMERICAN ACADEMY OF POLITICAL AND SOCIAL SCIENCE
     419 (May 1975):  36-49.

     Federal revenue sharing will apparently improve the com-
     petitive fiscal position of central cities relative to their
     suburbs.  In addition it is likely to allow the lowering of
     local taxes.


703  Mitchell, Robert E., and Smith, Richard A.  "Race and Housing:
     A Review and Comments on the Content and Effects of Federal Policy."
     ANNALS OF THE AMERICAN ACADEMY OF POLITICAL AND SOCIAL
     SCIENCE   441 (January 1979):  168-85.

     Housing and community development policies attack the causes
     of racial segregation in urban communities.  Federal antidis-
     criminatory policies have resulted in some success in achieving
     a stable, interracial society and in protecting individual rights.
     Future success will depend on a number of factors not easily
     influenced by public policy.


704  Moynihan, Daniel P.  MAXIMUM FEASIBLE MISUNDERSTANDING.
     New York:  Free Press, 1969.  218 p.

     This is a selective history of the war on poverty and the "Maxi-
     mum Feasible Participation" clause.  His conclusions about the
     utility of arousing the poor to protest at the local level of
     government are basically negative.


705  Newton, Robert D.  "Towards an Understanding of Federal Assistance."
     PUBLIC ADMINISTRATION REVIEW  35 (July-August 1975):  372-77.

     Current concern with federal assistance programs includes
     their outputs, a desire for more decentralized program author-
     ity, and a belief that the consolidation of single-purpose pro-
     grams will solve some problems.


706  Porter, Douglas R.  "Regions and Federal Policy:  The Orphan Annie
     of New Federalism."  BUREAUCRAT  2 (Spring 1973):  36-44.

     Regional agencies appear to be on the way to becoming impor-
     tant actors in the governance process.  Anticipated changes
     in federal support will test their linkages to local governments.


707  Reuss, Henry S.  "Should We Abandon Revenue Sharing?"  ANNALS
     OF THE AMERICAN ACADEMY OF POLITICAL AND SOCIAL SCIENCE
     419 (May 1975):  88-99.

     The 1960s view of revenue sharing was to use federal revenue
     surpluses to improve the delivery of government services to
     local populations.  After it became a Republican campaign
     tool, the formula for distribution guaranteed funds to almost
     all governments regardless of need.


708  Smith, Bruce L.R.  "The Non-Governmental Policy Analysis Organization."
     PUBLIC ADMINISTRATION REVIEW  37 (May-June 1977):  253-57.

This is a review of the role of nongovernmental policy analysis organizations in the evaluation of public policy. Smith concludes that the ranks of private analysts will be thinned out, leaving a smaller group of more highly qualified firms.

709 Smith, Bruce L.R., and LaRoue, George R., eds. "Urban Decentralization and Community Participation, A Symposium." AMERICAN BEHAVIORAL SCIENTIST 15 (September–October 1971): 3–129.

Seven articles that deal with the federal role in urban decentralization, citizen involvement in law enforcement, school decentralization, ghetto health care, and the political economy of decentralization.

710 Van Horn, Carl E. "Evaluating the New Federalism: National Goals and Local Implementors." PUBLIC ADMINISTRATION REVIEW 39 (January–February 1979): 17–22.

Revenue sharing, CETA, and community development block grant programs are considered to determine the pattern of benefits resulting from the new federalism.

711 Van Horn, Carl E., and Van Meter, Donald S. "The Implementation of Intergovernmental Policy." In PUBLIC POLICY MAKING IN A FEDERAL SYSTEM, edited by Charles O. Jones and Robert D. Thomas, pp. 39–62. Beverly Hills, Calif.: Sage, 1976.

A model of intergovernmental policy implementation is developed that allows policy analysts to point to variables that might be changed to improve the delivery of public services.

712 Warner, David G. "Fiscal Federalism in Health Care." PUBLIUS 5 (Fall 1975): 79–100.

The health policy area is noted for its intractability to policy direction. Several variables combine to produce fiscal chaos accompanied by resource allocation and service deterioration.

713 Wright, Deil S. "Intergovernmental Relations: An Analytical Overview." ANNALS OF THE AMERICAN ACADEMY OF POLITICAL AND SOCIAL SCIENCE 416 (1974): 1–16.

The distinguishing features of the U.S. intergovernmental relations system are profiled and the policy trends of the last half-century are viewed through an intergovernmental relations perspective.

714 _____. "Intergovernmental Relations and Policy Choice." PUBLIUS 5 (Fall 1975): 1–24.

Intergovernmental relations and policy choice enjoy timeliness but their significance is unrealized. This article explores the character and content of the terms and looks at the utility of policy choice as a focus for addressing public problems in the intergovernmental relations area.

715    _____, ed.   "Problems of Policy Choice in Intergovernmental Relations."
       PUBLIUS   5 (Fall 1975):   entire issue.

   The seven articles are concerned with urban growth policies,
   responsiveness to citizen-consumers, health care, categorical
   grants and local services, and the expenditure effects of federal aid.

# Chapter 7

# IMPLEMENTATION AND EVALUATION

716   Abert, James G. "Bridging Some Gaps Between Policy-Related Research and Its Generation and Use by the Public Sector." BUREAU-
CRAT 5 (October 1976): 273-94.

Most observers of the interface between the "knowledge buyers"
and the "knowledge sellers" would agree that analysis often
misses the point, is late, or not utilized. Much of the trouble
is caused by rigidity in the institutional arrangements within
which the government and the knowledge-analysis industry
operate. Gap 1 addresses the problem of more effectively
and equitably utilizing the potential of individual researchers
in the academic community. Gap 2 deals with selected tax-
exempt, nonprofit firms; gap 3 is the problem of waste and
inefficiency in competitive contracting.

717   Abt, Clark C., ed. THE EVALUATION OF SOCIAL PROGRAMS.
Beverly Hills, Calif.: Sage, 1977. 504 p.

Abt has collected twenty-nine papers and accompanying discussions from a conference on Social Programs Evaluation
held September 23-24, 1974, in Cambridge, Massachusetts.
Principal topics covered were: evaluation of social experiments, political impact of evaluation research, payoffs of
evaluation research, research versus decision requirements,
evaluation of health programs, evaluation of educational programs, research allocation strategies.

718   Aiken, Michael, and Alford, Robert. "Community Structure and Innovation: The Case of Public Housing." AMERICAN POLITICAL SCI-
ENCE REVIEW 64 (September 1970): 843-64.

This article focuses on three aspects of community innovation:
(1) the presence or absence of federally financed public housing
program in a city; (2) the speed of innovation of such a program; and (3) the level of output or performance of this innovative activity.

719   Altman, Stan. "Performance Monitoring Systems for Public Managers."
PUBLIC ADMINISTRATION REVIEW 39 (January-February 1979):
31-35.

It is now well accepted that a commitment of dollars and personnel to the solution of social problems does not guarantee success. Improved management techniques must be developed if state and local governments are to live up to their potential and to citizen demands. This article describes efforts at developing management information systems as a part of the development of performance monitoring systems in state and local government.

720  Alwin, Duane F., and Sullivan, Michael J. "Issues of Design and Analysis in Evaluation Research." SOCIOLOGICAL METHODS AND RESEARCH 4 (August 1975): 77-100.

The analysis of data in social policy evaluation where true experimental designs for research are either impossible or impractical has led to debate over the issues involved in making policy inferences from these data. Problems of selection threaten sound empirical evaluation research in such settings; the evaluation of social programs is ineffectual in the absence of comparison groups.

721  Anderson, Charles W. "The Logic of Public Problems: Evaluation in Comparative Policy Research." In COMPARING PUBLIC POLICIES: NEW CONCEPTS AND METHODS, edited by Douglas E. Ashford, pp. 19-41. Sage Yearbooks in Politics and Public Policy, vol. 4. Beverly Hills, Calif.: Sage, 1978.

Anderson concerns himself with the evaluation of public policy. Before different public policies can be compared, we must know what problems each policy is trying to solve.

722  Armour, Philip K.; Estes, C.L.; and Noble, Maureen L. "Problems in the Design and Implementation of a National Policy on Aging." In POLICY STUDIES REVIEW ANNUAL, vol. 2, edited by Howard E. Freeman, pp. 616-33. Beverly Hills, Calif.: Sage, 1978.

This paper seeks to answer the question why there is a continuing debate over the effectiveness and appropriateness of the Older Americans Act of 1965 as the national strategy for developing and funding aging services. The authors attempt to clarify the distinctions among policy intent, programmatic intervention strategies, and the implementation apparatus of the act. The basic conclusion is that there are inherent problems in the incremental nature of the implementation portion of the act and only time, not legislative fine tuning, can resolve them.

723  Awerbuch, Shimon, and Wallace, William A. POLICY EVALUATION FOR COMMUNITY DEVELOPMENT. New York: Praeger, 1976. 286 p.

Municipal services have been expanded, but the comprehensive plans of the last twenty years have concentrated on physical planning rather than fiscal and socioeconomic issues. Simple and effective plan-evaluation tools are needed to enable municipal policymakers to rapidly evaluate the impacts of alternative development strategies. An evaluation tool must have the following characteristics: interactive design, usable output, data limitations, fiscal outputs, other indicators regarding quality of life, and ease of implementation. The Community Development Impacts Model (CODIM) is an automated cost-revenue analysis tool which enables a planner to base his or her actions on a broad information base without the manual analysis previously required to determine the impact of development projects.

724   Badawy, M.K. "Applying MBO to the Public Sector." BUREAUCRAT 6 (Fall 1977): 3-18.

This essay has several purposes: (1) to examine some of the problems faced in implementing MBO in public sector service organizations; (2) to show that the problems are not un-solvable and to present a set of conditions for implementing MBO in service organizations.

725   Baer, William C. "On the Making of Perfect and Beautiful Social Programs." PUBLIC INTEREST, no. 39 (Spring 1975): pp. 80-98.

Current thinking attributes the failure of 1960s social programs to the "quality of their craftsmanship," not to the concept of the craftsmanship itself. This essay analyzes a perfect social program, designed by no one, with very positive social effects, the homeowner deduction provisions of the income tax laws which make up the most successful housing subsidy program in the nation.

726   Bardach, Eugene. THE IMPLEMENTATION GAME: WHAT HAPPENS AFTER A BILL BECOMES A LAW. Cambridge: MIT Press, 1977. 323 p.

There are three principal perils in public policy implementa-tion: under-achievement of stated objectives, delay, and ex-cessive financial cost. The implementation process involves pressure politics, intergovernmental bargaining, and adminis-trative control. The goals in a policy statement can be trimmed back, distorted, prevented, or expanded. An agency can meet with tokenism or massive resistance in its efforts to implement programs. Energies are often dissipated in defending a program against its opponents, resulting in delay and under-performance. Delays occur in assembling program elements as well as in reaching collective decisions. Nego-tiation is inefficient and often increases delays.

727   Barmack, Judith A. "The Case Against In-Kind Transfers: The Food Stamp Program." POLICY ANALYSIS 3 (Fall 1977): 509-30.

This paper reviews criteria for the evaluation of public income transfer programs and applies them to an analysis of the Food Stamp Program. Barmack concludes that the Food Stamp Pro-gram intensified and worsened the basic inequity and ineffi-ciency of the American welfare system. As such, it should not be viewed as welfare reform.

728   Baum, Lawrence. "Implementation of Judicial Decisions: An Organi-zational Analysis." AMERICAN POLITICS QUARTERLY 4 (January 1976): 86-114.

Baum contends that organizational analysis provides a promising framework for analyzing the implementation of judicial
decisions. The paper presents an analytic model of the judicial implementation process based on a framework of organizational hierarchy. The author claims that what is new in
the model is its general fragment and perspective on the implementation process and the combination of variables it employs.

729     Behn, Robert D. "How to Terminate a Public Policy: A Dozen Hints
        for the Would-Be Terminator." POLICY ANALYSIS 4 (Summer 1978):
        393–413.

        Public policies are difficult to terminate. The author suggests
        some political strategies that may help policy terminators
        achieve their objectives, but these suggestions are drawn from
        a necessarily limited collection of termination studies. He
        also raises some ethical issues concerning the terminator's
        obligation both to the democratic process and to the conse-
        quences of his policy actions. He feels a better understanding
        of the termination process would not only be intellectually
        interesting, but could have significant practical consequences
        as well.

730     Behn, Robert D., and Clark, Martha A. "The Termination of Beach
        Erosion Control at Cape Hatteras." PUBLIC POLICY 27 (Winter 1979):
        99–127.

        Termination of the beach erosion control policy at Cape
        Hatteras National Seashore suggests several characteristics
        of a successful policy termination: (1) demonstration that
        the policy is harmful; (2) lack of compromise between con-
        tinuation and termination; (3) a broadening of the policy's
        constituency; (4) an active terminator to denigrate the policy
        and implement the termination.

731     Beigel, Allan, and Levenson, Alan I. "Program Evaluation on a Shoe-
        string Budget." In EVALUATION OF HUMAN SERVICE PROGRAMS,
        edited by C. Clifford Attkisson et al., pp. 97–124. New York: Aca-
        demic Press, 1978.

        The authors consider some of the principal ideological and
        pragmatic problems faced by the human service program adminis-
        trator who does not immediately have access to specified eval-
        uation staff and adequate budgetary resources. Evaluation
        strategies that are useful and easily deployed are described.
        These will enable the administrator with few readily available
        budgetary supports to begin some aspects of a comprehensive
        evaluation strategy and will result in the development of infor-
        mation that is useful for policy decisions.

732     Berger, Peter L., and Neuhaus, Richard John. TO EMPOWER PEOPLE:
        THE ROLE OF MEDIATING STRUCTURES IN PUBLIC POLICY. Wash-
        ington, D.C.: American Enterprise Institute for Public Policy Research,
        1978. 45 p.

The authors look at a new way of thinking about public policies designed to meet human needs. The mediating structures of family, neighborhood, church, voluntary associations, and ethnic and racial subcultures are viewed. Public policy should not only protect and foster such institutions, it should use them in advancing social goals.

733    Bergstrom, Theodore C., and Goodman, Robert P. "Private Demands for Public Goods." AMERICAN ECONOMIC REVIEW 63 (June 1973): 280-96.

The authors develop a method for estimating demand functions of individuals for municipal public services. Demand depends on price, income, and demographic characteristics of the individual and the city in which he lives.

734    Berman, Paul. "The Study of Macro- and Micro-Implementation." PUBLIC POLICY 26 (Spring 1978): 157-84.

The implementation analysis field lacks a conceptual framework for doing general research on what goes wrong in the social policy and how to improve policy performance. This essay offers building blocks for such a framework. It assumes that implementation problems stem mostly from the interaction of a policy with its institutional setting. There is a complex adaptive process affecting federal and local policy, creating uncertainty in how policy will be implemented. The uncertainty cannot be eliminated without removing the local flexibility that is necessary if policy is to work.

735    Birnberg, Jacob G., and Ghandi, Natwar M. "The Accountants Are Coming! How Accountants Can Help Policymakers in Social Program Evaluation." POLICY SCIENCES 8 (December 1977): 469-82.

This article assesses the usefulness of expanding traditional accountant activities to include the assessment of social programs. While the question has been raised in several publications, little agreement has been reached on the desirability or usefulness of it.

736    Blodgett, Terrell. "Zero-Base Budgeting Systems: Seventeen Steps to Success." NATIONAL CIVIC REVIEW 67 (March 1978): 123-29.

ZBB is not a complex process and is a logical approach to arriving at a budget which feasibly maintains services. The implementation process requires special attention. To work successfully, a ZBB implementation process must include: clearly stated goals; criteria for accurate workload measurement; and an accounting system which generates budget data from a professional budget staff.

737    Bowman, James, and Eisenhart, Susan. "Program Implementation in Nebraska: The Safe Streets Act." MIDWEST REVIEW OF PUBLIC ADMINISTRATION 6 (February 1972): 14-28.

Reviews, via survey research and other techniques, the impact of the 1968 Safe Street Act with respect to federal rule making and its impact, state organization, state planning agencies, and funding levels.

738    Bradley, Valerie J. "Policy Termination in Mental Health: The Hidden Agenda." POLICY SCIENCES 7 (June 1976): 215-24.

Three policy termination objectives can be analyzed in the field of mental health: the move to phase down or close large state institutions for the mentally disabled; the elimination in some states of involuntary commitment procedures; and the attempt to transfer responsibility for the provision of direct services from the state level to local government and/or private providers of care. Termination in this field, however, has met with increasing resistance because of the failure in many instances to pair these objectives with positive program development. In some states, the result has been the dismantling of one system without the commitment of resources necessary to encourage the development of an alternative system.

739    Brook, Robert H. "Quality of Care Assessment: Policy Relevant Issues." POLICY SCIENCES 5 (1974): 317-41.

After a review of the quality assessment literature, this paper presents a study of five different methods of assessing quality of care and makes policy recommendations. Results are (1) most quality care assessment issues are a century old; (2) results of quality care assessment are dependent upon the methods used; (3) a wrong choice of assessment techniques could result in the decline in efficiency of the system; (4) any national program must be prospectively evaluated; and (5) a quality assessment system must be concerned with populations who did and did not receive the services.

740    Brooks, Gary H. "The Utility of Downs' Analysis of Bureau Territoriality for Policy Evaluation: The Case of Kansas Energy Policy." MID-WEST REVIEW OF PUBLIC ADMINISTRATION 8 (July 1974): 178-90.

Two problems are addressed: development and implementation of an effective energy policy at state level; and development of a systematic approach to policy evaluation. Emphasis of study is evaluation of existing and alternate energy policy decision-making structures in Kansas. Downs's analysis is useful in that it forces the analyst to consider policy feasibility questions in policy evaluation processes.

741    Brownstein, Charles N. "The Experimental Evaluation of Public Policy." In PUBLIC POLICY MAKING IN A FEDERAL SYSTEM, edited by Charles O. Jones and Robert D. Thomas, pp. 19-37. Beverly Hills, Calif.: Sage, 1976.

A growing interest in policy impact analysis has led to the development of experimental evaluation research. The purpose of this research is to provide decision makers with reliable information gathered while observing the effects of test policy alternatives on the existing flow of events. Policy impact experimentation requires that researchers carefully define policy and impact and that they specify the administrative levels at which the experimental alternative is expected to work. In contrast to passive correlation studies of natural-istic data in which the analyst searches among plausible independent variables for the cause of a single observed dependent variable, an experimental study requires the analyst to be an active participant in the events at hand, assigning the role of independent variable to a controllable test policy and viewing impacts as dependent variables. In the world of applied evaluation research, the experimental approach can enhance established techniques which rely on anecdotal evidence, managerial records, and sample surveys.

742   Bullock, Charles S. III, and Rodgers, Harrell R., Jr. "Impediments to Policy Evaluation: Perceptual Distortion." SOCIAL SCIENCE QUARTERLY 57 (December 1976): 506-19.

The feedback loop has been a little studied component of the systems available model. School officials in thirty-one Georgia school systems which instituted terminal desegregation plans between 1968 and 1970 were interviewed. By comparing the desegregation explanation offered by school officials with what was actually required, the accuracy of the information passed on to the regulators could be determined. A statewide suit enjoining the payment of state education funds to districts was the most effective desegregation motivation, but Office for Civil Rights respondents considered federal fund im-poundment to be the most effective techniques. The idea of enjoining state funds came from two state officials, and the Justice Department did not recognize the value of this tech-nique until it was successful. This study suggests that those responsible for carrying out a program will rarely be able to critically evaluate their own performance because of feed-back distortion.

743   Bunker, Douglas R. "Policy Sciences Perspectives on Implementation Processes." POLICY SCIENCES 3 (March 1972): 71-80.

Implementation is an integral part of the policymaking process. It is examined as a sociopolitical process, an administrative task, a follow-on from systematic analysis, a problem in the diffusion and utilization of knowledge, and a basic capacity which is differentially distributed among organizations and subject to change.

744   Canfield, Monte, Jr., and Sieminski, Adam E. "If You're So Smart, Why Ain't You Rich? An Analysis of Impediments to Implementing Energy Conservation in the United States." PUBLIC ADMINISTRATION REVIEW 35 (July-August 1975): 322-27.

This paper describes the energy predicament that the nation has gotten itself into, analyzes the major barriers to conser-vation, and offers a few suggestions on how the nation can make some progress in the direction of rational energy con-servation policies.

745 Caputo, David A. "The Citizen Component of Policy Evaluation." In METHODOLOGIES FOR ANALYZING PUBLIC POLICIES, edited by Frank P. Scioli, Jr. and Thomas J. Cook, pp. 25-32. Lexington, Mass.: D.C. Heath, 1975.

> There is no right or one way to conceptualize and subsequently operationalize the citizen component. The optimum strategy is to develop a methodology broad enough to incorporate citizen evaluation of widely differing policies in order to increase compatibility and to permit individual methodological adaptations to meet the specific needs of the policy or program being evaluated. This middle-range approach will provide maximum returns and increase comparability. Such an approach will include five variables: participation characteristics; program impact; future needs; resolution of impact and needs conflict; and continuing time perspectives. Without full consideration of these variables and of their impact on one another and the policy process itself, policy evaluation will remain less than optimal and will continue to provide evaluation results reflecting static rather than dynamic attributes of public policy.

746 _____. "Evaluating Urban Public Policy: A Developmental Model and Some Reservations." PUBLIC ADMINISTRATION REVIEW 33 (March-April 1973): 113-19.

> This article begins by considering the need for effective techniques for evaluating policies, and then develops a model for evaluating urban public policy. The model consists of five variables (program evaluator, group interaction, citizen evaluation, academic and professional evaluation, and the policy being evaluated) and a time variable.

747 Caro, Francis G., ed. READINGS IN EVALUATION RESEARCH. New York: Russell Sage, 1977. 418 p.

> Thirty chapters are included with brief selections covering: basic issues in program development and scientific inquiry; establishing and maintaining the evaluation research role; methodological issues of measurement and design. The second half includes specific case materials with commentary on the evaluation efforts.

748 Cary, Charles D. "An Introductory Course in Evaluation Research." POLICY ANALYSIS 3 (Summer 1977): 429-44.

> Public administrators and policy analysts in government are increasingly expected to evaluate the operation of public program. To meet this need, the master of art degree program in public affairs at the University of Iowa now includes an introductory course in evaluation research. The course provides an overview of what is involved in program evaluation and is intended to train students to manage competitively rather than to conduct evaluation research.

749 Churchman, C.W., and Schainblatt, A.H. "PPB: How Can It Be Implemented?" PUBLIC ADMINISTRATION REVIEW 29 (March-April 1969): 178-88.

If a debate develops over the implementation of PPB between experts and politicians, there may well be no winner as the whole system may be destroyed. This article describes the background and processes of systems analysis and illustrates how several kinds of issues might be fruitfully debated between system analyst and political leader.

750    Clark, Lawrence P. DECISIONS FOR EVALUATING SOCIAL PRO-
        GRAMS. Learning Packages in the Policy Sciences, PS 11. Croton-
        on-Hudson, N.Y.: Policy Studies Associates, 1976. 42 p.

        This package is designed to acquaint students with the con-
        cepts and designs used to evaluate social programs. It
        requires students to recognize the need for systematic evalua-
        tion of social programs, identify designs used for the evalua-
        tion of social programs, distinguish between poorly designed
        and well-designed social programs, and select most appropriate
        evaluation design given the constraints of time, money, and
        knowledge.

751    Clark, Robert F. "Program Evaluation and the Commissioning Entity."
        POLICY SCIENCES 7 (March 1976): 11-16.

        Program evaluation must contend with many different actors
        and interests. In particular, the interest commissioning
        the evaluation expects to get some benefit from it. Evaluation
        intended as an aid to decision making cannot afford to separate
        the program under study from its organizational and political
        context.

752    Clark, Terry Nichols. "Policy Outputs." In his COMMUNITY POWER
        AND POLICY OUTPUTS: A REVIEW OF URBAN RESEARCH, pp.
        53-67. Beverly Hills, Calif.: Sage, 1973.

        Satisfaction with the traditional concern of "who governs?"
        led to an emphasis on "with what effects?" This shift away
        from the process of decision making and governance toward
        policy consequences has characterized work in many substan-
        tive areas, especially among political scientists. The eco-
        nomic theory of democracy is a general admonition to look
        at some values as influencing leadership and policy outputs.
        The theory of Banfield and Wilson (AMERICAN POLITICAL
        SCIENCE REVIEW 58 [1964]) distinguished public and private
        regardingness value configurations. Lineberry and Fowler
        (AMERICAN POLITICAL SCIENCE REVIEW 61 [1967]) hypo-
        thesized that citizen values concerning public policies were gener-
        ally related to census measures such as home and education, and
        they found that reform cities seem less responsive to citizen de-
        mands.

753    Coleman, James S. "Problems of Conceptualization and Measurement
        in Studying Policy Impacts." In PUBLIC POLICY EVALUATION,
        edited by Kenneth M. Dolbeare, pp. 19-40. Beverly Hills, Calif.:
        Sage, 1975.

        This paper questions whether policy research may require
        a different foundation and practice from that familiar in dis-
        ciplinary grounded research. Drawing on the experience

developed in his education study, Coleman presents a set of principles that should guide in policy research. Essentially, they invoke guidelines for serving the policymaker's needs with the tools presently available.

754   Cook, Thomas J., and Scioli, Frank P., Jr. "Impact Analysis in Public Policy Research." In PUBLIC POLICY EVALUATION, edited by Kenneth M. Dolbeare, pp. 95-118. Beverly Hills, Calif.: Sage, 1975.

This paper suggests some specific ways to overcome shortcomings in implementation analysis. The authors develop an elegant model and then show how it can be drawn upon to inform policy impact research.

755   _____. "A Research Strategy for Analyzing the Impacts of Public Policy." ADMINISTRATIVE SCIENCE QUARTERLY 17 (September 1972): 328-39.

A neglected aspect of policy research has been the systematic analysis of policy impacts. This paper presents a research strategy for measuring policy impacts based upon the principles of experimental design methodology. The strategies are illustrated through the application of a multivariant factorial design to the area of air pollution control. The overall approach is discussed in terms of its general utility for policy impact analysis.

756   _____. "Value Assumptions Underlying Evaluation Research." JOURNAL OF POLITICAL SCIENCE 4 (Spring 1977): 110-17.

This paper discusses several of the major assumptions and their relevance to the conduct of an evaluation analysis. It discusses the potential impact of these assumptions on such issues as the scope of the evaluation, the choice of evaluative criteria, and the type of research design employed.

757   deLeon, Peter. "Public Policy Termination: An End and a Beginning." POLICY ANALYSIS 4 (Summer 1978): 369-92.

The termination of public organizations, policies, and programs has generally been neglected by policy researchers. The author defines what is meant by policy termination and discusses why it has received so little analytical attention and why it warrants more. He addresses this oversight by posing a series of questions about policy termination: "What is it? Where and how does it fit into a general model of the policy process? Is termination important and, if so, why? And how might one make the termination option more accessible?" He examines reasons for the longevity of government organizations and policies and suggests some general strategies for making the termination option more available. He points out that though policy termination may be difficult, the potential payoffs of policy termination are such that successful termination strategies should and could be devised to overcome these obstacles.

758    Dolbeare, Kenneth, ed. PUBLIC POLICY EVALUATION. Sage Year-
       books in Politics and Public Policy, vol. 2. Beverly Hills, Calif.:
       Sage, 1975. 288 p.

       Dolbeare provides a critical assessment of the state of evalua-
       tion research covering a wide range of social problems and
       policies. New methodological tools and new developments in
       policy methodology are discussed.

759    Durham, T.R. AN INTRODUCTION TO BENEFIT-COST ANALYSIS
       FOR EVALUATING PUBLIC PROGRAMS. Learning Packages in the
       Policy Sciences, PS 14. Croton-on-Hudson, N.Y.: Policy Studies
       Associates, 1977. 67 p.

       This package is designed to introduce the student to benefit-
       cost analysis. This approach is a type of systems analysis.
       Both benefits and costs are quantified in comparable dollar
       terms in an effort to evaluate the total costs and consequences
       of a program in a systematic manner. Certain important prac-
       tices and key concepts have emerged through this type of anal-
       ysis. This learning package is concerned with presenting
       these concepts by providing the student with examples of
       benefit-cost studies, major difficulties, and pitfalls in iden-
       tifying the benefits and costs of a particular project, and a
       critical attitude in designing cost-benefit studies. Another
       important aspect of cost-benefit studies is their application
       to public program. Examination of services rendered versus
       fees paid and benefits derived provides a valuable efficiency
       index to government.

760    Finsterbusch, Kurt. "The Potential Role of Social Impact Assessments
       in Instituting Public Policies." In METHODOLOGY OF SOCIAL IMPACT
       ASSESSMENT, edited by Kurt Finsterbusch and C.P. Wolf, pp. 2-20.
       Stroudsburg, Pa.: Dowden, Hutchinson and Ross, 1977.

       The primary goal of social impact assessment (SIA) is to
       facilitate decision making by determining the full range of
       costs and benefits of alternative proposed courses of action.
       The most important secondary goal is to improve the design
       and administration of policies in order to ameliorate the dis-
       benefits and to increase the benefits. SIA design includes
       (1) policy selection (selection and description of alternatives,
       research design and operation, data analysis, and conclusions
       and recommendations), (2) policy design (specification of policy
       provisions, modification of provisions, and supplementation
       of the policy to ameliorate disbenefits), and (3) policy adminis-
       tration (implementation by administrators, monitoring the policy
       by identifying its consequences, and revision of the harmful
       features of the policy). Political forces may cause SIAs to
       deviate from the ideal type or may nullify the influences of
       SIAs on policy decisions, yet SIAs can increase the social
       utility of policy decisions.

761    Floden, Robert E., and Weiner, Stephen S. "Rationality to Ritual:
       The Multiple Roles of Evaluation in Governmental Process." POLICY
       SCIENCES 9 (February 1978): 9-18.

The disillusion with social science evaluation can be partly attributed to an overly narrow view of the function of evaluation. In the accepted model, evaluation functions to provide information needed by rational design makers for discrete decisions. Evaluations often cannot perform this function, evaluation but often does serve other functions. In one such function, it acts as a means for managing conflict and promoting social change. It often also stimulates program staff to critically examine their assumptions and behavior. Consideration of these additional functions leads to suggestions for changes in recruitment of evaluators and in the definition of the evaluator's role. Finally, one can view evaluation as a social ritual whose function is to calm the citizenry and to perpetuate an image of government rationality.

762    Frederickson, H. George, and Reagan, Michael D. "Administering Public Policy." POLICY STUDIES JOURNAL 1 (Winter 1972): 72–75.

This short piece traces the linkage between public administration and public policy, lists several issues in the study of policy (legislative-administrative relations, power, and the relationships between administrators and citizens), and lists several sources of information in the field of policy studies.

763    Froomkin, Joseph. "Needed: A New Framework for the Analysis of Government Programs." POLICY ANALYSIS 2 (Spring 1976): 341–50.

The four types of difficulties faced by policy analysts in the evaluation of federal programs are: (1) the limitations of program objectives, (2) absence of an overall model to test the effects of new programs, (3) failure to understand the scope of a program, and (4) lack of planning. The contribution of human resource programs to productivity must be considered. Groups that deal with program planning and evaluation in different departments should be given the resources to do more macro analysis instead of merely justifying existing programs.

764    Fucik, William C. "The Challenge of Implementing Federally Assisted New Communities." PUBLIC ADMINISTRATION REVIEW 35 (May-June 1975): 249–62.

The Title VI program of the Housing and Urban Development Act of 1970 has suffered from insufficient intergovernmental cooperation, insufficient financial support, bureaucratic problems, developer weaknesses, and inadequate monitoring and evaluation. Most of the federally assisted new community endeavors are satellite types. The village, city, or county having jurisdiction often lacks the experience and fiscal capacity to deal with the new community. County planning has not generally reflected compatible priorities, which can result in future urban sprawl. Developers anticipated that HUD would play a greater financial assistance role than it has to date. Local and state governments working in conjunction with the developer have found it difficult to obtain grant assistance from other federal departments, and the developer has sometimes had to contribute funds to the local government.

765    Galvin, Donald E. "Program Evaluation in Michigan VR Services." SOCIAL AND REHABILITATION RECORD 1 (November 1974): 28-31.

As part of a statewide reform effort of vocational rehabilitation, the state of Michigan contracted to assess its general program of administration. The conclusions were that the agency did not know its capacity to effectively serve the people and that it had only vague ideas of the severity of the disabilities its clients faced and the amounts of time and money necessary to serve them well. It also concluded that most decision making was highly intuitive and not usually based on facts.

766    Goldfarb, Robert S. "Learning in Government Programs and the Usefulness of Cost-Benefit Analysis: Lessons from Manpower and Urban Renewal History." POLICY SCIENCES 6 (September 1975): 281-99.

The large element of uncertainty which attends social programs could be reduced if more attention were paid to evaluation methods which make possible "learning by doing." Administrators, particularly those trained in cost-benefit analysis, do not regard their programs as experiments or as parts of a learning process but tend to concern themselves only with immediate results. These features are examined in the recent history of two types of programs, manpower and urban renewal. There is much more evaluation and learning in urban renewal programs, because the results are more visible and measurable. Cost-benefit analysis should be trained to exploit more effectively the learning potential in their programs.

767    Graham, George J., Jr., and Graham, Scarlett G. "Macro-Evaluation: Framework for a Policy System." POLICY STUDIES JOURNAL 3 (Spring 1975): 262-68.

Macroanalysis of the policy system is prerequisite for macroevaluation. Macroanalysis links the determinants and the consequences of social policy, including comparative investigation of the relationship between policy processes and such system-characterizing variables as the social structure, political institutions, governmental policy making and policy executing structures, and constitutional and ideological constraints. The effects of real world distortions on the functioning of the policy system are cumulative, emphasizing their importance in explaining or prescribing policy outcomes. These distortions can be called policy system drift, problem drift, institutional drift, political drift, and value drift, and must be taken into account in every macro-evaluative effort.

768    Guthrie, Harold W.  "Microanalytic Simulation Modeling for Evaluation
       of Public Policy."  URBAN AFFAIRS QUARTERLY  7 (June 1972):
       403-18.

       This paper describes a socioeconomic simulation model de-
       signed to evaluate alternative public policies at federal level.
       The primary purpose of the model is to provide decision
       makers with a tool to give them information not previously
       available about alternative programs within given policy areas.
       He uses as a case example the goal of reducing poverty and
       income inequality.  Some specific programs to implement are
       discussed, the simulation model is viewed, and some hypo-
       thetical applications of policy evaluation in different policy en-
       vironments are attempted.

769    Guttentag, Marcia, and Snapper, Kurt. "Plans, Evaluations, and
       Decisions."  EVALUATION  2, no. 1 (1974):  58-74.

       Planning and evaluation are closely linked.  The decision-
       theoretic approach, which permits the specification and quan-
       tification of values, was found to be useful in the Office of
       Child Development in planning and evaluating research and
       development programs through the use of a multiattribute
       utilities refinement.

770    Guttentag, Marcia, ed.  EVALUATION STUDIES REVIEW ANNUAL.
       Vol. 2.  Beverly Hills, Calif.: Sage, 1977.  736 p.

       Here are thirty-two papers covering the topics of:  evalua-
       tion methodology; evaluation impact on poverty; and evaluation
       research in education, crime, and human services.

771    Haveman, Robert H., and Weisbrod, Burton A.  "Defining Benefits of
       Public Programs:  Some Guidance for Policy Analysis."  POLICY ANAL-
       YSIS  1 (Winter 1975):  169-96.

       Before any sound cost-benefit analysis of public programs
       can be undertaken, a clear understanding of the meaning of
       the financial and nonfinancial characteristics of benefits must
       be achieved.

772    Henig, Jeffrey; Lineberry, Robert L.; and Milner, Neal A.  "The Policy
       Impact of Policy Evaluation:  Some Implications of the Kansas City
       Patrol Experiment."  In PUBLIC LAW AND PUBLIC POLICY, edited
       by John A. Gardiner, pp. 225-41.  New York:  Praeger, 1977.

       While the virtue of a policy-relevant social science has long
       been touted, there is confusion and disappointment over the
       apparent failure of policy evaluations and experiments to have
       their expected impact.  As a superior example of a policy
       experiment, the Kansas City police patrol study provides a
       focus for an investigation of the factors that intervene between
       the completion of such a study and the incorporation of its
       findings in public policy.  This case study, coupled with a
       review of the literature on judicial impact, policy implemen-
       tation, and policy evaluation, concludes that though the impact
       of policy experimentation is problematic and indirect and the

costs high and clear, one should not infer that zero impact
has occurred. Rather, one should realize that neither the
policy process nor experimentation stops with the enuncia-
tion of dicta and policies. Evaluation and experimentation
are political processes, directly touching organizations,
their goals, and their constituents. What happens after the
experiment is concluded may be more important than experimental findings in determining its ultimate impact.

773    Hood, Christopher. THE LIMITS OF ADMINISTRATION. New York:
John Wiley and Sons, 1976. 213 p.

In this book Hood explores the intersection between organization theory and policy analysis. At a time when policy
implementation is of increasing concern, Hood offers an analysis of the pitfalls and dilemmas attendant to the art of administering public policies. Beginning with a conception of
a perfect organization, he goes on to relax the assumptions
and analyze both external and internal limits to administration
in light of relevant theories and evidence drawn from case
studies of policy implementation.

774    Horst, Pamela, et al. "Program Management and the Federal Evaluator."
PUBLIC ADMINISTRATION REVIEW 34 (July-August 1974): 300-308.

Written from perspective outside the governmental bureaucracy,
and concerned with program evaluation as a tool of management,
this article identifies causes of ineffective program evaluation
and proposes solutions to meet the problems.

775    Kobrin, Solomon, and Lubeck, Steven G. "Problems in the Evaluation
of Crime Control Policy." In PUBLIC POLICY EVALUATION, edited
by Kenneth M. Dolbeare, pp. 219-52. Sage Yearbooks in Politics
and Public Policy, vol. 2. Beverly Hills, Calif.: Sage Publishers,
1975.

This essay addresses problems involved in the specification
and measurement of the goals of crime control, the responses
of criminal justice agencies, and the predictive contributions
of social and demographic characteristics of the jurisdiction
being studied.

776    Larkey, Patrick D. "Process Models of Governmental Resources Allocation and Program Evaluation." POLICY SCIENCES 8 (September 1977):
269-301.

Conceptually, the evaluation of social programs is difficult
when programs are not planned experiments and depend on
the activities of numerous individuals and organizations. In
addition, evaluation is difficult when one does not know what
would have happened without the program. This paper uses
the revenue sharing program as a case of program evaluation
of a social program and considers the role of process models
in evaluation. It concludes that when good descriptive models
of programs are available, classic experimental research designs are not necessary.

777   Lewis, Frank L., and Zarb, Frank G. "Federal Program Evaluation from the OMB Perspective." PUBLIC ADMINISTRATION REVIEW 34 (July–August 1974): 308–17.

> Beginning with the premise that program evaluation is one of the most useful and essential tools for assuring rational policy decisions and effective program management, this article provides some perspective on the evaluation effort in the executive branch and describes some of the activities planned by OMB in cooperation with other federal agencies to improve the quality of evaluation as an aid to the decision process.

778   Mechling, Jerry. "Analysis and Implementation: Sanitation Policies in New York City." PUBLIC POLICY 26 (Spring 1978): 263–84.

> New York City's Environmental Protection Agency's experience in implementing new programs indicates that implementation problems result either from technical uncertainty or internal conflict. Successful implementation requires clear delegation of responsibilities and persistent monitoring efforts.

779   Meyers, William R. "The Politics of Evaluation Research: The Peace Corps." JOURNAL OF APPLIED BEHAVIORAL SCIENCE 11 (July–September 1975): 261–80.

> This article analyzes the political problems evaluation research must solve if it is to be effective as an innovative agency. The Peace Corps is the case example and the article describes the role of the inside researcher and the outside researcher. Finally, Meyers discusses the impact that careful research can have on an innovative agency's program and mission.

780   Morehouse, Thomas A. "Program Evaluation: Social Research vs. Public Policy." PUBLIC ADMINISTRATION REVIEW 32 (November–December 1972): 868–74.

> The failure of evaluation research can be explained in large part as a consequence of the researchers' attempts to respond to divergent and conflicting political and technical imperatives.

781   Nielsen, Victor G. "Why Evaluation Does Not Improve Program Effectiveness." POLICY STUDIES JOURNAL 3 (Summer 1975): 385–90.

> Nielsen tries to determine why the products of program evaluations are seldom used by people responsible for operating programs. Based on a study of three social service agencies, it was determined that program managers need nonquantitative descriptive information while evaluations tend to emphasize the quantitative.

782   Ortiz, Isidro D. "The Politics of Collective Bargaining in Agriculture." POLICY STUDIES JOURNAL 6 (Summer 1978): 510–13.

This article outlines some of the implementing problems faced by the California Agricultural Labor Relations Act of 1975. Obstacles to implementation included administrative deficiencies, the resistance of key participants, and gubernatorial intransigence.

783 Patton, Michael Q.  UTILIZATION-FOCUSED EVALUATION.  Beverly Hills, Calif.: Sage, 1978.  280 p.

Patton reviews how and why to conduct evaluations.  He reviews the history of the development of evaluation research and presents a model for evaluation, the utilization focused approach.  The book presents twelve chapters on evaluation and its usefulness.

784 Phillips, D.C.  "When Evaluators Disagree:  Perplexities and Perspectives."  POLICY SCIENCES  8 (June 1977):  147-59.

When evaluators of social policy or education programs disagree as to their findings, the policymaker is in a bind because he does not possess the technical expertise to resolve the dispute.  The article states that if an administrator's concern is with making a rationally defensible decision, then he should select his evaluation panel so that all members share the same theoretical orientation.

785 Poland, Orville F., ed.  "Program Evaluation: A Symposium."  PUBLIC ADMINISTRATION REVIEW  34 (July-August 1974):  299-338.

This is a symposium concerned with making government more accountable via the technique of program evaluation.  Four of the five papers are by practitioners and deal with evaluation from an Office of Management and Budget perspective, state legislative use of evaluation, Congress, and evaluation and administrative theory.

786 Pressman, Jeffrey L., and Wildavsky, Aaron.  IMPLEMENTATION.  Berkeley and Los Angeles: University of California Press, 1973.  182 p.

Building on the Economic Development Administration efforts in Oakland, California, the authors explain how the initial policy agreement slowly dissolved into a host of disagreements over the details of implementation.

787 "Program Evaluation:  A Cautious Perspective."  BUREAUCRAT  5 (April 1976):  3-100.

The public policy forum of this issue deals with the uses of program evaluation at the federal level.  Articles include: program evaluation for Congress, legislative oversight and program evaluation, PE in an unquantified world, using performance measures for long range planning and policy formulation, and progress reporting in public administration.

788 Pugh, Robert E.  EVALUATION OF POLICY SIMULATION MODELS: A CONCEPTUAL APPROACH AND CASE STUDY.  Washington, D.C.: Information Resources Press, 1977.  320 p.

This book deals with evaluating the usefulness of policy
simulation models. The emphasis is on models intended to
support analyses of broad, complex policy problems. Chapter
1 develops a conceptual approach that the authors claim is
appropriate for evaluating complex policy models. Later
chapters discuss various aspects of the evaluation process
in detail.

789    Rein, Martin, and Rabinovitz, Francine F.   IMPLEMENTATION:   A
       THEORETICAL PERSPECTIVE. Working Paper, no. 43. Cambridge,
       Mass.:   Joint Center for Urban Studies of MIT and Harvard University,
       1977.   44 p.

       If implementation is understood as (1) a declaration of govern-
       ment preferences, (2) mediated by a number of actors who (3)
       create a circular process characterized by reciprocal power
       relations and negotiations, then the actors must take into
       account three potentially conflicting imperatives.   They are:
       legal imperative to do what is legally required; the rational-
       bureaucratic imperative to do what is rationally defensible;
       and the consensual imperative to do what can attract agree-
       ment among contending influential parties who have a stake
       in the outcome.   The politics of implementation may be best
       understood as an attempt to resolve any conflicts among these
       imperatives.   The way in which conflicts are resolved is a
       function of the purposes (their clarity, saliency, and consis-
       tency); resources (kind, level, and timing); and the complexity
       of the administrative process of implementation.

790    Rocheleau, Bruce.   "Evaluation, Accountability, and Responsiveness
       in Administration."   MIDWEST REVIEW OF PUBLIC ADMINISTRATION
       9 (October 1975):   163-72.

       Examines the relationships which exist among three concepts:
       evaluation, accountability, and responsiveness.   Data is drawn
       from a study of the role and impact of evaluation in fourteen
       mental health organizations in Florida.   It notes that the suc-
       cess of any evaluation depends upon (1) the kinds of values
       held by evaluations and the people being evaluated; (2) motiva-
       tion behind the evaluation; (3) authority exercised by evalua-
       tions; and (4) extent to which information necessary to deter-
       mining if the evaluation is achieving its intended impact is
       available.

791    Roffman, Roger A.   "Borrowing from the National Environmental Policy
       Act:   A Model for Accountable Drug Abuse Policy-Making."   CONTEM-
       PORARY DRUG PROBLEMS   6 (Fall 1977):   373-95.

       The National Environmental Policy Act acknowledged that the
       very existence of competing value systems concerning the use
       of the environment warranted a systematic multiple-input plan-
       ning process through which those values would be surfaced,
       assessed, and balanced.   The profit motive and preservation
       of the environment were often recognized as conflicting forces
       in relation to uses of physical resources.   The thrust toward
       greater rationality in the human resources sphere is similar
       in purpose.   Beliefs about human nature that favor controlling,

treating, educating, punishing, rehabilitating, coercing, or facilitating are potential underlying and competing forces in the human resources domain. The question being asked in both fields, however, is whether the decision—making mechanisms currently in operation have evolved sufficiently to make planning both rational in process and accountable as to out—come.

792   Roos, Noralou P. "Contrasting Program Evaluation with Social Experimentation——A Health Care Perspective." PUBLIC POLICY 23 (Spring 1975): 241–57.

> This paper reviews the difficulties inherent in any program evaluation effort. It is specifically concerned with the strengths and weaknesses of social experimentation and retrospective evaluation. Finally, it discusses alternative roles by which these different approaches to evaluation can be conducted.

793   _____. "Proposed Guidelines for Evaluation Research." POLICY STUDIES JOURNAL 3 (Autumn 1974): 107–11.

> In designing an effective evaluation strategy, two sets of factors must be kept in mind. First is that the appropriate behavioral, political, structural, and methodological problems must be addressed. Second is that the evaluation strategy must be matched to the needs of the particular program.

794   Roos, Noralou P., and Roos, Leslie L., Jr. "Reducing Potential Conflicts between Evaluators and Administrators." POLICY STUDIES JOURNAL 6 (Summer 1978): 548–51.

> Conflicts between evaluators and administrators are a natural part of policy research. Although considerable attention has been paid to problems of administrator acceptance of research designs involving randomization, the more mundane problems arising from day—to—day interaction between evaluators and administrators have received less attention. This article treats a number of the problems which can generate friction in the evaluator—administrator relationship.

795   Rose, Richard. "Implementation and Evaporation: The Record of MBO." PUBLIC ADMINISTRATION REVIEW 37 (January–February 1977): 64–71.

> Introducing a management technique to solve a problem in the public sector does not dispose of problems but substitutes the implementation of the solution for the problem as originally defined. This article shows the limitations of applying management techniques that do not take into account the political priorities that dominate government.

796   Rossi, Peter H., and Wright, Sonia R. "Evaluation Research: An Assessment of Theory, Practice, and Politics." EVALUATION QUARTERLY 1 (February 1977): 5–52.

The main difficulties limiting the application of social research techniques to policy evaluation are methodological in character and include the problem of designing research capable of answering the questions posed by policymakers. The distinctive features of evaluation research are as follows: precise definition of the program itself, its goals, and the criteria for its success can only be supplied by the policymakers, not by the researcher; evaluation research takes place in an "action-setting," so that the evaluation researcher may have to forego considerable control over the problem specification, the variables to be included, and the sample to be used; and findings must be reported in a form and style such that policymakers and their staffs can understand them. A survey of existing research designs and accompanying techniques is presented along with brief assessments of their usefulness for different social programs. Well-known program evaluators (e.g., the Coleman Report) are compared and the use of field experiments is stressed as a sound method for the assessment of prospective social policies and programs.

797    Rutman, Leonard. EVALUATION RESEARCH METHODS: A BASIC GUIDE. Beverly Hills, Calif.: Sage, 1977. 232 p.

This guide explains the fundamental procedures of planning and conducting a program evaluation. It is designed to help the evaluator achieve a high degree of technical competence in research methodology. The nine chapters include: planning an evaluation study, evaluability assessment, formative research, measurement problems in criminal justice, experimental design, benefit-cost analysis, and others.

798    Salamon, Lester M. "Follow-Ups, Letdowns, and Sleepers: The Time Dimension in Policy Evaluation." In PUBLIC POLICY MAKING IN A FEDERAL SYSTEM, edited by Charles O. Jones and Robert D. Thomas, pp. 257-84. Beverly Hills, Calif.: Sage, 1976.

The impact of a government program may not appear for a considerable amount of time, yet this time factor is frequently neglected by evaluation researchers. For analytical purposes, there are three types of time-related effects, each one likely to be produced by a certain type of program. The first is the letdown effect, which diminishes over time; this is produced by programs aimed at imparting skill or knowledge to program participants. The second is the latent effect, which increases over time; this is produced by programs aimed at changing values or attitudes of program participants. The third is the sleeper effect, which does not appear during a program's operation but shows up later. This is produced by programs aimed at changing external social and political conditions.

799    _____. "The Time Dimension in Policy Evaluation in the Case of the New Deal Land-Reform Experiments." PUBLIC POLICY 27 (Spring 1975): 129-84.

Potential biases are built into policy evaluation by the limited time frame used in most evaluation research. The article identifies three types of time related effects (staying-power effect, staying effect, sleep effect) and offers a framework for presenting the types of programs likely to be associated with each. The model is illustrated using the New Deal's resettlement program which, while branded a failure in its time, transformed a group of landless black tenants into a landed middle class by the 1960s. It shows how the passage of time can affect the kind and amount of program impact.

800    Scheirer, Mary Ann. "Program Participants' Positive Perceptions: Psychological Conflict of Interest in Social Program Evaluation." EVALUATION QUARTERLY 2 (February 1978): 53-70.

This paper attempts to address the problem confronted by an outside evaluator when outsiders' quantitative judgments and insiders' intuitive judgments are at odds. The author concludes that the source of conflict is the participation of individuals in new programs.

801    Schick, Allen. "From Analysis to Evaluation." ANNALS OF THE AMERICAN ACADEMY OF POLITICAL AND SOCIAL SCIENCE 394 (March 1971): 57-71.

The difference between analysis and evaluation is tied to the policymaking context within which social science operates. The uses of analysis are most in demand when underutilized slack resources are available, when there is a great deal of confidence in the efficacy of public action and when policy-makers want to forge new program initiatives. When these conditions change, the dominant tone of both social science and public policy shifts to evaluation.

802    Schmidt, Richard E., et al. SERVING THE FEDERAL EVALUATION MARKET. Washington, D.C.: Urban Institute, 1977. 93 p.

Adopting the perspective of those responsible for a federal evaluation office, the authors discuss the resources and organizational requirements necessary to serve three different markets: policymakers, program management, and individual government officials.

803    Scioli, Frank P. "Problems and Prospects for Policy Evaluation." PUBLIC ADMINISTRATION REVIEW 39 (January-February 1979): 41-45.

Proposition 13 has led to a nationwide call for improving the efficiency and effectiveness for government services at all levels. This paper discusses several of the problems inhibiting policy evaluation at state and local levels as well as the prospects for overcoming them.

804    Scioli, Frank P., Jr., and Cook, Thomas J. "Experimental Design in Policy Impact Analysis." SOCIAL SCIENCE QUARTERLY 54 (September 1973): 271-80.

The essay provides a presentation of the issues involved in selecting an optimal methodology for examining what (if any) impacts a public policy has on achieving its intended objectives. Authors discuss the advantages and disadvantages of experimental design and present a compromise design alternative focusing on the impact of program alternatives across specific time periods in different locations.

805  Smith, Thomas B. "The Policy Implementation Process." POLICY SCIENCES 4 (June 1973): 197-209.

Smith claims that there is an implicit assumption in most policy studies that, once formulated, a policy is certain to be implemented. He presents a model of the policy implementation process as a tension-generating force in society. By applying the model, policymakers can attempt to minimize the disruptive tendencies caused when outcomes fail to match expectations.

806  "Termination of Policies, Programs, and Organizations." POLICY SCIENCE 7 (June 1976): 123-200.

The issue contains nine articles on various aspects of program and organization reduction or termination. Specific topics include termination as a political process, design considerations in termination, schools, war, veterans benefits, police, and federal research and development programs.

806A  Tuncer, Yalcin. "Some Aspects of Science-Based Technological Promotion." POLICY SCIENCES 6 (September 1975): 267-80.

When scientific research is used for nonscientific purposes, its evaluation is based on criteria other than those associated with science. Criteria are developed by which science-based technological promotion can be evaluated.

807  Van Meter, Donald S., and Van Horn, Carl E. "The Policy Implementation Process: A Conceptual Framework." ADMINISTRATION AND SOCIETY 6 (February 1975): 445-88.

The authors create a model of policy delivery systems that: creates an environment that stimulates government officials and reviews their work; presents demands and resources that carry stimuli from the environment to the policymakers; develops a conversion process; presents policies that represent formal goals, intentions, or statements of government officials; includes policy performance as it is delivered to clients; and creates a feedback.

808  Weiss, Carol H. "The Politicization of Evaluation Research." JOURNAL OF SOCIAL ISSUES 26, no. 4 (1970): 57-68.

This paper describes the growing visibility of evaluation research and the effects of its overt entry into the political arena on the evaluator. Ways of dimming the political implications of evaluation, particularly when conclusions about program success are negative, are discussed. Negative conclusions can be highly significant. When findings of many action program evaluations are added together, the result is a serious critique of current approaches to social programming.

809 Whitaker, Gordon P. "Who Puts the Value in Evaluation." SOCIAL SCIENCE QUARTERLY 54 (March 1974): 759-61.

Whitaker reviews the possible ways to determine who should establish evaluation standards and what they should be. Whitaker says equity and responsiveness can best be measured by direct citizen satisfaction with services. Consumers of services are in the best position to determine the effectiveness of services.

810 Wholey, Joseph S. "What Can We Actually Get from Program Evaluation." POLICY SCIENCES 3 (September 1972): 361-69.

The paper assesses the role program evaluation can play in assisting decisions on public programs. Wholey looks at evaluation from the perspective of decision makers trying to find the right answer to their questions.

811 _____. ZERO BASE BUDGETING AND PROGRAM EVALUATION. Lexington, Mass.: Lexington Books, 1978. 157 p.

Wholey attempts to show how simplified ZBB and program evaluation can be used by policymakers to control government costs and achieve policy objectives without creating a massive flow of irrelevant paper work. The basic conclusion is that the key to efficient, effective government is the personal involvement of top management in setting realistic objectives and then mobilizing needed support.

812 _____, et al. FEDERAL EVALUATION POLICY: ANALYZING THE EFFECTS OF PUBLIC PROGRAMS. Washington, D.C.: Urban Institute, 1976. 134 p.

A survey and assessment of the extent and quality of social policy evaluation by federal administrative agencies is presented.

813 Williams, Walter [L]. "The Capacity of Social Science Organizations to Perform Large-Scale Evaluative Research." URBAN AFFAIRS QUARTERLY 7 (June 1972): 431-72.

The principal concern of the paper is with the capacity of social organizations to perform large-scale evaluative research in support of social policymaking. Two basic issues of the paper are: (1) organizational changes that might be made with government and the social science community to increase the number of policy-relevant researchers and to improve the tools and techniques available to researchers; (2) to highlight the possible deleterious consequences for society and social scientists in performing studies directly relevant to social agency policy.

814       . "Implementation Analysis and Assessment." POLICY ANALY-
SIS 1 (Summer 1975): 531-66.

> Implementation is a bureaucratic and political problem.
> Generally speaking, the higher the initiator is in the hier-
> archical chain, the more complex will be the bureaucratic
> layers that must be worked through. The most difficult prob-
> lems are likely to be jurisdictional disputes and lower-level
> resistance. Implementation process weakness may also relate
> to the fundamental issues of management responsibility. Changes
> needed for improved implementation may be even more difficult
> to make than those for policy analysis because the implemen-
> tation process moves so widely and deeply in an organization.
> Both the systematic study of implementation and the develop-
> ment of better techniques for such study are needed.

815       . SOCIAL POLICY RESEARCH AND ANALYSIS: THE EX-
PERIENCE IN FEDERAL SOCIAL AGENCIES. New York: American
Elsevier, 1971. 204 p.

> This is an introduction to the systematic evaluation of social
> policies.

816 Williams, Walter, and Elmore, Richard F., eds. SOCIAL PROGRAM
IMPLEMENTATION. Quantitative Studies in Social Relations Series.
New York: Academic Press, 1976. 304 p.

> This work consists of articles of two types: (1) case studies
> of the implementation of federal programs in education, com-
> munity development, and income transfer; and (2) implemen-
> tation as a conceptual problem for policy analysts and ad-
> ministrators.

817 Williams, Walter, and Evans, John A. "The Politics of Evaluation:
The Case of Head Start." ANNALS OF THE AMERICAN ACADEMY
OF POLITICAL AND SOCIAL SCIENCE 385 (September 1969): 118-32.

> Much of the philosophy behind the war on poverty was that
> effective programs could be developed quickly and launched
> full scale. This approval was being called into question by
> the type of evaluation called for by PPBS. This paper traces
> the events leading up to the controversy and the controversy
> itself to look at the implications for future policy.

818 Yin, Robert K., and Heald, Karen A. "Using the Case Survey Method
to Analyze Policy Studies." ADMINISTRATIVE QUARTERLY 20
(September 1975): 371-81.

> Evaluation research often involves the assessment of existing
> policy studies. The three methods used are propositional,
> cluster, and case survey. The latter is only in its forma-
> tive stage, but for reviewing policy studies it may be the
> most appropriate of the three methods. Until recently, the
> main shortcoming of case studies was that the insights could
> not be aggregated in any sense. The case survey calls for
> a reader-analyst to answer the same set of closed-ended
> questions for each case study; the answers can thus be ag-

gregated for further analysis. The most important limitation is that the results of the survey are of no better quality than the original case studies.

# Chapter 8
# POLICY ISSUES

## BUSINESS, LABOR, AND ECONOMIC POLICY

819  Aaron, Henry J.  WHO PAYS THE PROPERTY TAX: A NEW VIEW.
Washington, D.C.:  Brookings Institution, 1975.  110 p.

This is a review of the property tax, suggested reforms, and
some new evidence on its incidence.  In view of the incidence of
the tax, most of the suggested reforms are found to be un-
acceptable.

820  Break, George F., and Pechman, Joseph A.  FEDERAL TAX REFORM,
THE IMPOSSIBLE DREAM?  Washington, D.C.:  Brookings Institution,
1975.  142 p.

The authors explain the controversial elements in the federal
tax system and a review of the suggested proposals for reform.

821  Brown, Peter G., and Shue, Henry, eds.  FOOD POLICY: THE RE-
SPONSIBILITY OF THE UNITED STATES IN THE LIFE AND DEATH
CHOICES.  New York:  Free Press, 1977.  336 p.

A group of articles representing all views on malnutrition and
poverty, including perspectives on food producers, consumers,
and the types of government policies available.

822  Bulmer, Charles, and Carmichael, John L., Jr.  "Labor and Employment Policy:  An Overview of the Issues."  POLICY STUDIES JOUR-
NAL  6 (Winter 1977):  255-62.

Here is a review of developments in the labor field including
labor law reform, right-to-work laws, common-situs picketing,
good-faith bargaining, organizing in the public sector, and
others.

823  Cebula, Richard J.  "A Brief Note on Economic Policy Effectiveness."
SOUTHERN ECONOMIC JOURNAL  43 (October 1976):  1174-76.

Discusses the effectiveness of monetary and fiscal policies
in pursuing full employment in a closed economy.  Under certain conditions fiscal policy is a better tool than monetary
policy for achieving full employment.

824 _____. "Local Government Policies and Migration: An Analysis for SMSAs in the United States." PUBLIC CHOICE 19 (Fall 1974): 85–93.

> Cebula examines the racial impact of local government taxation, income redistribution, and expenditure policies on migration to SMSAs in the United States from 1965 to 1970.

825 Clark, Terry Nichols. "Can You Cut a Budget Pie?" POLICY AND POLITICS 3 (December 1974): 3–31.

> Presenting a voter with a budget pie and asking him to divide it into sections corresponding to the proportion of a budget that he would allocate to various activities yields valuable information about preferences and values.

826 Crandall, Robert M., and MacRae, C. Duncan. "Economic Subsidies in the Urban Ghetto." SOCIAL SCIENCE QUARTERLY 52 (December 1971): 492–508.

> Capital subsidies are not the answer to the problem of unemployment and underemployment in the ghetto. Labor subsidies—offering rebates on wages paid—might prove to be a better solution to the problem.

827 Douglas, Stephen A. "Policy Issues in Sports and Athletics." POLICY STUDIES JOURNAL 7 (Autumn 1978): 137–51.

> The article raises issues about the business of sport in America. Issues considered are equal opportunity, athletes' rights, drugs, safety, consumers' rights, gambling, and others.

828 Dunlop, John T. "Inflation and Income Policies: The Political Economy of Recent U.S. Experience." PUBLIC POLICY 23 (Spring 1975): 136–66.

> The inflation of 1973 and 1974 was traumatic for all Western societies. A number of governments were shaken and fell over energy issues. Argues that inflation might change economic policy analysis in as basic a way as did the Depression of the 1930s.

829 _____. "Policy Decision and Research in Economics and Industrial Relations." INDUSTRIAL AND LABOR RELATIONS REVIEW 30 (April 1977): 275–82.

> The bulk of academic research in economics and industrial relations has had little impact on public or private policy decisions. If scholarly research is to be influential, greater attention must be paid to the institutional settings in which decisions are made.

830 Esseks, Richard. "The Politics of Farmland Preservation." POLICY STUDIES JOURNAL 6 (Summer 1978): 514–19.

This paper is concerned with why some farmland preservation techniques are adopted and later sustained by state and local governments. It presents and discusses four techniques in the preservation of farmland.

831    Fechter, Alan. PUBLIC EMPLOYMENT PROGRAMS. Washington, D.C.: American Enterprise Institute for Public Policy Research, 1977. 40 p.

Public employment programs are being looked at as possible solutions to current social problems. A large program, while politically attractive, would probably be an undesirable use of public resources.

832    Ferrell, O.C., and LaGrace, Raymond, eds. PUBLIC POLICY ISSUES IN MARKETING. Lexington, Mass.: Lexington Books, 1975. 192 p.

Combining public policy analysis with marketing, the editors deal with such issues as truth in advertising, the unfairness doctrine, corrective advertising, self-regulation of business, consumerism, and future marketing techniques.

833    Frank, S.A., and Noah, J.W. "Costs of Federal Assistance to Distressed Areas." POLICY ANALYSIS 1 (Fall 1975): 719-30.

Economic Development Administration loans tend to have high administrative and opportunity costs. Even so, the study reaches no conclusion with respect to the value of the programs of the EDA.

834    Friedman, Lewis. "How to Save Money with Policy Analysis." POLICY ANALYSIS 1 (Fall 1975): 755-57.

In eighty-eight cities, using policy analysis as part of the budgetary decision-making process was positively related to a high credit rating. Policy analysis can help to save money.

835    Garson, G. David, and Smith, Michael P. "On Public Policy for Self-Management: Toward a Bill of Rights for Working People." ADMINISTRATION AND SOCIETY 7 (May 1975): 107-28.

There is a need to reevaluate public policy toward private government based on the need to guarantee human rights in the workplace.

836    Gordon, Lawrence A., and Schick, Allen. "Executive Policy-Making Authority and Using Zero-Base Budgeting for Allocation Resources." POLICY STUDIES JOURNAL 7 (Spring 1979): 554-68.

A comparison of incremental policymaking to scientific policy-making shows that the use of ZBB will result in greater policy-making authority in the hands of senior management and less power to agencies and bureaus.

837    Hadwinger, Don; Fraenkel, Richard; and Browne, William, eds. THE NEW POLITICS OF FOOD. Lexington, Mass.: Lexington Books, 1979. 324 p.

Deals with the change in American agricultural policy from a concern with farm income to one that emphasizes the problems of food production. It focuses on new authority relationships that have emerged.

838 Hale, George E. "The Political Implications of American National Manpower Policy." AMERICAN BEHAVIORAL SCIENTIST 17 (March-April 1974): 555-71.

To date, manpower programs have ignored the problems associated with institutional change and the improvement of ghetto labor markets. They have done little to improve worker employability or hourly wages.

839 Hardin, Charles M. "Agricultural Price Policy: The Political Role of Bureaucracy." POLICY STUDIES JOURNAL 6 (Summer 1978): 467-72.

This article traces the historical role of the bureaucracy in agriculture, outlines changes in the structure of agriculture policymaking, and in price policy, and provides an evaluation of agricultural policymaking.

840 _____. FOOD AND FIBER IN THE NATION'S POLITICS. Washington, D.C.: Government Printing Office, 1967. 236 p.

A former secretary of agriculture provides an insider's view of the politics of agriculture policy formation and administration.

841 Harman, Sidney. "Implications for Public Policy: The Role of Government in the Enhancement of Human Development in the World of Work." JOURNAL OF APPLIED BEHAVIORAL SCIENCE 13 (July-September 1977): 458-62.

This is the testimony by Dr. Sidney Harman, Under Secretary of Commerce, before the Subcommittee on Economic Stabilization of the House of Representatives in March 1977. Harman testified in support of H.R. 2596, the Human Resources Development Act, which has as its goals economic stability and job security.

842 Hartman, Robert W. "Next Steps in Budget Reform: Zero-Base Review of the Budgetary Process." POLICY ANALYSIS 3 (Summer 1977): 387-94.

The key to workable zero-base budget reforms is that it be selective and that multiyear budgeting be approached in an evolutionary manner.

843 Hazleton, Jared E. "Public Policy Toward Bank Mergers: A Legal and Economic Evaluation." SOCIAL SCIENCE QUARTERLY 51 (September 1970): 295-308.

Public policy toward the banking industry has undergone great change since 1960. In contrast to over a century of regulatory policy designed to restrict competition in banking, the new merger policy seeks to promote competition among banks.

844 Holden, Matthew, Jr., ed. "Policy Content and the Regulatory Process." AMERICAN BEHAVIORAL SCIENTIST 19 (September–October 1975): entire issue.

The issue is devoted to five essays on regulatory policy. Included are articles on energy, technology assessment, low income housing policy, pricing policy in the delivery of health care services, and medicine.

845 Kau, James B., and Kau, Mary L. "Social Policy Implications of the Minimum Wage Law." POLICY SCIENCES 4 (1973): 21–27.

The minimum wage law has played a major role in causing unemployment among the most disadvantaged groups. Thus, further increases in the minimum wage should be blocked.

846 Kohlmeier, Louis J. THE REGULATORS. New York: Harper and Row, 1969. 339 p.

This is a journalist's account of the policy actions of several federal administrative regulatory agencies.

847 Laird, Roy D. "Grain as a Foreign Policy Tool in Dealing with the Soviets." POLICY STUDIES JOURNAL 6 (Summer 1978): 533–37.

The author reviews his and other writers' conclusion that food should not become a diplomatic weapon. Under certain circumstances, it might be politically and ethically proper to use it as any other weapon would be used.

848 LeLoup, Lance. "Discretion in National Budgeting: Controlling the Controllables." POLICY ANALYSIS 4 (Fall 1978): 455–75.

The controllable–uncontrollable dichotomy does not provide an adequate understanding of budgetary expenditures. Using projections of current policies and services, the author estimates baselines and boundaries for annual budget change.

849 Lindbeck, Aaron. "Stabilization Policy in Open Economics with Endogenous Politicians." AMERICAN ECONOMIC REVIEW 66 (May 1976): 1–19.

While it is an important factor, aggregate demand management is insufficient as a successful stabilization policy in open economics with high levels of capacity utilization. Lindbeck presents four additional types of national stabilization policy.

850 McCalla, Alex F. "The Politics of the U.S. Agricultural Research Establishment: A Short Analysis." POLICY STUDIES JOURNAL 6 (Summer 1978): 479–83.

This is a discussion of the organizations that fund and/or do agricultural research in the United States to unravel the politics of the agricultural establishment. The establishment is a loosely related set of organizations that defies simple description.

851 Morrison, Peter A. MIGRATION AND RIGHTS OF ACCESS: NEW PUBLIC CONCERNS OF THE 1970S. Santa Monica, Calif.: Rand Corporation, 1977. 17 p.

Morrison presents a demographic perspective on migration and the issue of access as they are visible in two community types: energy boom towns and growth-limiting communities.

852 Nadel, Mark. "Economic Power and Public Policy: The Case of Consumer Protection." POLITICS AND SOCIETY 1 (May 1971): 313-26.

Nadel analyzes proposed consumer protection legislation from the perspective of the politics of a policy emerging from interests that are widely dispersed, of low intensity, and frequently opposed to each other.

853 Natchez, Peter B., and Cupp, Irwin C. "Policy and Priority in the Budgetary Process." AMERICAN POLITICAL SCIENCE REVIEW 67 (September 1973): 951-72.

Priority setting in the federal government resembles the nineteenth century capitalistic market, with aggressive entrepreneurs struggling to build and maintain support for their programs.

854 Nichols, Albert L., and Zeckhauser, Richard. "Government Comes to the Workplace: An Assessment of OSHA." PUBLIC INTEREST, no. 49 (Fall 1977), pp. 39-69.

This is a review of the early years, successes, and failures of the Occupational Safety and Health Administration. While OSHA's decisions affect the allocation of resources, it has adopted a missionary stance rather than an economic identity.

855 Paarlberg, Robert. "The Failure of Food Power." POLICY STUDIES JOURNAL 6 (Summer 1978): 537-42.

The power of food as a weapon is much less than first assumed. He cites several examples where the attempt to use food as a weapon has failed.

856 Peters, B. Guy. "Determinants of Tax Policy." POLICY STUDIES JOURNAL 7 (Summer 1979): 787-93.

This article identifies three major functions of tax policies adopted by governments and tries to find the determinants of those policy choices. Economic development is important in explaining redistributive tax patterns while political factors were related to attempts to make taxes invisible.

857    Phyrr, Peter A. "Zero-Based Budgeting." HARVARD BUSINESS
       REVIEW 37 (November-December 1970): 111-21.

       This article is the first appearance of the ZBB concept.
       Phyrr outlines the "how-to" of a ZBB process, explains
       the decision package concept, provides ranking mechanisms,
       and provides a method for identifying packages.

858    Pierce, Lawrence C. THE POLITICS OF FISCAL POLICY FORMA-
       TION. Pacific Palisades, Calif.: Goodyear, 1971. 225 p.

       Pierce gives an analysis of the processes and politics of
       fiscal policy formation with special concern for the develop-
       ment of policy proposals by fiscal agencies.

859    "Planning-Programming-Budgeting System Reexamined: Development,
       Analysis, and Criticism, A Symposium." PUBLIC ADMINISTRATION
       REVIEW 29 (March-April 1969): 111-202.

       This is a second look at PPBS, the first being a similar
       symposium in 1966. The eight articles cover PPBS at the
       federal, state, and local levels, examine its strengths and
       weaknesses, and project its future.

860    Price, Don K. "Money and Influence: The Links of Science to Public
       Policy." DAEDALUS 103 (Summer 1974): 97-114.

       An analysis of the causes of the decline in governmental support
       for scientific research and the decreased public faith in scien-
       tific leaders. Events outside of the control of scientists, such
       as self-governance, professional ethics, and political obliga-
       tions, probably account for the problems faced by scientists.

861    Quigley, John M., and Schmenner, Roger. "Property Tax Exemption
       and Public Policy." PUBLIC POLICY 23 (September 1975): 259-98.

       This is a discussion of the different levels of property tax
       exemption, why taxing of property has become a more impor-
       tant issue in recent years, and alternative directions for
       public policy in the treatment of tax exempt properties.

862    Richard, John. "The Scramble for Water: Agriculture Versus Other
       Interests in Wyoming." POLICY STUDIES JOURNAL 6 (Summer 1978):
       519-23.

       Richard argues the importance of adequate water resources
       in relation to agriculture and food supplies. Food needs
       place heavy demands on the water supplies of Western states
       while the concern for the environment often place agricultural
       and environmental interests in conflict.

863    Rosenthall, Gerald. "Manpower Policy: The Role of the Federal
       Government." AMERICAN BEHAVIORAL SCIENTIST 15 (May-June
       1972): 697-711.

This is a review of the evolution of federal manpower policy to its current status as a matter of separate policy concern. Future trends will require a closer coordination between manpower needs and education policy.

864   Rothblatt, Donald N. "National Development Policy." PUBLIC ADMINIS-TRATION REVIEW   34 (July–August 1974):   369–76.

Rothblatt discusses the goals and means of a national development policy for urban and regional areas and the potential conflicts between and among these goals.

865   Sabatier, Paul A.   "Regulatory Policy-Making:   Toward a Framework of Analysis."   NATURAL RESOURCES JOURNAL   17 (July 1977):   415–60.

This is a first step at developing a framework for the study of regulatory policy.   A typology of regulatory policy is suggested, the variables affecting policymaking by regulatory agencies are discussed, and some hypotheses concerning each variable are presented.

866   Schick, Allen.   "Systems Politics and Systems Budgeting."   PUBLIC ADMINISTRATION REVIEW   29 (March–April 1969):   137–51.

This is an analysis of PPBS from a process-systems dichotomy.   The article covers:   (1) elements of old and new budget systems; (2) process politics and systems politics; (3) the ability of politics and budgeting to use the systems view; and (4) a taxonomy of political process deficiencies.

867   Stahrl, Edmund A.   "Who Pays the Costs of Inflation?"   POLICY STUDIES JOURNAL   7 (Spring 1979):   568–77.

Inflation from 1965 to 1975 was seventeen times greater for families earning less than $5,000 a year than on those earning in excess of that.   Meanwhile the inflationary effect for families earning over $50,000 was a bonus of 1 percent.

868   Stigler, George J.   "The Law and Economics of Public-Policy:   A Plea to the Scholars."   JOURNAL OF LEGAL STUDIES   1 (January 1972):   1–12.

Stigler describes the cooperation that must exist between lawyers and economists in such areas as the regulation of monopolies and the protection of the consumer.   The amount of current cooperation is very low resulting in lower quality public policy.

869   Talbot, Ross B.   "The Three U.S. Food Policies:   An Ideological Perspective."   FOOD POLICY   2 (February 1977):   3–16.

Three ideologies are contesting for dominance in the area of food policy in the United States:   the market economy, public economy, and an interest group perspective.

870    Ulman, Lloyd. "The Uses and Limits of Manpower Policy." PUBLIC
INTEREST, no. 34 (Winter 1974), pp. 83-105.

> 1960s' manpower policies have not reached their intended goals
> and it is currently understood that such policies alone cannot
> be seen as alternatives to wage-price controls, the enforce-
> ment of antidiscrimination laws, or direct income transfers
> to the poor.

871    U.S. Congress. Senate. Committee on Government Operations. Subcommittee on Intergovernmental Relations. COMPENDIUM OF MATERIALS
ON ZERO-BASE BUDGETING IN THE UNITED STATES. 95th Cong.,
1st sess. Washington, D.C.: Government Printing Office, 1977. 384 p.

> This is an assessment of state efforts to implement ZBB.
> While about twelve states use some variant of ZBB, their
> methods are so varied that it is hard to identify a common
> core of practices.

872    Wanat, John. "Bureaucratic Politics in the Budget Formulation Area."
ADMINISTRATION AND SOCIETY 7 (August 1975): 191-212.

> Wanat discusses the interbureaucratic political process of
> budget formulation in the Labor Department from 1959 through
> 1968. It deals with the allocation of money by the inter-
> action of agencies, Department of Labor, and Budget Bureau.

873    Weiss, Thomas G., and Jordan, Robert S. "Bureaucratic Politics
and the World Food Conference: The International Policy Process."
WORLD POLITICS 28 (April 1976): 422-39.

> The World Food Conference shows how an international organi-
> zation can help to order interdependence. Existing international
> institutions can act responsibly and governmental elites can
> be influenced to recognize international responsibility.

874    Wildavsky, Aaron. "Rescuing Policy Analysis from PPB." PUBLIC
ADMINISTRATION REVIEW 29 (March-April 1969): 189-202.

> Since PPB cannot be undertaken for a variety of reasons,
> the real need for good policy analysis is jeopardized. Wildavsky
> assesses the damage done to policy analysis by PPB and
> suggests ways for the policy analyst to survive in the bureau-
> cracy.

875    Wooley, John T. "Monetary Policy, Instrumentation, and the Relationship of Central Banks and Government." ANNALS OF THE AMERICAN
ACADEMY OF POLITICAL AND SOCIAL SCIENCE 434 (November
1977): 151-73.

> Political scientists have ignored important political questions
> involving monetary policy and central banks. This essay
> organizes information about central banks and bankers.

## CITIZEN PARTICIPATION AND PLANNING

876     Adams, John S.   URBAN POLICYMAKING AND METROPOLITAN DY-
NAMICS:   A COMPARATIVE GEOGRAPHICAL ANALYSIS.   Cambridge,
Mass.:   Ballinger Publishing Co., 1976.   576 p.

> This volume is designed to assess the degree to which basic
> human needs were being met in America's twenty largest
> metropolitan areas.   Chapters include a discussion of the
> environment, housing, environmental goals, schools, crime,
> health care delivery, open space programs, transportation,
> and others.

877     "Alienation, Decentralization, and Participation:   A Symposium."
PUBLIC ADMINISTRATION REVIEW   29 (January–February 1969):
3–64.

> This symposium contains articles on alienation, including
> discussions of administration, decentralization, and political
> power; participation, poverty, and administration; self-fulfill-
> ment in bureaucratic society; the dialectical organization as
> alternative to bureaucracy; and the participative process.

878     Anderson, James E., ed.   CASES IN PUBLIC POLICY–MAKING.
New York:   Praeger Publishers, 1976.   329 p.

> Created to accompany his text in public policy, this collection
> of seventeen essays covers the problems and agendas of policy-
> making, policy formulation, policy adoption, implementation,
> and policy evaluation.

879     Bridge, Gary.   "Citizen Choice in Public Services:   Voucher Systems."
In ALTERNATIVES FOR DELIVERING PUBLIC SERVICES, edited
by E.S. Savas, pp. 51–109.   Boulder, Colo.:   Westview Press, 1978.

> Bridge addresses the policy questions in the delivery of sub-
> sidized goods to individuals.   The voucher system should be
> used to permit people to purchase goods in the open market.

880     Brown, Steven R., and Coke, James G.   PUBLIC OPINION ON LAND
USE REGULATION.   Columbus, Ohio:   Academy for Contemporary Problems, 1977.   19 p.

> American attitudes on the issue of land–use regulation are
> divided between environmentalists and localists on where
> land–use decisions ought to be made.

881     Choguill, Charles L.   "Regional Planning in the United States and the
United Kingdom."   REGIONAL STUDIES   11, no. 3 (1977):   135–45.

> Choquill focuses on the efforts associated with regional eco-
> nomic and social development in the United States and United
> Kingdom.   Attention is devoted to regional efforts directed
> to broad geographical areas.

882     Crecine, John P.   "University Centers for the Study of Public Policy:
Organizational Visibility."   POLICY SCIENCES   2 (March 1971):   7–32.

Crecine explains some of the problems encountered in creating
and maintaining university centers of public policy. Most of
the difficulties arise from the distinctions between pure and
applied research.

883    Cupps, Stephen D. "Emerging Problems of Citizen Participation."
PUBLIC ADMINISTRATION REVIEW 37 (September–October 1977):
478–87.

The problems associated with citizen participation include
the possible shortsightedness of the administrative response
to citizen demands, problems of representation and legitimacy,
the style and tactics of citizen groups, and the absence of
cost–benefit analysis of such programs.

884    Deutschler, Irwin. "Social Research and Public Policy: Some Comments
Inspired from the Papers on Applied Sociology." SOCIOLOGICAL
SYMPOSIUM 21 (Winter 1978): 46–58.

Policy research is a political enterprise and the research
must adopt a political perspective if the research is to have
any value to the policymaker.

885    Drucker, Peter F. "Managing the Public Service Institution." PUBLIC
INTEREST, no. 33 (Fall 1973), pp. 43–60.

Public service institutions can be managed. The reason that
they perform poorly is because they have a budget that is not
related to their actual performance. Development of an MBO
system would do wonders for public agency performance.

886    _____. "The Sickness of Government." PUBLIC INTEREST, no. 14
(Winter 1969), pp. 3–23.

Government has failed, it is not responsive to the needs of
the people and many of the government's functions ought to
be returned to the private sector.

887    Dunn, Delmer D. "Policy Preferences of Party Contributors and Voters."
SOCIAL SCIENCE QUARTERLY 55 (March 1975): 983–90.

Dunn compares the policy preferences of political party contributors in presidential elections from 1956 through 1968.

888    Freeman, Howard E. POLICY STUDIES REVIEW ANNUAL. Vol. 2.
Beverly Hills, Calif.: Sage, 1978. 750 p.

The articles are divided into perspectives on the policy process, the public sector, the economy, human resources, environmental issues, and "pervasive" issues.

889    Friedmann, John. "The Public Interest and Community Participation:
Toward a Reconstruction of Public Philosophy." JOURNAL OF THE
AMERICAN INSTITUTE OF PLANNERS 39 (January 1973): 2–12.

The idea of a public interest cannot be discarded except at risk to the community. It must be reconstructed to meet the challenges facing the nation.

890 Friedmann, John, and Abonyi, George. "Social Learning: A Model for Policy Research." ENVIRONMENT AND PLANNING 8 (1976): 927-40.

The results of policy research are not more widely utilized because of the incompatibility between the academic and governmental worlds.

891 "The Future of Policy-Making." MIDWEST REVIEW OF PUBLIC ADMINISTRATION 9 (January 1975): 43-77.

Included are fifteen articles on policymaking. Topics include: elite and pluralist policymaking, policy and administration, how not to be dominated by sophisticated management techniques, and others.

892 Gazell, James A. "Empirical Research in American Public Administration and Political Science: Is the Estranged Relative Outstripping the Rest of His Former Household?" MIDWEST REVIEW OF PUBLIC ADMINISTRATION 7 (October 1973): 229-44.

Public administration research has not advanced the behavioral frontier of political science. It is too normative, prescriptive, and institutional.

893 Gluck, Peter G. "Governance Arrangement and Governmental Performance: The Impact of Organizational Arrangements." MIDWEST REVIEW OF PUBLIC ADMINISTRATION 9 (October 1975): 173-86.

Gluck reviews major traditions of reform of urban government in terms of expectations and accomplishments.

894 Goodstein, Leonard D., and Boyer, Ronald K. "Crisis Intervention in a Municipal Agency: A Conceptual Case Study." JOURNAL OF APPLIED BEHAVIORAL SCIENCE 6 (May-June 1972): 318-40.

The authors provide a case report of the consulting process in the Health Department, Cincinnati, Ohio. An issue was to whom the consultants were responsible, the department, or the community at large.

895 Goodwin, Leonard. "PRESENT SHOCK: Bridging the Gap Between Social Research and Public Welfare, A Case in Point." JOURNAL OF APPLIED BEHAVIORAL SCIENCE 9 (January-February 1973): 85-114.

A form of social research on national problems that bridges the gap between social science and social practice is suggested.

896 Greenberg, Edward S. SERVING THE FEW: CORPORATE CAPITALISM AND THE BIAS OF GOVERNMENT. New York: John Wiley and Sons, 1974. 275 p.

Greenberg argues that public policy in the United States is
designed to serve the interest of big business.

897   Greenberg, Stanley B.   "The Alienated Politics of Poor Neighborhoods."
      In POLITICS AND POVERTY:   MODERNIZATION AND RESPONSE
      IN FIVE POOR NEIGHBORHOODS, edited by Stanley B. Greenberg,
      pp. 104-30. New York: John Wiley and Sons, 1974.

      Political alienation involved not just a positive or negative
      identification with a political system but feelings of political
      ineffectiveness, poor evaluations of government performance,
      and negative attitudes toward the entire political community.

898   Hollingsworth, J. Rogers, ed.   "Social Theory and Public Policy."
      ANNALS OF THE AMERICAN ACADEMY OF POLITICAL AND SOCIAL
      SCIENCES   434 (November 1977):   1-198.

      Contains twelve original essays on the application of social
      theory to public policy.   Topics include integrating social
      theory, policy, national health services, educational policy
      research, the fiscal crisis of U.S. cities, and juvenile de-
      linquency.

899   Hudson, Robert B.   "Rational Planning and Organizational Imperatives:
      Prospects for Area Planning in Aging."   ANNALS OF THE AMERICAN
      ACADEMY OF POLITICAL AND SOCIAL SCIENCE   415 (September
      1974):   41-54.

      This paper argues that because the new legislation is based
      on a rational goal model and conceptualizes the area agencies
      accordingly, it neglects important requisites of organizational
      life.   Given social realities, these agencies will concern
      themselves with issues other than those mandated in the legis-
      lation.   Their embarking upon incremental or goal-displacement
      activities may result in substantial modifications in the national
      policy strategy.

900   James, Dorothy B., ed.   OUTSIDE LOOKING IN:   CRITIQUES OF
      AMERICAN POLICIES AND INSTITUTIONS, LEFT AND RIGHT.
      New York:   Harper and Row, 1972.   439 p.

      This is an anthology of twenty-three critiques of American
      politics and institutions from the ideological Left and Right.
      The papers discuss capitalism, racism, poverty, the en-
      vironment, urban policy, and others.

901   Jones, Bryan D.; Greenberg, Saadia R.; Kaufman, Carole; and Drew,
      Joseph.   "Bureaucratic Response to Citizen-Initiated Contacts:   En-
      vironmental Enforcement in Detroit."   AMERICAN POLITICAL SCIENCE
      REVIEW   71 (March 1977):   148-65.

      The authors examine the nature of citizen contact and its
      results with respect to environmental enforcement in Detroit.
      The agency generally responds to citizen demands, but the
      nature of the response is varied according to the social
      characteristics of neighborhoods.

902     Jones, Mary Gardiner. "The Consumer Interest: The Role of Public Policy." CALIFORNIA MANAGEMENT REVIEW 16 (Fall 1973): 17-24.

> Consumer activism has demanded new types of responses on the part of business and government. This article reviews some of the new avenues for citizen–consumer activism.

903     Kaplan, Abraham. "On the Strategy of Social Planning." POLICY SCIENCES 4 (March 1973): 41-61.

> The philosophical question in social planning is whether facts can provide a logical basis for values since a planner concerns himself with facts and values only in the specific context with which he is working.

904     Karl, Barry D. "Philanthrophy, Policy Planning, and the Bureaucratization of the Democratic Ideal." DAEDALUS 105 (Fall 1976): 129-50.

> There has been a long–standing American hostility to management elites, but their utility for the democratic process is uncontestable. Whatever planning has been done for the society has been done by the professional managers.

905     Karnig, Albert. "Private Regarding Policy, Civil Rights, Groups, and the Mediating Impact of Municipal Reforms." AMERICAN JOURNAL OF POLITICAL SCIENCE 19 (February 1975): 91-106.

> Data from 417 cities are used to test the proposition that municipal reforms blunt the impact of private–regarding demands for public policy.

906     Keller, Lawrence, and Heatwole, Craig G. "Action Research in Policy Analysis: A Rejoinder to Frank Sherwood." ADMINISTRATION AND SOCIETY 8 (August 1976): 193-200.

> Shifting focus to public affairs does little to change what Sherwood identifies as the basic elements of action research-- problem orientation, real–time basis, and involving participants in both action and research.

907     King, Lauriston R., and Melanson, Philip H. "Knowledge and Politics: Some Experiences from the 1960s." PUBLIC POLICY 20 (Winter 1972): 83-101.

> The paper illustrates ways in which knowledge becomes involved in policy questions by examining cases in social welfare, national security,and foreign policy. Expert knowledge is rarely used as intended when it becomes tied up in political questions.

908     Kirkpatrick, Samuel A., and Morgan, David R. "Policy Support and Orientations toward Metropolitan Political Integration among Urban Officials." SOCIAL SCIENCE QUARTERLY 52 (December 1971): 656-71.

> The article tests a model of public officials' evaluation of urban policies and the effects of their orientations on metropolitan political integration.

909    Kirp, David.    "Growth Management, Zoning, Public Policy and the
       Courts."    POLICY ANALYSIS    2 (Summer 1976):    431-58.

       There are many legal bases on which land-management laws
       can be challenged including the claim that property has been
       taken, equal protection, the right to travel, general welfare,
       and the due process clause.

910    Khelshus, Ben, ed.    "Public Administration Forum:    The Future of
       Policy-Making."    MIDWEST REVIEW OF PUBLIC ADMINISTRATION
       9 (January 1975):    43-70.

       The fifteen articles cover elite versus participatory policy-
       making, politics and administration, the decision-making pro-
       cess, and changes in the policy process.

911    Kloman, Erasmus H.    "Public Administration in Technology Assessment."
       PUBLIC ADMINISTRATION REVIEW    34 (January-February 1974):
       52-61.

       Making and administering laws to govern present-day society
       is challenged on two fronts:    new laws must reflect the com-
       plexities encountered in unleashing new technologies while
       there are pressures to make the governing process more
       participatory.

912    Krieger, Susan.    "Prospects for Communication Policy."    POLICY
       SCIENCES    2 (1971):    305-19.

       At stake in communications policymaking is control and use of
       technologies used in the governance process.    Future policies
       must admit a broader range of social goals than present ones.

913    Krone, Robert M.    "Policy Sciences and Civil-Military Systems."
       JOURNAL OF POLITICAL AND MILITARY SOCIOLOGY    3 (Spring 1975):
       71-84.

       Policy sciences concepts have not yet had an effect on civil-
       military relations issues.    Political feasibility is probably
       the most difficult area to confront.

914    Lasswell, Harold D.    "Communications Research and Public Policy."
       PUBLIC OPINION QUARTERLY    36 (Fall 1972):    301-10.

       If public opinion-communications research is to become pro-
       fessionalized, it should report more on the quality and quan-
       tity of information entering into the policy process.

915    Lewin, Melvin R.    COMMUNITY AND REGIONAL PLANNING:    ISSUES
       IN PUBLIC POLICY.    New York:    Praeger Publishers, 1969.    305 p.

       Lewin examines community and regional planning ranging from
       neighborhood poverty programs to Appalachia.    It points out
       the consequences of creating complex federal programs before
       assuring that an adequate staff is able to implement them.

916    Lineberry, Robert L. "Equality, Public Policy, and Public Services: The Underclass Hypothesis and Limits to Equality." POLICY AND POLITICS 4 (December 1975): 67-84.

        The highest value that needs to be increased in the production and delivery of government services is equality. Neighborhoods should have enough resources to make their own services decisions.

917    _____. "Who Is Getting What?" PUBLIC MANAGEMENT 58 (August 1976): 13-18.

        If local government services are to be delivered equitably, they cannot be delivered according to need or demand. This research shows that who is getting what differs from city to city and that delivery decisions are the result of numerous previous decisions.

918    Lyden, Fremont J. "Psychological Research for Public Policy Formation." PUBLIC ADMINISTRATION REVIEW 36 (May-June 1976): 316-17.

        Psychologists have a unique expertise that could be contributed to policy analysis if the proper opportunity was provided.

919    Lyden, Fremont J., and Thomas, Jerry V. "Citizen-Participation in Policy Making: A Study of a Community Action Program." SOCIAL SCIENCE QUARTERLY 50 (December 1969): 631-42.

        A report of a nineteen-month study of a community action program board. It tries to determine if the representatives of the poor were able to contribute effectively to policy-making processes.

920    McConnell, Grant. PRIVATE POWER AND AMERICAN DEMOCRACY. New York: Alfred A. Knopf, 1966. 397 p.

        McConnell examines the role of private interest groups in policy formation and how pluralism and decentralization have often made them the dominant force.

921    Mazziotti, Donald F. "The Underlying Assumptions of Advocacy Planning: Pluralism and Reform." JOURNAL OF THE AMERICAN INSTITUTE OF PLANNERS 40 (January 1974): 38-48.

        The author examines the underlying assumption of political pluralism of advocacy planning. It has become the prevailing social myth for all planning activites in the United States.

922    Miller, S.M., and Roby, Pamela. THE FUTURE OF INEQUALITY. New York: Basic Books, 1970. 272 p.

        This is a study of the social indicators of inequality in the area of program development. In the future the distance between our expectations and realizations and the structural strain brought about by the failure of our social institutions will be the source of new social problems.

923    Murray, Edwin A., Jr. "Strategic Choice as a Negotiated Outcome."
MANAGEMENT SCIENCE   24 (May 1978):   960-72.

> With increasing pressures for public accountability by private
> enterprise, the autonomy of corporate managers to make
> decisions is being reduced.   As outside parties become more
> involved in corporate decision making, the idea of corporate
> strategy formulation will need to change.

924    Newland, Chester.  "MBO Concepts in the Federal Government."
BUREAUCRAT   2 (Winter 1974):   354-61.

> Newland summarizes key elements of MBO with an emphasis
> on setting objectives, tracking progress, and evaluating re-
> sults.   Newland also summarizes public administration con-
> cepts as they affect MBO objectives.

925    _____, ed.  "Management by Objectives in the Federal Government.
A Symposium."   BUREAUCRAT   2 (Winter 1974):   351-426.

> Eight articles on aspects of MBO applications in the federal
> government.   They cover general MBO ideas, the management
> conference, the promise of MBO, and the challenges it presents
> to the federal government.

926    Nichols, David A.  "Pluralism and Post-Pluralism in the Study of
Public Policy."   POLITY   10 (Winter 1977):   274-80.

> Nichols provides a review of six public policy texts.   A
> common failure in policy studies is their avoidance of the
> basic structure of social power and its importance.   Until
> policy studies give full consideration to all the forces affect-
> ing policy, they will be incomplete.

927    Nielsen, Richard P.; McQueen, Charles; and Nielsen, Angela B.  "Public
Policy and Attitudes on Tax Support for Live Artistic Communications
Media."   AMERICAN JOURNAL OF ECONOMICS AND SOCIOLOGY   35
(April 1976):   149-60.

> Hypothesized direct and interaction relationships among the
> dependent variable and the independent variables are tested.
> Past enjoyment makes people more favorably disposed to tax
> support.

928    Orbell, John M., and Uno, Toro.  "A Theory of Neighborhood Problem
Solving:   Political Action vs. Residential Mobility."   AMERICAN PO-
LITICAL SCIENCE REVIEW   66 (June 1972):   471-89.

> People have three ways of responding to a neighborhood prob-
> lem: leaving, doing something, and doing nothing.   Doing
> something is more likely to improve the situation than either
> of the other alternatives.

929    Owen, Bruce M.  "Public Policy and Emerging Technology in the Media."
PUBLIC POLICY   18 (Summer 1970):   539-52.

Public policy is too often the slave of defunct technology and bad decisions. The mass communications field provides an opportunity to change this situation. The paper explores the future of communications technology and discusses the role of Congress and the regulatory agencies in shaping a regulatory policy.

930　Park, Rolla Edward. "The Role of Analysis in the Formation of Cable Television Regulation Policy." POLICY SCIENCES 5 (March 1974): 71-81.

A prominent concern in FCC rulemaking is the impact of cable on over-the-air broadcasting. Analysis has an important effect on FCC policymaking.

931　Peterson, Richard A. THE INDUSTRIAL ORDER AND SOCIAL POLICY. Englewood Cliffs, N.J.: Prentice Hall, 1973. 159 p.

A sociologist views the consequences of technology and the continuing industrialization of social institutions.

932　Rider, Robert W. "Transition from Land Use to Policy Planning: Lessons Learned." JOURNAL OF THE AMERICAN INSTITUTE OF PLANNERS 44 (January 1978): 25-36.

Honolulu's new charter mandates a change in the existing land use plan to make it more policy oriented. This article reviews the lessons learned in making those changes.

933　Rondinelli, Dennis A. "Adjunctive Planning and Urban Development." URBAN AFFAIRS QUARTERLY 7 (September 1971): 13-30.

Modern planning is inadequate to deal with current governmental problems because of its intellectual development. Adjunctive planning would recognize the ecological, organizational, and institutional variables which affect the planning process.

934　_____. "The Dynamics of Policy Making." In URBAN AND REGIONAL DEVELOPMENT PLANNING: POLICY AND ADMINISTRATION, edited by Dennis A. Rondinelli, pp. 186-211. Ithaca, N.Y.: Cornell University Press, 1975.

Planning theorists advocating management science principles assume that rational policies cannot be made through noncentrally located decision making structures. Effective planning has to assume that a single organization can rarely control the outcome of the policymaking process.

935　_____. "Politics, Policy Analysis, and Development: The Future of Urban and Regional Planning." In URBAN AND REGIONAL DEVELOPMENT PLANNING: POLICY AND ADMINISTRATION, edited by Dennis A. Rondinelli, pp. 237-66. Ithaca, N.Y.: Cornell University Press, 1975.

Changes will have to occur in planning theory if it is to be reconciled with the realities of policy making. Planning is not the sole province of one trained group but the product of numerous interests and actors operating in a political structure.

936    Rutledge, Philip J. "Policy Analysis and Human Resources Management." PUBLIC MANAGEMENT 56 (September 1974): 16-19.

State and local human resources policy has been reactive to federal funding and municipalities have not been given a major responsibility in making or implementing national human resource policy.

937    Schumaker, Paul D. "Policy Responsiveness to Protest Group Demands." JOURNAL OF POLITICS 37 (May 1975): 486-521.

The article describes a model of the factors explaining the responsiveness of urban political systems to protest group demands. Government responsiveness to group demands is a function of group cohesiveness and the behavior and attitudes of the community towards the group.

938    Shellow, Robert. "Social Scientists and Social Action from within the Establishment." JOURNAL OF SOCIAL ISSUES 26, no. 1 (1970): 207-20.

The responsible roles of social scientists include those of interpreter and researcher, critic and participant in the reformation of social institutions. The existence of such roles allows social scientists to affect the formation of public policy.

939    Sindler, Allan P. POLICY AND POLITICS IN AMERICA: SIX CASE STUDIES. Boston: Little, Brown and Co., 1973. 244 p.

Six original case studies on welfare reform, the direct election of the president, public school financing, model cities, education, and the reelection of a congressman are included.

940    Smith, Richard W. "A Theoretical Basis for Participatory Planning." POLICY SCIENCES 4 (September 1973): 275-95.

Arguments are presented for the reconsideration of models which guide planning behavior and structure planning organizations. Participation is discussed as a form of legitimacy, which is presented as a fundamental basis for justifying planning action.

941    Vosburgh, William W., and Hyman, Drew. "Advocacy and Bureaucracy: The Life and Times of a Citizen's Advocacy Program." ADMINISTRATIVE SCIENCE QUARTERLY 18 (December 1973): 433-48.

This is an examination of a citizen's advocacy office in ghetto areas of Pennsylvania during a four-year period. The experiment raises issues about the possibility for success of an advocacy program subject to bureaucratic forces.

942    Weissman, Stephen R. "The Limits of Citizen Participation: Lessons from San Francisco's Model Cities Program." WESTERN POLITICAL QUARTERLY 31 (March 1978): 32-47.

> Weissman seeks to determine the impact of neighborhood participation on the identification and solution of urban social programs. Neighborhood mobilization strategies fail to recognize the constraints of the larger urban environment.

943    Yin, Robert K., and Lucas, William A. "Decentralization and Alienation." POLICY SCIENCES 4 (September 1973): 327-36.

> The reduction of citizen alienation is one goal in decentralizing public services. Decentralization of public services may be one of many steps to reduce citizen alienation toward government, but it will not have a significant impact on alienation by itself.

944    Zellman, Gail L. "Antidemocratic Beliefs: A Survey and Some Explanations." JOURNAL OF SOCIAL ISSUES 31 (Spring 1975): 31-53.

> Here is a presentation of data about the tolerance for civil liberties and dissent in the American public. Support is less in the concrete case than in the abstract. Few efforts are made to socialize Americans as true civil libertarians.

## CIVIL RIGHTS, CRIMINAL JUSTICE

945    Baum, Lawrence. "Police Response to Appellate Court Decisions: Mapp and Miranda." POLICY STUDIES JOURNAL 7, no 3 (1978): 425-31.

> The Mapp and Miranda decisions created considerable procedural requirements in the gathering of evidence. While the police would like to minimize the impact of these decisions on their practices, they have had little success in doing so.

946    Beutel, Frederick K. "Experimental Jurisprudence and Systems Engineering in Determining Policy." In POLICY STUDIES AND THE SOCIAL SCIENCES, edited by Stuart S. Nagel, pp. 249-63. Lexington, Mass.: Lexington Books, 1975.

> The task of experimental jurisprudence and social systems engineering is to rearrange laws and government policies so that tragedies can be prevented and progress can be continuous.

947    Brintnall, Michael A. "Police and White Collar Crime." POLICY STUDIES JOURNAL 7, no. 3 (1978): 431-36.

> White collar crime has seldom been formally addressed by police departments, partially because of the specialized organization necessary to investigate such crimes.

948     "The Burger Court:  New Directions in Judicial Policy–Making."
        EMORY LAW JOURNAL   23 (Summer 1974):   643–786.

        The issue contains five articles on the Burger–headed Supreme
        Court and judicial policymaking.  Topics include:  substantive
        equal protection, one–man, one–vote, Congress and the
        courts, and others.

949     "Civil Liberties Policy, A Symposium."   POLICY STUDIES JOURNAL
        4 (Winter 1976):   103–79.

        Issue contains sixteen articles on the following aspects of
        civil liberties:  the First Amendment, new areas of civil
        liberties, civil liberties and policymaking, and methodology.

950     Cook, Beverly B.  "Public Opinion and Federal Judicial Policy."
        AMERICAN JOURNAL OF POLITICAL SCIENCE   21 (August 1977):
        567–600.

        The representative model is used to determine the relation-
        ship between public opinion on the Vietnam war and the sen-
        tences handed down by federal judges from 1967 to 1975.
        Over the period the correlation between national opinion and
        sentencing was .957; between regional opinion and sentencing
        was .849; and between state opinion and sentencing .697.

951     Culver, John H.  "Television and the Police."  POLICY STUDIES
        JOURNAL   7 (1978):   500–505.

        Television programs give a misleading picture of the police
        function by underestimating the obstacles and frustrations
        they face.  As a result, the public receives a misleading
        picture.

952     Doig, James.  "Public Policy and Police Behavior:  Patterns of Diver-
        gence."  POLICY STUDIES JOURNAL   7 (1978):   436–42.

        Doig examines the difficulty police administrators have in
        controlling behavior in the field.  Doig reviews policy goals,
        police culture, legal restrictions, and appropriate adminis-
        trative responses.

953     Eisenstein, James, and Jacob, Herbert.  "Measuring Performance and
        Outputs of Urban Criminal Courts."   SOCIAL SCIENCE QUARTERLY
        54 (March 1974):   713–24.

        This is an effort to explain the obstacles to obtaining reliable
        and valid measures relating to the outputs of urban criminal
        courts.  It is based on the authors' experiences during the
        planning of a study of the disposition of felony charges in
        Baltimore, Chicago, and Detroit.

954     Fairchild, Erika S.  "Organizational Structure and Control of Discre-
        tion in Police Operations."  POLICY STUDIES JOURNAL   7 (1978):
        442–49.

Fairchild makes an effort to relate the control of police discretion to models of organizational structure. It is suggested that approaches which will increase officer decision-making capability should be tried.

955    Gardiner, John A., and Mulkey, Michael A., eds. "Crime and Criminal Justice Policy, A Symposium." POLICY STUDIES JOURNAL 3 (Autumn 1974): 5-96.

Thirteen articles on crime and criminal justice policy are divided into the following categories: the setting of criminal justice decision making, criminal justice agencies, and problems in research policy analysis.

956    Giles, Michael W., and Walker, Thomas G. "Judicial Policy-Making and Southern School Segregation." JOURNAL OF POLITICS 37 (November 1975): 917-36.

Four hypotheses are tested to discover possible correlates of desegregation decisions: the social backgrounds of judges, environmental variables, community linkages, and school district variables.

957    Graber, Doris. "The Media and the Police." POLICY STUDIES JOURNAL 7 (1978): 493-500.

Favorable reports about police departments received less media coverage than did sensational crime stories; thus, citizens in a survey knew little about police operations and used their own social views to reach judgments about the police.

958    Green, Justin J. "Judicial Policy-Making, 1973-1974." WESTERN POLITICAL QUARTERLY 28 (March 1975): 167-92.

During its 1973-74 term, the U.S. Supreme Court rendered opinions in 140 cases. The major policy areas considered were the scope of federal court jurisdiction, desegregation, search and seizure rights, and the rights of persons accused of crimes.

959    Hanson, Roger A., and Crew, Robert E., Jr. "The Policy Impact of Reapportionment." LAW AND SOCIETY REVIEW 8 (Fall 1973): 69-94.

This is an attempt to determine the effect of reapportionment on government institutions. The data indicate that reapportionment preceded changes in the pattern of policy outcomes.

960    Kelly, Michael. "Social Science Evaluation and Criminal Justice Policy-Making: The Case of Pre-Trial Release." In PUBLIC POLICY EVALUATION, edited by Kenneth M. Dolbeare, pp. 253-82. Beverly Hills, Calif.: Sage, 1975.

Kelly addresses the problems inherent in the evaluation of pre-trial release programs and the weaknesses of available quantitative data as guides to the institutional realities of lower court activities.

961     Levin, Martin A. URBAN POLITICS AND THE CRIMINAL COURTS.
Chicago: University of Chicago Press, 1977. 332 p.

> The focus is on criminal justice policy, especially sentencing
> and the relationship of judicial selection to judicial sentencing-
> decision behavior.

962     Levin, Martin A., and Dornbusch, Horst D. "Pure and Policy Social
Sciences: Evaluation of Policies in Criminal Justice and Education."
PUBLIC POLICY 21 (Summer 1973): 383–424.

> The authors provide a discussion of the problems in moving
> social science research into policy evaluation and program
> decisions. There are important differences and distinctions
> between the needs of pure and policy social science.

963     Levine, James P. "The Ineffectiveness of Adding Police to Prevent
Crime." PUBLIC POLICY 23 (Fall 1975): 523–45.

> Increasing the number of police on the street has little effect
> on reported crime rates. More attention ought to be placed
> on organizing and deploying the police more effectively.

964     Lovrich, Nicholas P., Jr. "Reducing Crime through Policy–Community
Relations: Evidence of the Effectiveness of Police–Community Relations
Training from a Study of 161 Cities." POLICY STUDIES JOURNAL
7 (1978): 505–12.

> The value of police–community relations programs as effective
> crime reduction policy is investigated in 161 U.S. cities.
> In cities that have committed themselves to police–community
> relations training, reporting crimes to the police is higher
> and the rate of crime increase has been lower than in cities
> that have not adopted police–community relations training.

965     McIver, John P. "The Relationship between Metropolitan Police Industry Structure and Interagency Assistance: A Preliminary Assessment."
POLICY STUDIES JOURNAL 7 (1978): 406–13.

> Interdepartmental and interjurisdictional assistance occurs
> with greater frequency in metropolitan areas with structural
> fragmentation. More assistance also occurs in metropolitan
> areas that lack a dominant central city policy agency.

966     Marks, Raymond F. "Some Research Perspectives for Looking at Legal
Need and Legal Service Delivery Systems." LAW AND SOCIETY RE-
VIEW 11 (Spring 1976): 191–205, 399–415.

> Marks looks at empirical research about the need for and
> use of delivery systems for legal research. A perspective
> is developed that would make existing research useful in
> determining what research ought to be undertaken in the future.

967     Morgan, David R., and Swanson, Cheryl. "Analyzing Police Policies:
Impact of Environment, Politics, and Crime." URBAN AFFAIRS
QUARTERLY 11 (June 1976): 489–510.

The authors are concerned with the relationship between city characteristics and the adoption of new procedures and programs by public departments. The goal is to discover what environmental and political valuables might be associated with crime rates and citizen satisfaction with police services.

968  Nagel, Stuart S., and Neef, Marian. LEGAL POLICY ANALYSIS. Lexington, Mass.: Lexington Books, 1977. 327 p.

The authors apply optimizing techniques to decision problems faced by judges, legislators, administrators, interest groups, and others involved with political and legal decision making.

969  Ostrom, Elinor, et al. "The Public Service Production Process: A Framework for Analyzing Police Services." POLICY STUDIES JOURNAL 7, no. 3 (1978): 381-89.

Accurate and comprehensive evaluation of agency performance requires a clear theoretical understanding of the process by which police services are produced. The article presents a model for conceptually identifying the elements of the service production process.

970  Payne, William C. "Implementing Federal Non-Discrimination Policies in the Department of Agriculture." POLICY STUDIES JOURNAL 6 (Summer 1978): 507-9.

Minority persons in rural areas have been the victims of an agricultural policy whose effects have been to deny them the alternative that were and are available to nonminorities and to preclude minorities from control over the forces that shape their lives.

971  Percy, Stephen L. "Conceptualizing and Measuring Citizen Co-Production of Community Safety." POLICY STUDIES JOURNAL 7 (1978): 486-93.

Citizens play an important role in the provision of community safety. This role as coproducers can be distinguished along two dimensions: cooperation with police and cooperation with other citizens.

972  Rhodes, Robert P. "Electronic Surveillance, Organized Crime, and Civil Liberties." POLICY STUDIES JOURNAL 7 (1978): 419-25.

Rhodes offers an examination of the policy issues surrounding the use of informants and electronic surveillance to control organized crime. Rhodes suggests that the effectiveness of these devices is fairly substantial in otherwise difficult cases.

973  Rudoni, Dorothy; Baker, Ralph; and Meyer, Fred A., Jr. "Police Professionalism: Emerging Trends." POLICY STUDIES JOURNAL 7 (1978): 454-60.

The essay is an examination of the ambiguity surrounding the idea of police professionalism. Models of professionalism are examined as well as the symbolic significance of the use of the term professional by the police.

974 Scharf, Peter. "Deadly Force: The Moral Reasoning and Education of Police Officers Faced with the Option of Legal Lethal Violence." POLICY STUDIES JOURNAL 7 (1978): 450-54.

There are significant differences among police officers of differing moral beliefs in conceptions of what they see as legitimate deadly force. The authors propose a training program designed to facilitate officer reasoning on a range of types of discretionary justice.

975 Skogan, Wesley G. "Citizen Satisfaction with Police Services: Individual and Contextual Effects." POLICY STUDIES JOURNAL 7 (1978): 469-79.

Skogan presents a model for examining the effects of variations in police policies and performance on citizen satisfaction with police services.

976 Smith, Russell L., and Uhlman, Thomas M. "Police Policy and Citizen Satisfaction: Evidence from Urban Areas." POLICY STUDIES JOURNAL 7 (1978): 480-86.

Two programs in fourteen cities are designed to improve public evaluations of the police.

977 Talarico, Susette M., and Swanson, Charles R., Jr. "Styles of Policing: A Preliminary Mapping." POLICY STUDIES JOURNAL 7 (1978): 398-405.

The authors study the relationship between organizational and individual styles of policing. The style of the immediate supervisor was more clearly associated with police styles than was that of the work group.

978 Wasby, Stephen L. "Police Training about Court Procedures: Infrequent and Inadequate." POLICY STUDIES JOURNAL 7 (1978): 461-68.

Despite the increase in training offered to police officers, there are still significant deficiencies in the level of training devoted to the law of criminal procedure.

979 Wilson, James. THINKING ABOUT CRIME. New York: Basic Books, 1975. 221 p.

Crime should be controlled by controlling criminals. Wilson suggests that the detention of convicted criminals and the alteration of their expectation of punishment might have some positive impact.

# EDUCATION POLICY

980     Bishop, John. "The Effect of Public Policies in the Demand for Higher Education." JOURNAL OF HUMAN RESOURCES 13 (Summer 1977): 285-307.

> Tuition, high admissions standards, travel costs, and room and board costs have significant negative effects on attendance. The highest elasticities of demand are found in the low-income and lower-middle ability range.

981     Boss, Michael O., and Zielger, Harmon. "Experts and Representatives: Comparative Basis of Influence in Educational Policy-Making." WESTERN POLITICAL QUARTERLY 30 (June 1977): 255-62.

> Decisions are the result of exchanges among participants vying for influence over the context of decisions. The less the community consensus about educational policy, the greater is the conflict over educational decision making.

982     Cebula, Richard J. "An Analysis of Migration Patterns and Local Government Policy Toward Public Education in the United States." PUBLIC POLICY 32 (Winter 1977): 113-21.

> The paper seeks to determine the impact of differential local government policies toward public education on migration patterns. The basic conclusion is that migration patterns and local government policies are highly interdependent.

983     Conant, James Bryant. SHAPING EDUCATIONAL POLICY. New York: McGraw Hill, 1964. 139 p.

> Conant examines who should determine educational policy for America. It is critical of the education establishment, and Congress is urged to establish an interstate commission for planning nationwide education policy.

984     Culbertson, Jack, ed. "Education and Public Policy." PUBLIC ADMINISTRATION REVIEW 30 (July-August 1970): 331-75.

> Seven articles on the public policy aspects of education covering: education in large cities, schools for low-income children, relationships between education and industry, the state and education policy, and others.

985     Down, George, and Rocke, David. "Bureaucracy and Juvenile Corrections in the States." POLICY STUDIES JOURNAL 7 (Summer 1979): 721-28.

> This study examines: (1) the extent to which variations in bureaucratic characteristics are tied to socioeconomic environments; (2) the relative impact of these characteristics on three different policy outputs; (3) the stability of their effect across outputs; and (4) the degree to which they interact with themselves and other variables.

986     Epps, Edgar G. "Educational Policy-Making for Urban Schools."
        JOURNAL OF NEGRO EDUCATION 44 (Summer 1975): 308-15.

        The article discusses what blacks can do to play a more
        influential role in the policymaking processes that go on
        in the education field.

987     Gove, Samuel, and Wirt, Frederick, eds. "Educational Policy Research,
        A Symposium." POLICY STUDIES JOURNAL 4 (Summer 1976): 335-407.

        This issue contains five articles dealing with adaptive schools
        and the limits of innovation, school superintendents and interest
        groups, efforts to reform school finance, policymaking and
        post-secondary education, and the educational policy implica-
        tions of Rawls's A THEORY OF JUSTICE (1971).

988     Greenberg, Deborah M. "Public Policy Issues in the Quota Controversy."
        EDUCATION AND URBAN SOCIETY 8 (November 1975): 73-85.

        Abstractly, issues like affirmative action, reverse discrimina-
        tion, and the like are subject to widespread disagreement.
        The more concrete the issue becomes, the more the dis-
        agreement disappears.

989     Hawley, Willis D., and Hill, Paul T. "Developing Adaptive Schools
        and the Limits of Innovation." POLICY STUDIES JOURNAL 4, no. 4
        (1976): 334-51.

        The capacity for innovation is highly overrated and the study
        of innovation yields too little that would be helpful for improving
        schools to warrant the resources devoted to its study.

990     Hirsch, Paul M. "Public Policy Toward Television: Mass Media and
        Education in American Society." SCHOOL REVIEW 85 (August 1977):
        481-512.

        The paper addresses several questions: What are some of the
        meanings of a successful perpetual image machine, how did it
        come about and how might it change?

991     Ornstein, Allen C., and Miller, Steven I., eds. POLICY ISSUES IN
        EDUCATION. Lexington, Mass.: D.C. Heath and Co., 1976. 159 p.

        This work includes eleven chapters and covers the full range
        of interests in education. Papers are grouped into three
        broad categories: issues in evaluating educational programs,
        conflict in the organization and control of schools, and efforts
        to deal with discrimination and its consequences.

992     Pettigrew, Thomas F. "Public Policy and Desegregation Research."
        INTEGRATED EDUCATION 10 (January-February 1972): 18-22.

        This is a summary of the policy implications for public educa-
        tion of racial desegregation of southern schools, white resis-
        tance to racial change in northern schools, and issues of
        parental control in education.

993  Spuck, Dennis W.; Hubert, Lawrence J.; and Lufler, Henry S., Jr. "Educational Policy Research: New Views on Methodology." EDUCATION AND URBAN SOCIETY 7 (May 1975): 211-349.

> Four articles deal with educational policy research, future research, the policy sciences, and methodological problems in economic policy research.

## HEALTH, WELFARE, AND POVERTY

994  Aday, LuAnn; Andersen, Ronald; and Anderson, Odi W. "Social Surveys and Health Policy: Implications for National Health Insurance." PUBLIC HEALTH REPORTS 92 (November-December 1977): 508-17.

> A review of the social surveys may contribute to the solution of health care delivery problems. Also discusses the acceptability to consumers of selected national health care insurance options.

995  Alford, Robert. HEALTH CARE POLITICS: IDEOLOGICAL AND INTEREST GROUP BARRIERS TO REFORM. Chicago: University of Chicago Press, 1975. 294 p.

> Alford contends that health care system is inadequate and that public and private programs designed to improve it have failed. The book is a case study of health care policy in New York City.

996  Anderson, Bernard E., and Wallace, Phyllis A. "Public Policy and Black Economic Progress: A Review of the Evidence." AMERICAN ECONOMIC REVIEW 65 (May 1975): 47-53.

> The essay summarizes and evaluates economic evidence to explain the pattern and determinants of change in the employment and income of blacks during the 1960s.

997  Baridon, Philip. ADDICTION, CRIME, AND SOCIAL POLICY. Lexington, Mass.: Lexington Books, 1976. 126 p.

> Heroin should be available in pharmacies to anyone over the age of eighteen who wants it. This book is an analysis of opium addiction in the United States and the crime associated with it.

998  Blackstone, Erwin A. "Misallocation of Medical Resources: The Problem of Excessive Surgery." PUBLIC POLICY 22 (Summer 1974): 329-52.

> There is a great deal of unnecessary surgery performed in this country; at the same time, there is a shortage of doctors. The reasons for this misallocation of resources are differential pricing behavior and entry conditions in surgery and general practice.

999    Boekmann, Margaret E.   "Policy Impacts of the New Jersey Income
       Maintenance Experiment."   POLICY SCIENCES   7 (March 1976):   53-76.

       New Jersey undertook an Income Maintenance and Family
       Assistance Plan.   This article evaluates the experiment's
       effect on decision makers, communication channels, and the
       impact of the findings on state-level decision makers.

1000   Bowler, M. Kenneth.   THE NIXON GUARANTEED INCOME PROPOSAL:
       SUBSTANCE AND PROCESS IN POLICY CHANGE.   Lexington, Mass.:
       Ballinger Books, 1974.   201 p.

       Bowler provides a chronological account of the Nixon adminis-
       tration's proposal for a guaranteed income for families with
       children, its fate in Congress, and other changes in the cash
       assistance program considered from 1969 to 1974.

1001   Brown, Lawrence.   "The Scope and Limits of Equality as a Normative
       Guide to Federal Health Care Policy."   PUBLIC POLICY   26 (Fall
       1978):   481-532.

       The idea that each citizen has a right to good medical care
       has become a popular political position.   Federal policy
       makers have been unable to decide between equal access for
       all or a more limited access keeping cost and other considera-
       tions in mind.

1002   Buntz, C. Gregory; Macaluso, Theodore F.; and Azarow, Jay Allen.
       "Federal Influence on State Health Policy."   JOURNAL OF HEALTH
       POLITICS, POLICY AND LAW   3 (Spring 1978):   71-86.

       States' political environments tailor program implementation
       to suit state preferences.   Federal programs facilitate rather
       than inhibit the attainment of state health goals.

1003   Burns, Eveline M.   "The Nation's Health Insurance and Health Services
       Policies, in Evolution Towards What?"   AMERICAN BEHAVIORAL
       SCIENTIST   15 (May-June 1972):   713-32.

       A historical review of the criticism is leveled against America's
       health care system in the past decades.   After reviewing the
       debate as far back as 1932, attention is turned to Family
       Assistance Plans and Health Maintenance Organizations as
       present policy and to some future possibilities.

1004   Cameron, James.   "Ideology and Policy Termination: Restructuring
       California's Mental Health System."   PUBLIC POLICY   26 (Fall 1978):
       533-70.

       Cameron explores the process of policy and organizational
       change that occurred with mental health reform.   Consequences
       of the new mental health policy are related to the manner in
       which the previous policy was terminated.   An experimental
       approval to the development of public policy is outlined, con-
       trasting it with policy innovation justified on the basis of
       ideology.

1005  Carroll, Stephen J., and Pascal, Anthony H. "Toward a National
      Youth Employment Policy: Mapping the Route from Problems to Pro-
      grams." POLICY SCIENCES 2 (June 1971): 159-75.

> The United States has not had a consistent, comprehensive
> youth employment policy. Program objectives are not clear
> and are often in conflict with the objectives of other programs
> aimed at the same target population. The primary needs
> are a clearly specified policy objective and a method for
> identifying the ways in which potential intervention can help
> attain that objective.

1006  Clark, Kenneth, and Hopkins, Jeanette. A RELEVANT WAR AGAINST
      POVERTY: A STUDY OF COMMUNITY ACTION PROGRAMS AND
      OBSERVABLE SOCIAL CHANGE. New York: Harper and Row,
      1970. 275 p.

> An analysis of the definitions and goals of war on poverty
> programs in twelve U.S. cities. The problems of poverty
> cannot be resolved if isolated from the whole pattern of
> American life.

1007  Cohen, Wilbur J. "Government Policy and the Poor: Past, Present,
      and Future." JOURNAL OF SOCIAL ISSUES 26, no. 3 (1970):
      1-7.

> The role of government in the United States in relation to
> the poor is examined in historical perspective, with emphasis
> on the shifting of responsibility from local and state agencies
> to the larger units of the federal government, on the influences
> of certain popular formal programs (e.g., Social Security),
> and on the effects of the recent long period of general pros-
> perity.

1008  Coppedge, Robert O., and Davis, Carlton G., eds. RURAL POVERTY
      AND THE POLICY CRISIS. Ames: Iowa State University Press, 1977.
      220 p.

> The focus in several chapters is on rural areas, but the
> authors are concerned with the issues and problems of poverty
> regardless of location.

1009  Derthick, Martha. UNCONTROLLABLE SPENDING FOR SOCIAL SER-
      VICES GRANTS. Washington, D.C.: Brookings Institution, 1975. 139 p.

> Derthick analyzes a provision of the Social Security Amend-
> ments of 1962 which allowed for virtually unlimited grants-
> in-aid to the states for social services under the public
> assistance titles of the Social Security Act.

1010  Eisele, Frederick R., ed. "Political Consequences of Aging." ANNALS
      OF THE AMERICAN ACADEMY OF POLITICAL AND SOCIAL SCIENCE
      415 (September 1974): entire issue.

> Thirteen articles in this issue are devoted to policy issues
> and the aging. Topics include income maintenance for the
> aged, area-wide planning, social services for the elderly,
> reforming private pensions, and others. There are seven
> additional essays dealing with other age-related concerns.

1011  Etzioni, Amitai. "Old People and Public Policy." SOCIAL POLICY
      7 (November–December 1976): 21–29.

> Viewing older persons as a status group with unique specialized
> needs tends to set up a dysfunctional tension between older
> Americans and the rest of society. The tension would be
> much reduced if more general, society-wide policies replaced
> categorical programs in taking care of older persons' special
> needs.

1012  _____. "Public Policy Issues Raised by a Medical Breakthrough."
      POLICY ANALYSIS 1 (Winter 1975): 69–76.

> Amniocentisis which detects mongolism and other serious
> abnormalities in a fetus, will prevent the birth of thousands
> of afflicted children a year once its widespread acceptability
> is established. This genetic intervention raises numerous
> public policy questions including who is to be tested, what
> shall the test be used for, and who shall decide?

1013  Falkson, Joseph L. "Minor Skirmish in a Monumental Struggle: HEW's
      Analysis of Mental Health Services." POLICY ANALYSIS 2 (Winter
      1976): 93–119.

> In 1972, HEW produced an analysis of the federal role in
> the delivery of health services. This article examines that
> analysis from its inception to its impact (disappointing in the
> view of the author), against the background of the new feder-
> alism that prevailed in HEW, and against the political environ-
> ment that surrounded mental health policy. In such a context,
> analysis has little hope of influencing policy outcome.

1014  Fanshel, Sol. "The Welfare of the Elderly: A System Analysis View-
      point." POLICY SCIENCES 6 (September 1955): 343–57.

> A methodology is presented for the analysis of social services
> offered to the elderly. It is assumed that the goal of social
> services is to increase the elderly person's independence.

1015  Foltz, Anne-Marie; Chen, Milton; and Stoga, Alan. "Public Policy
      and Health Resource Distribution." POLICY SCIENCES 8 (September
      1977): 323–41.

> The authors find little evidence to support the hypothesis
> that Connecticut's town and state decision makers were
> following a rational model in allocating health resources. A
> more complex model, such as a bureaucratic politics model,
> would explain better public decisions in health resources in
> this area.

1016  Fox, Peter D. "Options for National Health Insurance: An Overview."
      POLICY ANALYSIS 3 (Winter 1977): 1–24.

> Based on a series of internal memos used for decision making
> by the secretary of HEW and the White House, this article
> discusses the basic options for national health care insurance
> as they are presented in the various pieces of legislation
> before Congress.

1017    Friedman, Kenneth.  PUBLIC POLICY AND THE SMOKING-HEALTH
        CONTROVERSY.  Lexington, Mass.:  D.C. Heath, 1975.  234 p.

        This is a detailed account of the controversies among govern-
        ment agencies, the tobacco industry and various health interest
        groups over the past twenty-five years.  Emphasis is on the
        United States, but some comparative material on Canada and
        Great Britain is included.

1018    Friedman, Lee S.  "An Interim Evaluation of the Supported Work Ex-
        periment."  POLICY ANALYSIS  3 (Spring 1977):  147-70.

        Friedman describes the setting of a supported work experiment,
        the interim results, and the limits of cost-benefit analysis
        as it affects program development.

1019    Furstenberg, Frank, Jr., and Thrall, Charles A.  "Counting the Job-
        less: The Impact of Job Rationing on the Measurement of Unemployment."
        ANNALS OF THE AMERICAN ACADEMY OF POLITICAL AND SOCIAL
        SCIENCE  418 (March 1975):  45-59.

        The official definition of unemployment is poorly designed to
        reflect the size of the population available for work.  One
        of the considerations affecting labor market behavior is
        how strongly an individual feels that he has the right to a
        job and the obligation to work.

1020    Glazer, Nathan.  "Reform Work, Not Welfare."  PUBLIC INTEREST,
        no. 40 (Summer 1975), pp. 3-10.

        The best welfare policy would be to make more attractive
        the kind of work that people on welfare might take.

1021    Greenfield, Harry I.  HOSPITAL EFFICIENCY AND PUBLIC POLICY.
        New York:  Praeger Publishers, 1973.  81 p.

        This book deals with the meaning and measurement of efficiency
        in the production of hospital services by focusing on the eco-
        nomic factors that influence health care in hospitals.  It in-
        dicates how public policy might be applied to produce health
        services which are qualitatively superior, more accessible,
        and more efficient.

1022    Gregg, Philip M., ed.  PROBLEMS OF THEORY IN POVERTY ANALY-
        SIS.  Policy Studies Organization Series.  Lexington, Mass.:  Lexing-
        ton Books, 1976.  186 p.

        This effort includes fifteen essays focusing on political in-
        quiry in policy analysis, models for policy analysis and de-
        sign, conceptual premises and policy studies, research tech-
        niques in policy studies, and resolutions of some questions
        facing policy studies.

1023    Gronbjerg, Kirsten A.  MASS SOCIETY AND THE EXTENSION OF
        WELFARE.  Chicago:  University of Chicago Press, 1977.  266 p.

In applying mass society theory to policy analysis, the author attempts to explain the welfare crisis as a democratization of social rights and expansion of economic or social citizenship.

1024 Gusfield, J.R. "The (F) Utility of Knowledge: The Relation of Social Science to Public Policy Towards Drugs." ANNALS OF THE AMERICAN ACADEMY OF POLITICAL AND SOCIAL SCIENCE 417 (1975): 1-15.

Gusfield discusses the ambiguities and levels of public policy with emphasis on the consequences of the visibility of policy statements.

1025 Hahn, Harlan, and Schmidt, Ronald J. "Policy Themes and Community Attitudes: A Research Note on the Anti-Poverty Program." SOCIAL SCIENCE QUARTERLY 52 (December 1971): 672-79.

Although policymakers portrayed the war on poverty as a major innovation in urban policy, the program seemed to attract more support from people who were oriented toward the status quo rather than from those who favored massive change or an increasing government role in the solution of urban problems.

1026 Hannan, Timothy H. "The Benefits and Costs of Methadone Maintenance." PUBLIC POLICY 24 (1976): 197-226.

This paper develops a benefit-cost analysis for methadone maintenance programs based on data from the country's largest program and then raises several policy issues resulting from the data.

1027 _____. THE ECONOMICS OF METHADONE MAINTENANCE. Lexington, Mass.: Lexington Books, 1975. 164 p.

Upon the basis of a cost-benefit analysis, this book concludes that methadone maintenance programs should be expanded. The author assumes that these drug control measures make the life of a heroin addict less desirable and effectively limit the growth of the addict population.

1028 Harrison, Bennett, and Osterman, Paul. "Public Employment and Urban Poverty: Some New Facts and a Policy Analysis." URBAN AFFAIRS QUARTERLY 9 (March 1974): 303-36.

Examines technical questions surrounding the designs of public employment programs; analyzes the Emergency Employment Act of 1971; and concludes that urban workers employed in the public sector are more likely to be poor than those with private jobs.

1029 Haveman, Robert H. "Poverty, Income Distribution, and Social Policy: The Last Decade and the Next." PUBLIC POLICY 25 (Winter 1977): 3-24.

The essay places the ten years of the war on poverty into perspective and speculates on the nature of social policy over the next decade.

1030   Holden, Gerald M. "The Nation's Income Maintenance Policies, Current Trends and Future Prospects." AMERICAN BEHAVIORAL SCIENTIST 15 (May–June 1972): 665–80.

Reviewing current income maintenance policies indicates that reform is needed. Holden concludes that the evidence is far from clear on what ought to be done or how to assure ourselves that it will improve on current policies.

1031   Hollister, Robinson. "Social Mythology and Reform: Income Maintenance for the Aged." ANNALS OF THE AMERICAN ACADEMY OF POLITICAL AND SOCIAL SCIENCE 415 (September 1974): 19–40.

This article reviews the debate over reform of Social Security. Reforms through the 1972 amendments are discussed, and it is concluded that they merely sharpen the debate between supporters of the system and opponents of present policies.

1032   James, Dorothy B. POVERTY, POLITICS, AND CHANGE. Englewood Cliffs, N.J.: Prentice Hall, 1972. 164 p.

James gives a critical analysis of public policy toward poverty and how it is shaped by American values.

1033   _____, ed. ANALYZING POVERTY POLICY. Lexington, Mass.: Lexington Books, 1975. 264 p.

A collection of essays originally published in the POLICY STUDIES JOURNAL, they cover such topics as research limitations in poverty policy, legislative behavior and poverty policy, administering poverty policy, courts and lawyers and poverty policy, and possible alternative for the poor.

1034   Khadduri, Jull; Lyall, Katharine; and Struyk, Raymond. "Welfare Reform and Housing Assistance: A National Policy Debate." JOURNAL OF THE AMERICAN INSTITUTE OF PLANNERS 44 (January 1978): 2–12.

A presidential mandate to HEW to reduce welfare expenditures resulted in a suggestion to cut back on current housing programs and use the resources to help support a general program of cash transfer to poor families. Exclusive reliance on cash transfer would be unsuccessful and inefficient.

1035   Krefatz, Sharon. WELFARE POLICY MAKING AND CITY POLITICS. New York: Praeger Publishers, 1976. 218 p.

This is a comparison of welfare policies in Baltimore and San Francisco with the finding that organizational inputs contribute substantially to differences in welfare policy output.

1036 Leman, Christopher. "Patterns of Policy Development: Social Security in the United States and Canada." PUBLIC POLICY 25 (Spring 1977): 261-91.

> Old age security policies in Canada and the United States have been profoundly affected by the political contexts in which they have developed. This article explores the differences in the political context of the two countries and their implications for the policymaking process.

1037 Lubliner, Jerry, and Bednarski, Mary W. AN INTRODUCTION TO MEDICAL MALPRACTICE AS A PUBLIC POLICY ISSUE. Croton-on-Hudson, N.Y.: Policy Studies Associates, 1976. 50 p.

> Because of the high incidence and cost of medical malpractice in the United States, malpractice has become a public policy issue. Steps which might improve the physician's performance are continuing education, relicensing requirements, and regulatory panels to inspect doctors' practices.

1038 Lynn, Laurence J., Jr., and Worthington, Mark D. "Incremental Welfare Reform: A Strategy Whose Time Has Passed." PUBLIC POLICY 25 (Winter 1977): 47-80.

> The authors argue that there is a demonstrated need for a comprehensive reform of income assistance programs. While incremental reform will improve the adequacy and equity of some existing programs, it will still leave us with a "welfare mess."

1039 Marmor, Theodore R. "The Politics of National Health Insurance: Analysis and Prescription." POLICY ANALYSIS 3 (Winter 1977): 25-48.

> Americans agree that a medical crisis exists, yet fewer than 10 percent are dissatisfied with their own health care. Few Americans advocate wholesale organizational changes to satisfy their specific complaints. The important considerations are the effects on the cost, organization, and distribution of medical care.

1040 Mead, Lawrence. "Health Policy: The Need for Governance." ANNALS OF THE AMERICAN ACADEMY OF POLITICAL AND SOCIAL SCIENCE 434 (November 1977): 39-57.

> If the health care cost crisis is to be resolved, public control of the health care system must be accepted. The success of public control will depend upon resolving the political tensions that will follow. Governance requires wrestling with provider and patient interests in which there can be no clear standards for the correct course of action.

1041 Navarro, Vincente. "Justice, Social Policy, and the Public's Health." MEDICAL CARE 15 (May 1977): 363-70.

> The expropriation of health care is part of, and derives from, the expropriation of power and control from the many by the few.

1042 Palley, Howard A. "Policy Formulation in Health: Some Considerations of Governmental Constraints on Pricing in the Health Delivery System." AMERICAN BEHAVIORAL SCIENTIST 17 (March-April 1974): 572-84.

> This is a review of public policy responding to the charges by providers of health care services. Changes have taken place in other national systems, and they should not be viewed as unrealistic if the inefficiency and high cost of America's health care delivery system are not sufficiently alleviated.

1043 Palley, Howard A., and Palley, Marian Lief. "The Determination of Pricing Policy in the Health Care Delivery System." AMERICAN BEHAVIORAL SCIENTIST 19 (September-October 1975): 104-21.

> The essay focuses on the interactions between the public and private sectors on determining reasonableness of costs and charges. The public sector is increasingly taking into account the interests of the consumers of health care services as well as the interests of the deliverers of the services.

1044 Palley, Marian Lief. "Current Issues in Welfare and Poverty Policy." POLICY STUDIES JOURNAL 6 (Spring 1978): 412-19.

> This article updates a 1974 poverty symposium published in the same journal. Its basic conclusion is that some changes in the way welfare income and services are delivered must be developed.

1045 Palley, Marian Lief, and Palley, Howard A. "A Call for a National Welfare Policy." AMERICAN BEHAVIORAL SCIENTIST 15 (May-June 1972): 681-95.

> The current social welfare system fails to establish a national social welfare policy with national programs, standards, and enforcement mechanisms. In part, the problem of equity and adequate social welfare standards is tied to state initiatives in the present system.

1046 Pfeiffer, David, and Glampietro, Michael. "Government Policy Toward Handicapped Individuals." POLICY STUDIES JOURNAL 6 (Autumn 1977): 93-100.

> This article relates some of the developments of the first White House Conference on Handicapped Individuals held in May 1977. It concerns itself with definitions of handicapped, their numbers, attitudes, technology, transportation, agricultural barriers, employment, housing, recreation, education, and other policy areas.

1047 Pious, Richard M. "Policy and Public Administration: The Legal Services Program in the War on Poverty." POLITICS AND SOCIETY 1 (May 1971): 365-92.

> This is an account of policymaking showing how interest groups at the national and local levels can influence the administrative structure of an organization and its policy outputs.

1048    Piven, Frances Fox, and Cloward, Richard. REGULATING THE POOR: THE FUNCTION OF PUBLIC RELIEF. New York: Pantheon, 1971. 389 p.

>  Piven and Cloward propose a theory of the relationship between systems of public welfare and society. Relief programs operate to regulate the behavior of the past and to increase social cohesion. The authors' own policy preferences would expand welfare until all low income individuals would be on welfare rolls.

1049    "The Political Science of Poverty and Welfare: A Symposium." POLICY STUDIES JOURNAL 2 (Spring 1974): 152-218.

>  This issue is devoted almost entirely to welfare and poverty. The articles treat limitations of available research, legislative behavior and poverty policy, administering poverty policy, courts and lawyers and poverty policy, and possible alternatives. There are fourteen articles devoted to this area.

1050    Preston, Michael B. "Blacks and Public Policy." POLICY SCIENCES JOURNAL 6 (Winter 1977): 245-55.

>  Major black gains in public policy have come via litigation and the electoral process. Task for black leaders today is to protect the gains of the past while accomplishing new gains for the future.

1051    "Prospects for Change in American Social Welfare Policy: A Symposium." AMERICAN BEHAVIORAL SCIENTIST 15 (May-June 1972): 645-729.

>  Seven original articles deal with policies and priorities in social welfare, income maintenance policies, the need for a national welfare policy, manpower policy, health insurance and health services policies, community participation and the corporation as a social welfare institution.

1052    Rachin, Richard L., and Czajkoski, Eugene H. DRUG ABUSE CONTROL. Lexington, Mass.: Lexington Books, 1975. 208 p.

>  This series of original essays focuses on the behavior of organizations and bureaucracies established to deal with drug abuse. Organizational imperatives have exacerbated the control problem.

1053    Radin, Beryl A. "Can We Learn From Experience? The Case of SSI." POLICY ANALYSIS 2 (Fall 1976): 615-21.

>  Many of the Supplemental Security Income program's difficulties are endemic to any national system of welfare administration and must be calculated as both fiscal and political costs of any new effort. The SSI program contains neither simple eligibility criteria, as initially intended, nor uniform payment amounts, making it neither politically nor historically possible for the program to be instituted.

1054  Randall, Ronald.  "The Consequences of Centralization for Welfare
      Policy."  WESTERN POLITICAL QUARTERLY  29 (September 1976):
      353-63.

      Of the nonfederal share of welfare funding, some states depend
      totally on state sources while others rely on both state and
      local sources.  Assuming that welfare is centralized in the
      states with state funding and decentralized in the states
      with mixed funding, community interests influenced decen-
      tralized states more than centralized ones.  Whether policy
      is more tolerant or more restrictive in the decentralized
      states depends on the constellation of pressures at the time
      of the analysis.

1055  Rein, Martin.  "Choice and Change in the American Welfare System."
      ANNALS OF THE AMERICAN ACADEMY OF POLITICAL AND SOCIAL
      SCIENCE  385 (September 1969):  89-109.

      Public welfare policy has come to assign priority to a cash-
      transfer policy.  To avoid several potential and real dilemmas,
      we need a wage-level policy which raises the wages in the
      marginal, low-wage economy to make it an alternative to
      welfare benefits.

1056  Roos, Noralou P.  "Influencing the Health Care System:  Policy Alter-
      natives."  PUBLIC POLICY  22 (Spring 1974):  139-68.

      Using health care policy as an example, this paper examines
      the differing traditions associated with the rational theory
      model and the behavioral theory model.  A policy-relevant
      integration of the rational and behavioral formulation is pro-
      posed and specific intervention strategies implied by this
      integration are discussed.

1057  Rossi, Peter H., and Bent, Richard A.  "Local Roots of Black Aliena-
      tion."  SOCIAL SCIENCE QUARTERLY  54 (March 1974):  741-58.

      This paper examines how inter-city variation in institutional
      performance and the reputation of local officials affects black
      residents' generalized assessments of their situation.

1058  Sapolsky, Harvey M.  "America's Socialized Medicine:  The Allocation
      of Resources Within the Veteran's Health Care System."  PUBLIC POLICY
      25 (Summer 1977):  359-82.

      The bureaucratic origins of Veterans Administration strategies
      for the delivery of health care to veterans are examined, as
      well as the implications for the nation's overall health policy.
      It is argued that professional incentives are at least as potent
      as are financial incentives in influencing the behavior of health
      care institutions.

1059  Schwartz, Joel J., and Tabb, David.  "Social Welfare:  Changing
      Priorities."  AMERICAN BEHAVIORAL SCIENTIST  15 (May-June
      1972):  645-64.

Whether one looks at welfare spending in the aggregate or
those programs that affect the poor, an increased national
commitment to the social sector can be seen. Had it not
been for Vietnam, an even greater amount would have been
spent on social welfare functions.

1060   Sharkansky, Ira. "Economic Theories of Public Policy: Resource-
Policy and Need-Policy Linkages between Income and Welfare Benefits."
MIDWEST JOURNAL OF POLITICAL SCIENCE   15 (November 1971):
722-40.

The comparative state politics literature hypothesizes important
relationships between economic levels and policy outputs, but
fails to systematically explain the relationships.

1061   Skidmore, Felicity. "Welfare Reform: Some Policy Alternatives."
TAX NOTES   3 (21 July 1975): 20-31.

While official interest in welfare reform is at a low ebb in
Washington, D.C., the problems of the welfare system have
been neither solved nor alleviated. This paper examines
the effects of past changes in the welfare system and some
policy alternatives for the future.

1062   Steiner, Gilbert Y.  SOCIAL INSECURITY: THE POLITICS OF
WELFARE.  Washington, D.C.: Brookings Institution, 1966.  270 p.

An analysis of welfare policymaking illustrates the relationship between the nature of the policy process and the substance of policy.

1063   Storey, James R.  "Systems Analysis and Welfare Reform:  A Case
Study of the Family Assistance Plan." POLICY STUDIES   4 (March
1973):  1-11.

Storey discusses the impact systems analysis has had on
welfare reform legislation since 1969. After a general discussion of welfare's objectives and constraints, the state of
the art as related to welfare problems is described. The
success and failure of a cost-effectiveness approach are
analyzed.

1064   Straayer, John A.  "The American Policy Process and the Problems
of Poverty and the Ghetto." WESTERN POLITICAL QUARTERLY   24
(March 1971):  45-51.

This paper examines why the American political system fails
to generate policy outputs designed to realize articulated
American values of equality. The conclusion is that the
nature of the process precludes the maximization of articulated values.

1065   Thompson, Mark, and Milunksy, Aubrey. "Policy Analysis for Prenatal
Genetic Diagnosis." PUBLIC POLICY   27 (Winter 1979):  25-78.

Public subsidy of prenatal testing can yield benefits substantially in excess of costs.

1066    Vickery, Clair. "The Changing Household: Implications for Devising
an Income Support Program." PUBLIC POLICY 26 (Winter 1978):
121-51.

Any income support program must consider the resources
and needs of households in terms of time and money. Low-
income families should be encouraged to take advantage of
the economies of scale observed for larger households.

1067    Williams, A.P., et al. POLICY ANALYSIS FOR FEDERAL BIOMEDICAL
RESEARCH. Santa Monica, Calif.: Rand Corporation, 1976. 283 p.

In reviewing proposals for research and evaluating research
performed, every funding agency attempts some assessment
of the quality of the scientific activity it sponsors. This
assessment might be improved through better understanding
of the qualitative dimensions of scientific activity, not the
creation of a single quality measure.

1068    Zubkoff, Michael, and Blumstein, James. FRAMEWORK FOR GOVERN-
MENT INTERVENTION IN THE HEALTH SECTOR. Lexington, Mass.:
Lexington Books, 1978. 274 p.

The volume deals with the role of government in the health
sector. Most of the discussion relates directly to the medical
care area. The view of the authors is that public policy
considerations transcend the normal focus of the delivery of
health services in determining the appropriate government
role in the health sector.

## HOUSING AND TRANSPORTATION

1069    Altshuler, Alan A. "Changing Patterns of Policy: The Decision Making
Environment of Urban Transportation." PUBLIC POLICY 25 (Spring
1977): 171-203.

The author traces the evolution of twenty-five years of urban
transportation policy to see how the unique pattern of American
urban transportation has developed. Our love affair with
the car results in a policy of not controlling citizen demands
and thus an ineffective transportation policy.

1070    _____. "The Politics of Urban Transportation Innovation." TECHNOL-
OGY REVIEW 79 (May 1977): 50-58.

,Altshuler creates a typology of the acceptance of transportation
innovations according to their level of political feasibility.

1071    _____, ed. "Symposium on Current Issues in Transportation Policy."
POLICY STUDIES JOURNAL 6 (Autumn 1977): 5-110.

Ten articles cover air transportation, equity issues, transportation and the environment, demonstration projects, and communications-transportation trade-offs.

1072    Avery, George A.   "Breaking the Cycle:   Regulation and Transportation Policy."   URBAN AFFAIRS QUARTERLY   8 (June 1973):   423-38.

The problem of urban public transportation is not rooted in regulatory issues.  Any useful analysis of the role of regulation must look to the basic causes for rising fares and declining ridership.

1073    Baer, William C.   "The Evolution of Housing Indicators and Housing Standards:   Some Lessons for the Future."   PUBLIC POLICY   24 (Summer 1976):   361-94.

Baer makes a general effort to discuss standards and indicators in the housing field, to determine decision-making processes, and to provide some guidance for the future.

1074    Bain, Henry.   NEW DIRECTIONS FOR METRO:  LESSONS FROM THE BART EXPERIENCE.   Washington, D.C.:   Washington Center for Metropolitan Studies, 1976.   47 p.

Bain provides an examination of the potential benefits to the Washington, D.C., area from the building of METRO based on data from the San Francisco BART system.  It is suggested that outlying suburban trackage be eliminated in favor of express buses.

1075    Briggs, Bruce B.   "Mass Transportation and Minority Transportation." PUBLIC INTEREST, no. 40 (Summer 1975), pp. 43-74.

The United States has the best mass transportation system in the world--the automobile which carries more people than any other system.

1076    Bryant, Coralie.   "The Politics of Housing and Housing Policy Research." POLICY STUDIES JOURNAL   3 (Summer 1975):   397-405.

Policy studies done by social scientists concerned with housing policy can be grouped into the categories of formulation, implementation, and evaluation.  Each category would be enriched by comparative research.

1077    Colcord, Frank C., Jr.   "Urban Transportation and Political Ideology: Sweden and the United States."   POLICY STUDIES JOURNAL   6 (Autumn 1977):   9-19.

Although transportation issues are rarely debated ideologically in either nation, their contrasting positions with respects to planning versus free enterprise are clearly reflected in transportation patterns.

1078    Convisser, Martin.   "Transportation and the Environment."   POLICY STUDIES JOURNAL   6 (Autumn 1977):   40-49.

Convisser reviews the ways that environmental laws have affected the operation of the U.S. Department of Transportation. Such concerns have been imposed on a well established structure of priorities, benefits, and demands.

1079    Davis, F.W., Jr., and Oen, K. SOLVING PUBLIC PASSENGER TRANSPORTATION PROBLEMS: A NEED FOR POLICY REORIENTATION. Knoxville: University of Tennessee, Transportation Center, 1977. 26 p.

If public transportation is to efficiently serve the transportation needs of a community, a consumer-oriented approach would be adopted.

1080    Davis, Sid; Holmes, Robert; and Fletcher, William. TRANSPORTATION POLICY AND PROGRAM IMPACT ANALYSIS PROCESS, CONFLICT AND CONFLICT RESOLUTION: ATLANTA CASE. Atlanta, Ga.: Atlanta University, School of Business, 1976. 128 p.

This is a review of federal urban transportation mandates and their impact at the local level. The focus is on how local areas respond to the policy environment established at the federal level.

1081    Domencich, Thomas A., and Kraft, Gerald. FREE TRANSIT. Lexington, Mass.: Lexington Books, 1970. 120 p.

Although free transit does generally increase usage, improved transit service is a more effective means of reaching the objective of increased patronage.

1082    Downs, Anthony. "The Successes and Failures of Federal Housing Policy." PUBLIC INTEREST, no. 34 (Winter 1974), pp. 124-45.

Downs evaluates federal housing policies of all types showing that they were effective in generating housing production, and economic stabilization; however, they were ineffective in stabilizing housing production and improving conditions in inner-city neighborhoods.

1083    Dunn, James A. "Railroad Policies in Europe and the United States: The Impact of Ideology, Institutions, and Social Conditions." PUBLIC POLICY 2 (Spring 1977): 205-40.

This is an examination of the support for private ownership of the railroads in the United States, which is virtually the only nation in the world with predominately privately owned railroads.

1084    Feldman, Elliot J. "Air Transportation Infrastructure as a Problem of Public Policy." POLICY STUDIES JOURNAL 6 (Autumn 1977): 20-28.

This is an analysis of the building of airports and the controversies surrounding their construction. Feldman is concerned with the pattern of protest across political cultures and why some airports were built and others were not.

1085   Friden, Bernard J. "The New Housing Cost Problem." PUBLIC INTEREST, no. 49 (Fall 1977), pp. 70-86.

Government should try to solve the problem of rising housing costs and take steps to eliminate those policies which make the problem worse.

1086   Gaffney, Mason. "Land Rent, Taxation, and Public Policy." AMERICAN JOURNAL OF ECONOMICS AND SOCIOLOGY 31 (July 1972): 241-58.

Primarily concerned with the taxing of ground rent, it discusses urban site rent, alternative ways of taxing rents, and intergovernmental relations.

1087   Goldstein, Gerald S., and Moses, Leon M. "Transport Controls, Travel Costs, and Urban Spatial Structure." PUBLIC POLICY 23 (Summer 1975): 355-80.

This is a discussion of different types of transportation strategies designed to reduce auto travel. An increase in auto travel costs is more likely to result in decreased auto travel than are improvements in public transportation.

1088   Haar, Charles, and Iatridis, Demetrius. HOUSING THE POOR IN SUBURBIA: PUBLIC POLICY AT THE GRASS ROOTS. Cambridge, Mass.: Ballinger Books, 1974. 438 p.

Five case studies designed to give a social policy perspective on the conflicts created by the presence of low income housing in middle class suburbs.

1089   Hartman, Chester W. HOUSING AND SOCIAL POLICY. Englewood Cliffs, N.J.: Prentice-Hall, 1975. 184 p.

Hartman discusses the obstacles preventing all Americans from obtaining decent housing. Attention is given to the private home builder whose concern is to maximize profit and the results of its intervention in the housing market.

1090   Hilton, George W. "The Urban Mass Transportation Assistance Program." In PERSPECTIVES ON FEDERAL TRANSPORTATION POLICY, edited by James C. Miller, pp. 131-44. Washington, D.C.: American Enterprise Institute for Public Policy Research, 1975.

While freeway express bus experiments have proven to be successful, other UMTA programs have a uniform record of failure. This essay explains the error in UMTA's definition of the cause of declining bus ridership.

1091   Hirten, John E. "Needed--A New Perception of Transportation." JOURNAL OF THE AMERICAN INSTITUTE OF PLANNERS 29 (July 1973): 277-82.

Hirten outlines eleven steps to be taken to achieve a comprehensive approach to transportation planning stressing the need to view urban planning and transportation as elements of the same process.

1092   Hodgson, M.J., and Doyle, P. "The Location of Public Services Con-
       sidering the Mode of Travel." SOCIO-ECONOMIC PLANNING SCIENCES
       12, no. 1 (1978): 49-63.

       Transit users are not as well served by many public facilities
       as are automobile users. This situation is investigated for
       the location of publicly funded child care centers.

1093   Kain, John F. "How to Improve Public Transportation at Practically
       No Cost." PUBLIC POLICY 20 (Summer 1972): 335-58.

       The most important available opportunity for improving public
       transportation is to use existing urban expressways for rapid
       transit. The paper looks at several shortcomings of the plan-
       ning process and then examines the freeway rapid transit idea.

1094   _____. WHAT SHOULD AMERICA'S HOUSING POLICY BE? Cambridge,
       Mass.: Harvard University Press, 1973. 42 p.

       Federal housing policies and programs should encourage
       minorities to locate outside of presently existing minority
       neighborhoods.

1095   Kendrick, Frank J. "Urban Transportation Policy, Politics, Planning,
       and People." POLICY STUDIES JOURNAL 3 (Summer 1975): 375-81.

       As a result of a transportation policy that favors automobiles,
       most people see transportation problems as merely one of
       moving and storing large numbers of cars. There is too
       little awareness of the effect transportation politics can
       have on development and quality of life.

1096   Kraft, Gerald. "Free Transit Revisited." PUBLIC POLICY 21
       (Winter 1973): 79-106.

       Free transit's proponents fail to see other alternatives and
       continue to disregard the arguments against free transit.

1097   Levinson, Herbert S. "Coordinating Transport and Urban Development."
       ITCC REVIEW 5 (October 1976): 23-29.

       Because of increased energy costs and scarcity, urban develop-
       ment and transportation decisions should be coordinated to
       assure as wide a distribution of benefits as possible.

1098   Louviere, Jordan J., and Norman, Kent L. "Applications of Information
       Processing Theory to the Analysis of Urban Travel Demand." ENVIRON-
       MENT AND BEHAVIOR 9 (March 1977): 91-106.

       Subjects evaluated the characteristics of various transportation
       systems. If multiplicative variables are at a near-zero psy-
       chological value, the system is doomed to failure regardless
       of its other attributes.

1099   Marcuse, Peter. "Social Indicators and Housing Policy." URBAN
       AFFAIRS QUARTERLY 7 (December 1971): 193-218.

Despite having great amounts of data available for housing analysis, indicators of housing quality are not simple, unambiguous to interpret, or accurate. Eight indicators that would have applicability to the housing policy field are listed.

1100 Margolis, Howard. "The Politics of Auto Emissions." PUBLIC INTEREST, no. 49 (Fall 1977), pp. 3-21.

This is a case study of the history and controversy surrounding standards imposed by the government on auto emissions. Political externalities have significantly affected the policy-making process.

1101 Mertins, Herman, ed. "The Impacts of Transportation Policy-Making." PUBLIC ADMINISTRATION REVIEW 33 (May-June 1973): 205-52.

Presented are six essays on the impacts of urban transportation policy. Included are discussions of BART, innovative approaches to urban transportation planning, transport investment and Appalachian development, and federal transportation policy and the new federalism.

1102 Meyerson, Martin, and Banfield, Edward C. POLITICS, PLANNING AND THE PUBLIC INTEREST: THE CASE OF PUBLIC HOUSING IN CHICAGO. New York: Free Press, 1964. 353 p.

The focus of the book is the decision to build public housing in Chicago. More generally, it is a study of public decision making processes and the strategies, tactics, maneuvers, and problems of the interests involved in the decision.

1103 Miller, David R., ed. URBAN TRANSPORTATION POLICY: NEW PERSPECTIVES. Lexington, Mass.: Lexington Books, 1972. 150 p.

This volume provides background for thinking about the policy process and the urban transportation problem in terms of the impact of specific programs, and relationships between transportation policy and other aspects of urban growth and development.

1104 Miller, James C. "An Economic Policy of the Amtrak Program." In PERSPECTIVES ON FEDERAL TRANSPORTATION POLICY, edited by James C. Miller, pp. 145-73. Washington, D.C.: American Enterprise Institute for Public Policy Research, 1975.

Amtrak has failed, given its original goals of improving rail service at competitive fares. It has failed because of a decline in the interest for rail travel and for other reasons.

1105 Murin, William J. MASS TRANSIT POLICY PLANNING, AN INCREMENTAL APPROACH. Lexington, Mass.: Lexington Books, 1971. 128 p.

This is a case study of the politics of the planning process for Washington, D.C.'s METRO system. Murin analyzes the system from the perspective of innercity residents who need public transportation as a means of travel.

1106 Myers, Sumner. "Public Policy and Transportation Innovation: The Role of Demonstration." POLICY STUDIES JOURNAL 6 (Autumn 1977): 62–73.

Government frequently confuses the idea of demonstration with experiment. Experiments have uncertain timetables and are best carried out away from the glare of publicity. Government officials operating under intense pressure are likely to oversell new technologies and demand tight timetables.

1107 NEIGHBORHOOD STABILITY AND PUBLIC POLICY: A RESEARCH PROGRAM. Denver: Office of Policy Analysis, City and County of Denver, Colorado, 1976. 25 p.

Housing deterioration and neighborhood decline are primarily caused by poverty. If low-income families outnumber the amount of public housing available, the private market will create housing for them.

1108 Oi, Walter Y. "The Federal Subsidy of Conventional Mass Transit." POLICY ANALYSIS 1 (Fall 1975): 613–58.

Oi establishes four criteria for choosing the most appropriate method of distributing the transit subsidy based on four formulas currently in use.

1109 Owen, Wilfred. "An Urban Transformation Through Transportation." NATION'S CITIES 15 (May 1977): 13–20.

If urban problems are to be solved, we need a broader view of the transportation function. By consolidating transportation programs with those of housing and urban services, a more comprehensive attack on urban problems would be possible.

1110 Pikarsky, Milton, and Christensen, Daphne. URBAN TRANSPORTATION POLICY AND MANAGEMENT. Lexington, Mass.: Lexington Books, 1976. 255 p.

The development of transportation management is improving the use and image of public transportation. Much of the book focuses on the Regional Transit Authority in the Chicago area.

1111 Pushkarev, Boris S., and Zupan, Jeffrey M. PUBLIC TRANSPORTA- TION AND LAND USE POLICY. Bloomington: Indiana University Press, 1977. 242 p.

Extending and upgrading existing transportation systems is more cost-effective than developing new ones. Land-use policies favoring mass transportation could assure that transportation needs are met.

1112 Rose-Ackerman, Susan. "On the Distribution of Public Program Benefits Between Landlords and Tenants." JOURNAL OF ENVIRONMENTAL ECONOMICS AND MANAGEMENT 4 (December 1977): 167–84.

Only under very narrow conditions can changes in land values be used to determine the benefits from public programs.

1113 Rosenbloom, Sandra, and Altshuler, Alan R. "Equity Issues in Urban Transportation." POLICY STUDIES JOURNAL 6 (Autumn 1977): 29-39.

Several concepts of equity compete for dominance in the urban transportation field. Most urban transportation systems channel their expenditures in ways that systematically favor those least in need.

1114 Sands, Gary. "Housing Turnover: Assessing Its Relevance to Public Policy." JOURNAL OF THE AMERICAN INSTITUTE OF PLANNERS 42 (October 1976): 419-26.

Housing turnover is not as strong a tool in the improvement of housing conditions as was once thought. This requires a change in much of our housing policy assumptions.

1115 Schmenner, Roger W. "Bus Subsidies: The Case for Route-by-Route Bidding in Connecticut." POLICY ANALYSIS 2 (Summer 1976): 409-30.

Of the several schemes available to subsidize bus operations, the best seems to be route-by-route bidding. This was tried during a strike in Connecticut with positive results.

1116 Schneider, Lewis M. "Urban Mass Transportation: A Survey of the Decision-Making Process." In THE STUDY OF POLICY FORMATION, edited by Raymond A. Bauer and Kenneth J. Gergen, pp. 239-80. New York: Free Press, 1968.

Beginning from the perspective that transportation is one of the most frustrating issues facing decision makers today, the author discusses the actors and institutions involved in the process.

1117 Sheldon, Nancy W., and Brandwein, Robert. THE ECONOMIC AND SOCIAL IMPACT OF INVESTMENTS IN PUBLIC TRANSIT. Lexington, Mass.: D.C. Heath and Co., 1973. 170 p.

The authors discuss the societal benefits that flow from good transit systems, the advantages of mass transit over automobile dominated systems, and the advantages of existing systems over new technologies.

1118 Smerk, George. URBAN TRANSPORTATION: A DOZEN YEARS OF FEDERAL POLICY. Bloomington: Indiana University Press, 1975. 388 p.

Smerk examines the creation and evaluation of urban mass transportation and the federal government's role. Legislation is examined, as are the railroads, financing trends, and ridership behavior.

1119 Snow, John W. "The Transportation Improvement Act of 1974." In PERSPECTIVES ON FEDERAL TRANSPORTATION POLICY, edited by James C. Miller, pp. 179-88. Washington, D.C.: American Enterprise Institute for Public Policy Research, 1975.

This legislation and its hoped-for impact on the railroad industry are examined. The general conclusion is that the
railroad industry would be helped considerably by this legislation.

1120   Solomon, Arthur P.   "Housing and Public Policy Analysis."   PUBLIC
POLICY   20 (Summer 1972):   443-72.

Several criteria are discussed that allow the measurement
of the adequacy of housing policy alternatives designed to
meet housing goals.   Their impact on housing the poor is
especially discussed.

1121   Steger, Wilbur A.   "Reflections on Citizen Involvement in Urban Transportation Planning:   Towards a Positive Approach."   TRANSPORTA-
TION 3 (July 1974):   127-46.

The article discusses several benefits that flow to an urban
transportation system from citizen involvement in the decision-
making process.

1122   Stegman, Michael A., and Sumka, Howard J.   NONMETROPOLITAN
URBAN HOUSING:   AN ECONOMIC ANALYSIS OF PROBLEMS AND
CHOICES.   Cambridge, Mass.: Ballinger, 1976.   304 p.

This volume contains an analysis of the rental housing market,
including its structural characteristics, the demand for rental
housing, the rental investment market, and housing allowance
programs.

1123   Stein, Martin.   "Social-Impact Assessment Techniques and Their
Applications to Transportation Decisions."   TRAFFIC QUARTERLY   31
(April 1977):   297-316.

Here is a discussion of four techniques that are available to
judge the human impact of proposed transportation facilities.

1124   Struyk, Raymond J.   "The Need for Local Flexibility in U.S. Housing
Policy."   POLICY ANALYSIS   3 (Fall 1977):   471-84.

Uniform federal program requirements ignore the different
needs existing throughout the nation.   The paper outlines
different outcomes which can be produced under different conditions and argues for greater local flexibility in future federal
housing programs.

1125   Taebel, Delbert A.   "Citizen Groups, Public Policy, and Urban Transportation."   TRAFFIC QUARTERLY   27 (October 1973):   503-15.

While the values traditionally considered in the transportation
planning process tend to favor the status quo, new values,
especially environmental, will probably change the nature of
transportation planning.

1126   Veatch, James F.   "Federal and Local Urban Transportation Policy."
URBAN AFFAIRS QUARTERLY   10 (June 1975):   398-422.

The attraction of federal capital grant assistance to local governments is so powerful that transportation expenditures are undertaken which should not be made. Local governments should be provided with transportation improvement dollars and left to decide for themselves how they will be used.

1127    Wachs, Martin. "Transportation Policy in the Eighties." TRANSPOR-
TATION 6 (June 1977): 103-20.

After discussing the characteristics of transportation planning in the 1970s Wachs suggests that 1980s planning will be concerned with physical facilities, institutional arrangements, financial plans, and user incentives and disincentives.

1128    Webber, Melvin M. "The BART Experience--What Have We Learned."
PUBLIC INTEREST, no. 45 (Fall 1976), pp. 79-108.

BART is carrying fewer people than projected at fares much higher than originally suggested. Most riders are former bus users and not automobile users. The mistake that system planners made was to emphasize vehicle speed and physical amenities instead of designing a system that was concerned with total travel time.

1129    Williams, J. Allen, Jr. "The Multifamily Housing Solution and Housing Type Preferences." SOCIAL SCIENCE QUARTERLY 52 (December 1971): 543-59.

Social acceptance of at least moderate density housing could be achieved by designing housing projects to include more amenities and by giving residents the option to purchase the unit.

1130    Wolman, Harold L., and Thomas, Norman C. "Black Interests, Black Groups, and Black Influence in the Federal Policy Process: The Cases of Housing and Transportation." JOURNAL OF POLITICS 32 (November 1970): 875-97.

The essay examines the federal policymaking processes to discover which groups had access, where, and at what point in the policy process that access occurred. It found an absence of black actors and effective black participation at crucial stages.

## POPULATION AND FAMILY POLICY

1131    Bachrach, Peter, and Bergman, Elihu. POWER AND CHOICE: THE FORMULATION OF AMERICAN POPULATION POLICY. Lexington, Mass.: Lexington Books, 1973. 120 p.

Consistent with most of Bachrach's writings on power, this book is about power and choice; specifically, how power is used in expanding or limiting policy choices in a process of policymaking for population.

1132 Back, Kurt W., and Fawcett, James T., eds. "Population Policy and the Person: Congruence or Conflict." JOURNAL OF SOCIAL ISSUES 30, no. 4 (1974): 1-296.

Virtually the entire issue is devoted to various aspects of population policy, including psychological aspects, effects of population studies, implementing population studies, and others. Thirteen articles comprise the effort.

1133 Ball, Carolyn Shaw. "Should Every Job Support a Family?" PUBLIC INTEREST, no. 40 (Summer 1975), pp. 109-18.

To deal with the problem of income distribution, worker income and household income must be distinguished. To require that every job be able to support a family of four rejects any idea of productivity and is inconsistent with any idea of full employment.

1134 Bernard, Jessie. WOMEN AND THE PUBLIC INTEREST: AN ESSAY ON POLICY AND PROTEST. Chicago: Aldine-Atherton, 1971. 293 p.

This is a sociological approach examining research, theory, and polemics surrounding functions of women, conflict within women themselves, the sexual division of labor, the strategy of protesters for women's rights.

1135 Bruce-Briggs, B. "Child Care: The Fiscal Time Bomb." PUBLIC INTEREST, no. 49 (Fall 1977), pp. 87-102.

Bruce-Briggs reviews the arguments for a greater federal role in subsidized day care for children and concludes that the arguments of the program's supporters are not convincing. The main beneficiaries of any increase in federal support will be the providers of the services and not the children or the working mothers.

1136 Crawford, Thomas J. "Theories of Attitude Change and the 'Beyond Family Planning' Debate: The Case for the Persuasion Approach to Population Policy." JOURNAL OF SOCIAL ISSUES 30, no. 4 (1974): 211-34.

Persuasion and incentives are the most widely used strategies in current population planning programs. While psychological theory is skeptical of persuasion to change behavior, this paper argues that recent findings in attitude theory show that persuasion may still be a useful tool.

1137 Cutler, Neal E. "The Impact of Population Dynamics on Public Policy: The Perspectives of Political Gerontology." POLICY STUDIES JOURNAL 6 (Winter 1977): 167-74.

The "graying of America" in addition to an increase in the number of older Americans also means a change in the characteristics of tomorrow's elderly. The article argues that age and aging are salient policy issues in the political process.

1138   Dye, Thomas R., and Caputo, David A. "Population Policy Research and Political Science." POLICY STUDIES JOURNAL 3 (Fall 1974): 97-106.

      A bibliographical essay on population policy divided into popular literature, population and world politics, national population policy, population research, and other topics.

1139   Fawcett, James T. "Psychological Research and Population Policy." JOURNAL OF SOCIAL ISSUES 30, no. 4 (1974): 31-38.

      One approach to defining population policy is to view it as a way of resolving potential conflict between the individual and society over demographic behaviors.

1140   Field, Marilyn J. "Determinants of Abortion Policy in the Developed Nations." POLICY STUDIES JOURNAL 7 (Summer 1979): 771-81.

      Variations in abortion law appear to be linked to several political-ideological differences across nations, including differences in the proportion of the Catholic population, the presence of governing Socialist parties, the type of regime, and the nature of nonelectoral policymaking institutions.

1141   Finkle, Jason L., and McIntosh, Alison. "Political Perceptions of Population Stabilization and Decline." POLICY STUDIES JOURNAL 6 (Winter 1977): 155-66.

      Many of the measures available to governments to stimulate fertility are the same as family welfare policies. U.S. response to low population growth will probably not involve explicit population policy but will be in the form of incremental adjustments to current policies.

1142   Hoffman, Ellen. "Policy and Politics: The Child Abuse Prevention and Treatment Act." PUBLIC POLICY 26 (Winter 1978): 71-88.

      In the case of the Child Abuse Prevention and Treatment Act, public hearings and the media focused attention on the problem of abused children, helping to create a favorable climate for congressional action. Incremental action was accepted by sponsors, since they felt that funding for a comprehensive funding was not available.

1143   Hunt, Joseph W., and Craig, Eleanor D. "Should We Provide More Government Funding for Day Care: A Statement of the Problem." PUBLIC POLICY 20 (Fall 1972): 565-76.

      This paper develops a cost-benefit framework to help guide policymakers in making decisions concerning day care.

1144   Kahan, James P. "Rationality, the Prisoner's Dilemma, and Population." JOURNAL OF SOCIAL ISSUES 30, no. 4 (1974): 189-210.

      The growth of the human population as a function of the desire to have more children is analyzed within the framework of the prisoner's dilemma game. A proposed solution is the adoption of a policy where families consider their own decisions in light of their common existence with other families.

1145 Knowles, John. "Public Policy on Abortion." SOCIETY 11 (July-August 1974): 15-21.

The Supreme Court's ruling on abortion requires government and the health system to develop a policy and program to insure that abortions are performed under the safest, most dignified and humane conditions.

1146 Kraft, Michael E., and Schneider, Mark, eds. "Symposium on Population Policy." POLICY STUDIES JOURNAL 6 (Winter 1977): 142-237.

The authors present eleven articles on population policy grouped under two general headings: political consequences of population change and population policy analysis.

1147 MacDonald, Maurice, and Sawhill, Isabel V. "Welfare Policy and the Family." PUBLIC POLICY 26 (Winter 1978): 89-119.

The first part of this paper discusses the difficulties of defining and implementing a more neutral family policy. The second part reviews the empirical evidence about the effects of income transfer programs on family behavior, finding that government policy is not a dominant influence.

1148 McLean, Edward L. "New Communities and Population Redistribution as Policy Issues." URBAN AND SOCIAL CHANGE REVIEW 4 (Spring 1971): 58-61.

This is a review of the possibilities of using "new communities" to redistribute central city ghetto residents to improve their life's chances and to lessen the problems of the central cities.

1149 Moroney, Robert M. "The Need for a National Family Policy." URBAN AND SOCIAL CHANGE REVIEW 10 (Winter 1977): 10-14.

The United States does not have a clearly stated position on the family, but existing policies still affect families. Many policies are developed on the assumption that the extended family is the dominant structure, while other policies recognize the nuclear family.

1150 North, David S. "The Growing Importance of Immigration to Population Policy." POLICY STUDIES JOURNAL 6 (Winter 1977): 200-207.

Immigration, at or a little above current limits, is good for the United States. We need a more rational immigration policy that makes decisions on the needs of society as a whole rather than on the needs of individual members.

1151 Petersen, William. "Population Policy and Age Structure." POLICY STUDIES JOURNAL 6 (Winter 1977): 146-54.

Zero population growth will bring about problems associated with the changed age structure of society. Changes in the age pattern will be less painful to the society if they can be made gradually.

1152  Prager, Edward. "Subsidized Family Care of the Aged: U.S. Senate Bill 1161." POLICY ANALYSIS 4 (Fall 1978): 477-90.

Senate Bill 1161 would encourage families to share their households with elderly kin as an alternative to skilled nursing care facilities. While the idea may have merit as social and political policy, the literature of family helping behavior lends little support to such a program.

1153  Reiner, Thomas A., and Scheff, Janet. "Care of City Children: A Rural Development Base?" POLICY ANALYSIS 4 (Summer 1978): 415-18.

Many inhabitants of rural and small town areas have little economic opportunity now and even less hope for such in the foreseeable future. At the same time, many city children lack adequate care. A program of benefit to both would subsidize the temporary housing of urban children in rural homes.

1154  Rice, Robert M. "Preamble to Family Policy: Issues of the Past and the Present." POLICY STUDIES JOURNAL 7 (Summer 1979): 811-20.

Family policy will develop slowly in the United States, and the comprehensive and cohesive family policy can better be considered a goal rather than a readily implemented public activity.

1155  Roberto, Eduardo. STRATEGIC DECISION-MAKING IN A SOCIAL PROGRAM: THE CASE OF FAMILY PLANNING DIFFUSION. Lexington, Mass.: Lexington Books, 1975. 182 p.

The book develops a framework for dealing with the problems of planning and evaluating the diffusion efforts of a family planning program. The framework can be used by those interested in family planning and in diffusion strategies for other social programs.

1156  Robins, Philip K., and Werner, Samuel. CHILD CARE AND PUBLIC POLICY. Lexington, Mass.: Lexington Books, 1978. 234 p.

This analysis of the economic and public policy issues of child care evaluates present facilities, determines who uses them and why, and looks at current methods of subsidizing child care.

1157  Shanas, Ethel, and Houser, Philip M. "Zero Population Growth and the Family Life of Old People." JOURNAL OF SOCIAL ISSUES 30 (1974): 79-92.

It is felt that zero population growth would accelerate the role of government in providing housing, recreation, health care, and income maintenance for the elderly.

1158 Stetson, Dorothy M. "Family Policy and Fertility in the United States." POLICY STUDIES JOURNAL 6 (Winter 1977): 223-30.

Stetson examines antinatalist state fertility policies and moderately pronatalist federal population policies. It discusses how policies regulating the family and providing services may affect fertility by changing childbearing patterns and by the consequences of policies for childbearing couples.

1159 Stycos, J. Mayone. "Some Dimensions of Population and Family Planning: Goals and Means." JOURNAL OF SOCIAL ISSUES 30 (December 1974): 1-30.

The convergence and divergence of population planning and family planning programs are discussed in terms of ultimate and immediate goals and the process by which the goals are reached.

1160 Taeuber, Cynthia M., and Taeuber, Richard C. "Population and Public Policy." STATE GOVERNMENT 48 (Summer 1975): 183-88.

This general essay shows how population size and demographics affect policy, how policy goals affect population size, and the data needs and capabilities of the states for population oriented policy decisions.

1161 Wilcox, Allen R. "Population and Urban Systems: The Blurring of Boundaries." POLICY STUDIES JOURNAL 3 (Summer 1975): 340-45.

Studies of the relationship of population to urban politics and policy have tended to be one of four types, depending on whether the orientation has been normative or empirical and whether population has been used as a dependent or independent variable.

# SCIENCE, TECHNOLOGY, ENERGY, AND THE ENVIRONMENT

1162 Allen, Edward H. HANDBOOK OF ENERGY POLICY FOR LOCAL GOVERN-MENTS. Lexington, Mass.: Lexington Books, 1975. 236 p.

Allen is concerned with the public policy issues surrounding energy issues from the perspective of local government. He includes a discussion of energy administration, policy essential for local government, and management of energy emergencies.

1163 Bardach, Eugene, and Pugliaresi, Lucian. "The Environmental Impact Statement vs. the Real World." PUBLIC INTEREST, no. 49 (Fall 1977), pp. 22-38.

The environmental impact statement process may get in the way of agencies taking a hard look at environmental problems. Consideration should be given to the idea of immunizing agencies from the legal proceedings arising out of the EIS requirement.

1164  Bar-Zakay, Samuel N.  "Policymaking and Technology Transfer:  The Need for National Thinking Laboratories."  POLICY SCIENCES  2 (Summer 1971):  213-27.

National thinking laboratories should be created to promote organized technology transfer and to act as catalysts for organized policymaking.

1165  Bauer, Raymond A., and Rosenblum, Richard A.  SECOND ORDER CONSEQUENCES:  A METHODOLOGICAL ESSAY ON THE IMPACT OF TECHNOLOGY.  Cambridge:  MIT Press, 1969.  240 p.

This is an attack on the problem of managing the consequences of technological change based on a strategy for evaluating their "second order" consequences.

1166  Bozeman, Barry.  "Straight Arrow Science Policy and Its Dangers."  PUBLIC ADMINISTRATION REVIEW  39 (March-April 1979):  116-21.

The notion of science as objective and value-free (straight arrow) has served science policy poorly and has contributed to many problems in contemporary policymaking.

1167  Bozeman, Barry, and Blankenship, L. Vaughn.  "Science Information and Governmental Decision-Making:  The Case of the National Science Foundation."  PUBLIC ADMINISTRATION REVIEW 39 (January-February 1979):  53-57.

Scientific and technical information has proven to be troublesome for decision makers.  This study provides insight into using scientific information in making science policy.

1168  Caldwell, Lynton K.  "Energy and Environment:  The Bases for Public Policies."  ANNALS OF THE AMERICAN ACADEMY OF POLITICAL AND SOCIAL SCIENCE  410 (November 1973):  127-38.

The only rational basis for an energy policy which is more than expedient is an examination of the energy problems confronting society and a projection of alternative courses of action to desired futures.

1169  _____.  "Environmental Policy and Public Administration."  POLICY STUDIES JOURNAL  1 (Summer 1973):  209-12.

How is society making and implementing decisions affecting environmental issues?  The emphasis is on issues in environmental policy that cause political and administrative difficulties.

1170  _____.  "Environmental Policy as a Catalyst of Institutional Change."  AMERICAN BEHAVIORAL SCIENTIST  17 (May-June 1974):  711-30.

Caldwell examines the ways in which environmental policy, as an aspect of the quality of life, is influencing institutional and behavioral change.

1171 _____, ed. "Environmental Policy: New Directions in Federal Action." PUBLIC ADMINISTRATION REVIEW 28 (July–August 1968): 301–47.

Includes seven articles dealing with aspects of environmental problems from the 1960s. Topics include the need for coordinated policy and action, Congress and environmental policy, water and land management, the marine environment, and several others.

1172 Carver, John A. "Energy Information and Public Policy: Reflections of a Former Policy Maker." AMERICAN BEHAVIORAL SCIENTIST 19 (January–February 1976): 279–85.

More and better energy information is irrelevant unless there is a clear understanding of the factors that constrain decision makers.

1173 Commoner, Barry. "The Link between Energy Policy and Unemployment." NATION'S CITIES 15 (February 1977): 13–15.

Many national problems could be solved if city governments would create new energy policies. They could reduce unemployment and revitalize themselves by turning to insulation and solar power.

1174 Cortner, Hanna J. "Formulating and Implementing Energy Policy: The Inadequacy of the State Response." POLICY STUDIES JOURNAL 7 (Autumn 1978): 24–29.

Cortner identifies an inertia in the state energy policy arena and a failure to innovate. Policy analysts should be concerned about the factors contributing to the inertia.

1175 Daddario, Emilio Q. "National Science Policy: Prelude to Global Cooperation." BULLETIN OF THE ATOMIC SCIENTISTS 27 (June 1971): 21–24.

How can science and technology be employed for the benefit of all people? A national science policy is needed to provide the goals, priorities, and needed direction for the nation's scientific enterprise.

1176 Daneke, Gregory A. "The Political Economy of Nuclear Development." POLICY STUDIES JOURNAL 7 (Autumn 1978): 84–90.

Daneke explores the controversies surrounding the nuclear power industry as a model of government involvement. The paper shows how an elaborate structure of artificial incentives has insulated an ailing industry from the world of economic realities.

1177    Dinkel, John J., and Erickson, Joyce E.  "Multiple Objectives in En-
        vironmental Protection Programs."  POLICY SCIENCES  9 (February
        1978):  87–96.

      The essay calls for a multidimensional approach to the manage-
        ment of environmental programs.  It describes an experiment
        in the determination of multidimensional objectives within three
        programs in a state environmental quality program.

1178    Doerksen, Harvey.  "Water, Politics, and Ideology:  An Overview of
        Water Resources Management."  PUBLIC ADMINISTRATION REVIEW
        37 (September–October 1977):  444–48.

      Water resources management is policymaking where agencies,
        laws, and political entities converge.  Currently, rational
        management is impossible, policies are the result of factors
        external to the agencies, and conflict over the decision is
        guaranteed.

1179    Dutton, William H., and Kraemer, Kenneth L.  "Technology and Urban
        Management:  The Power Payoffs of Computing."  ADMINISTRATION
        AND SOCIETY  9 (November 1977):  305–40.

      Data systems in local government are designed to provide
        management with information.  A "management oriented com-
        puting index" is developed to determine the degree to which
        a city's information system is oriented to the needs of manage-
        ment.

1180    Edgmon, Terry D.  "Energy as a Disorganizing Concept in Policy and
        Administration."  POLICY STUDIES JOURNAL  7 (Autumn 1978):  58–67.

      Edgmon reviews past energy organizing concepts, patterns
        of energy politics, and emerging energy ideologies used to
        assess the potential impact of recent federal energy reorgani-
        zation efforts.

1181    Engler, Robert.  THE POLITICS OF OIL.  2d ed.  New York:  Mac-
        millan, 1976.  565 p.

      This is an analysis of the impact of the petroleum industry
        on energy related policymaking.  Engler provides background
        reading on energy policy in the pre-energy crisis days as
        well as current developments.

1182    Erickson, Kenneth P.  "Public Policy and Energy Consumption in Indus-
        trialized Societies."  POLICY STUDIES JOURNAL  7 (Autumn 1978):
        112–21.

      An analysis of energy consumption patterns shows the United
        States can reduce its energy consumption without reducing
        its standard of living and that differences in nations' energy
        consumption is due to public policy choices.

1183    Ervin, Osbin L.  "Local Fiscal Effects of Coal Resource Development:
        A Framework for Analysis and Management."  POLICY STUDIES JOUR-
        NAL  7 (Autumn 1978):  9–17.

If small communities in coal-producing regions are to enjoy quality growth from increased demands for coal, then attention should be given to research on energy-related community impacts and on the management options of local officials.

1184 Eulau, Heinz. "Technology and the Fear of the Politics of Civility." JOURNAL OF POLITICS 35 (May 1973): 367-85.

Both technologists and antitechnologists envision antipolitical utopias. The article discusses behaviors which prevent the factions from engaging in compromise solutions.

1185 Ewald, William R. ENVIRONMENT AND POLICY: THE NEXT FIFTY YEARS. Bloomington: Indiana University Press, 1968. 459 p.

This is a collection of papers covering a wide range of environmental topics. The volume includes education, health, transportation, housing and manpower, and the "possible city."

1186 Furash, Edward C. "The Problem of Technology Transfer." In THE STUDY OF POLICY FORMATION, edited by Raymond J. Bauer and Kenneth J. Gergen, pp. 281-328. New York: Free Press, 1968.

Furash identifies the actors who participate in and influence the transfer of federally funded technology. The attitudes, predispositions, and context are identified to understand the kinds of research information needed.

1187 Garvey, Gerald. "Environmentalism Versus Energy Development: The Constitutional Background to Environmental Administration." PUBLIC ADMINISTRATION REVIEW 35 (July-August 1975): 328-33.

Government must be viewed as a secondary system to the market in the allocation of resources for the transfer of environmental rights.

1188 Gates, Bruce L. "Knowledge Management in the Technological Society: Government by Indicator." PUBLIC ADMINISTRATION REVIEW 35 (November-December 1975): 589-92.

Gates provides a justification of knowledge management as a way of improving organizational responsiveness to society's needs. Such techniques alter the nature of political dialogue within and between institutions.

1189 Gianos, Philip L. "Scientists as Policy Advisers: The Context of Influence." WESTERN POLITICAL QUARTERLY 27 (September 1974): 429-56.

Gianos focuses on the role of scientists and scientific organizations in the formulation and implementation of science policy in the federal government.

1190 Gilman, Glenn. "Technological Innovation and Public Policy." CALIFORNIA MANAGEMENT REVIEW 13 (Spring 1971): 13-24.

If we are to meet our national goals, we must have a continuing high level of innovation. Corporate laboratories and university research facilities cannot provide enough support for such activities. Public policy should support the individual inventor.

1191 Haberer, Joseph, ed. SCIENCE AND TECHNOLOGY POLICY. Lexington, Mass.: Lexington Books, 1977. 216 p.

This volume contains sixteen articles that originally appeared in the POLICY STUDIES JOURNAL. They are divided into the following areas: perspectives on science and technology policy, developments in science and technology policy, and making and managing policies.

1192 Hall, Robert E., and Pindyck, Robert S. "The Conflicting Goals of National Energy Policy." PUBLIC INTEREST, no. 47 (Spring 1977), pp. 3-15.

Our national energy policy has been based on maintaining low prices. As a result, our dependence on foreign oil is a problem of our own making. The authors discuss how current policies keep prices low, what energy policy should and should not do, and an energy outlook for the future.

1193 Hamilton, Mary A. "Energy Policy and Changing Public-Private Sector Relationships." POLICY STUDIES JOURNAL 7 (Autumn 1978): 90-96.

Government, and not the private sector, is taking the lead in energy activity by initiating projects and programs that will lead to achieving national energy policy objectives.

1194 Henry, Nicholas. "Bureaucracy, Technology, and Knowledge Management." PUBLIC ADMINISTRATION REVIEW 35 (November-December 1975): 572-77.

Bureaucracy and technology are facts of American life in the twentieth century, and the idea of "knowledge management" provides a useful intellectual perspective in analyzing the public's problems as they relate to bureaucracy and technology.

1195 Hy, Ron. "Futures Research and Public Policy." POLICY STUDIES JOURNAL 4 (Summer 1976): 416-23.

The techniques of futures' analysis can help policymakers face the pressures of technological change by forcing choices about what problems to study, what factors to concentrate upon, what groups to consider, and what alternatives to select.

1196 Jantsch, Eric. "Forecasting and the Systems Approach: A Critical Survey." POLICY SCIENCES 3 (December 1972): 475-98.

Long-range forecasting for social systems deals with feedback interactions between all elements and sectors of such systems. A survey of current approaches to forecasting attempts is used to discuss the state of the art and potential for future developments.

1197    Jones, Charles O. CLEAN AIR: THE POLICIES AND POLITICS OF
        POLLUTION CONTROL. Pittsburgh: University of Pittsburgh Press,
        1975.  372 p.

        This is a case study of the intergovernmental aspects of air
        pollution control at a U.S. steel plant in the Pittsburgh area.


1198    _____.  "Speculative Augmentation in Federal Air Pollution Policy-
        Making."  JOURNAL OF POLITICS  36 (May 1974):  438-64.

        Air pollution is an issue in which science and technology
        have a major impact on the cause and cure of the problem.
        Jones claims that incrementalism fails to explain federal air
        pollution policy after 1970 and he develops an alternative
        model.


1199    Kaplan, Max, and Bosserman, Phillip, eds.  TECHNOLOGY HUMAN
        VALUES, AND LEISURE.  Nashville, Tenn.:  Abingdon Press, 1971.
        256 p.

        The creative use of leisure is examined as a world problem,
        a concern for public policy and not just for the aged or
        elderly.  Twelve contributors discuss the effect of leisure
        and technology on political, economic, and social patterns.


1200    Keating, William T.  "Politics, Energy, and the Environment:  The Role
        of Technology Assessment."  AMERICAN BEHAVIORAL SCIENTIST
        19 (September-October 1975):  37-74.

        The issue is whether electricity ought to be generated by
        nuclear powered plants.  Suggestions are offered for organi-
        zational reform in order to improve the assessment of benefits
        and risks.


1201    Kneese, Allen V., and Schultz, Charles L.  POLLUTION, PRICES,
        AND PUBLIC POLICY.  Washington, D.C.:  Brookings Institution, 1975.
        125 p.

        Congress does not have the staff or technical assistance to
        develop or evaluate alternate approaches to complex economic
        and social questions.  A solution is to improve the technical
        qualifications of congressional committee staffs.


1202    Krutilla, John V., and Page, Talbot.  "Towards a Responsible Energy
        Policy."  POLICY ANALYSIS  1 (Winter 1975):  77-100.

        Short-term adjustments in energy demand will be painful and
        alternatives will take years to develop.  Decision-making
        institutions have not solved the problem of intergenerational
        equity as in the case of nuclear waste disposal.  Public
        participation needs to be increased to integrate economic
        and ethical considerations.


1203    Kuenne, Robert E., et al.  "A Policy to Protect the U.S. against
        Oil Embargoes."  POLICY ANALYSIS  1 (Fall 1975):  571-98.

Cost-benefit analysis is used to determine how much oil should be placed in reserve to guard against another oil embargo. While a ninety-day supply is currently available, analysis suggests a three-year reserve.

1204 Laird, Melvin R. ENERGY--A CRISIS IN PUBLIC POLICY. Washington, D.C.: American Enterprise Institute for Public Policy, 1977. 23 p.

Laird claims that we cannot solve the energy problem until we first understand what its components are. There are demand-created problems, government-created problems, and industry-created problems.

1205 Lambright, W. Henry. GOVERNING SCIENCE AND TECHNOLOGY. New York: Oxford University Press, 1976. 218 p.

Lambright focuses on the administrative-political interactions of science and technology. The main problems in science and technology governance is the constitutional division of powers.

1206 Lambright, W. Henry, and Teich, Albert H. "Policy Innovation in Federal R and D: The Case of Energy." PUBLIC ADMINISTRATION REVIEW 39 (March-April 1979): 140-47.

The essay expresses a concern for how change occurs in national research and development policy. The authors highlight the interplay of foreign policy, technological opportunities, and societal crises in national research and development decision making.

1207 LaPorte, Todd R. "The Changing Context of Technology Assessment: A Changing Perspective for Public Organization." PUBLIC ADMINISTRATION REVIEW 31 (January-February 1971): 63-73.

This is an exploration of the political and social changes that occur as a result of technological advancement. The emphasis is on the impact of change for the administration of public affairs.

1208 Lawrence, Robert M. "Higher Prices, Insecurity and Degradation: Trade Offs in U.S. Energy Policy." AMERICAN BEHAVIORAL SCIENTIST 19 (September-October 1975): 8-36.

Energy policy must be concerned with several costs to society: higher prices, environmental degradation, and national security. An increase in one throws the other out of balance. Lawrence outlines different combinations of change for policy and discusses combinations of interest groups that are important.

1209 Lerner, Allan W. EXPERTS, POLITICIANS, AND DECISION MAKING IN THE TECHNOLOGICAL SOCIETY. Morristown, N.J.: General Learning Press, 1976. 31 p.

Enlightened and rational behavior in the technological age requires control over a staggering amount of information pertaining to almost every sector of society.

1210    Levine, Arthur L. "The Role of the Technoscience Administrator in Managing National Science Policy." PUBLIC ADMINISTRATION REVIEW 39 (March–April 1979): 122–28.

Levine examines the role of technoscience administrators in such programs as national defense, energy, aviation and space, medicine, and others. It is concerned with the background and training, sources of influence, and their present and likely future impact on science policy.

1211    Light, Stephen S., and Groves, David L. "Policy Issues in Recreation and Leisure: An Overview." POLICY STUDIES JOURNAL 6 (Spring 1978): 404–11.

This is an overview of the policy concerns involved in the recreation and leisure industry. An analysis of three policy areas is provided: private versus public provision of outdoor recreation, measuring the benefits of recreation, and urban versus rural provision of outdoor recreation.

1212    Livingston, Dennis. "Little Science Policy: The Study of Appropriate Technology and Decentralization." POLICY STUDIES JOURNAL 5 (Winter 1978): 185–92.

Livingston discusses "little science policy" as an appropriate or mediating technology in a context of political or economic decentralization.

1213    Loucks, Daniel P. "Residuals––Environmental Quality Management: A Framework for Policy Analysis." NATURAL RESOURCES JOURNAL 11 (July 1971): 547–60.

Loucks develops an analytical residual management model to assist judgment in sorting out issues and objectives for environmental policy. Residual management does not seek optimization techniques but merely defines alternative solutions based on different sets of assumptions.

1214    Maass, Arthur. MUDDY WATERS. Cambridge, Mass.: Harvard University Press, 1951. 306 p.

This is a classic if slightly dated account of the role of the U.S. Army Corps of Engineers in water policy formation.

1215    Majone, Giandomenico. "Choice Among Policy Instruments for Pollution Control." POLICY ANALYSIS 2 (Fall 1976): 589–613.

Majone discusses the tools of pollution-control policy, their political characteristics, and the possibilities for increasing public participation in the process.

1216 _____. "Technology Assessment and Policy Analysis." POLICY SCI-
ENCES 8 (1977): 173-75.

> Technology assessment involves questions that are beyond
> the capacity of science to answer. The impact of a tech-
> nology depends on the institutional framework within which
> it is located.

1217 Martin, Dolores T. "Energy Policy, Information Costs, and Secondary
Demand Effects." POLICY STUDIES JOURNAL 5 (Spring 1977): 301-7.

> Martin looks at the spillover effects from the fifty-five mile-
> per-hour speed limit. While drivers have slowed down and
> saved gasoline, there have been increases in law violations
> and increases in expenditures for law enforcement.

1218 Mead, Walter J. ENERGY AND THE ENVIRONMENT: CONFLICT IN
PUBLIC POLICY. Washington, D.C.: American Enterprise Institute
for Public Policy Research, 1978. 38 p.

> Future energy policy will probably repeat the past as poli-
> ticians must be sensitive to the pressures around them. In
> addition, the author does not see evidence of monopoly in
> the energy industry.

1219 Milbrath, Lester W., and Inscho, Frederick R., eds. "The Politics
of Environmental Quality, A Symposium." AMERICAN BEHAVIORAL
SCIENTIST 17 (May-June 1975): 621-770.

> Essays cover environmental problems as political problems,
> the polity as a monitor of the quality of life, incentives for
> compliance with environmental law, and others.

1220 Morgan, Arthur E. THE MAKING OF THE TVA. New York: Prome-
theus, 1974. 205 p.

> Efforts to develop all-inclusive cultural and economic programs
> have been expanded in the TVA area, and the lives of people
> in the area have been enriched because of those efforts.

1221 Munns, Joyce Matthews. "The Environment, Politics, and Policy Literature: A Critique and Reformulation." WESTERN POLITICAL QUARTERLY
28 (December 1975): 646-67.

> The deficiences in studies based on Easton's model of the
> political process are so serious that it ought to be retired.
> The author presents two alternative models to explain politi-
> cal system behavior.

1222 Nelson, Richard; Peck, Merton J.; and Kalachek, Edward F. TECH-
NOLOGY, ECONOMIC GROWTH AND PUBLIC POLICY. Washington,
D.C.: Brookings Institution, 1967. 238 p.

> This volume is concerned with the relations among research,
> development, innovation, and economic growth. It considers
> economic adaptation to technological change and the problems
> of adapting to change.

1223  Novick, Sheldon.  "The Federal Energy Policy."  ENVIRONMENT  18 (October 1976):  17-20.

> If the United States has anything approximating an energy policy, it is complete reliance upon the private sector. Market forces are gradually forcing a return to more efficient energy use, but reliance on the electric power industry could have negative consequences.

1224  O'Leary, John F.  "Nuclear Energy and Public Policy Issues."  In ENERGY SUPPLY AND GOVERNMENT POLICY, edited by Robert J. Kalter and William A. Vogel, pp. 235-54.  Ithaca, N.Y.:  Cornell University Press, 1976.

> The basis for public concern about the future of nuclear power comes from three issues:  safety, safeguards, and storage. The most useful outcome of the present debate would be to permit the nation to have the benefits of such power while addressing the major issues.

1225  Orlans, Harold, ed.  SCIENCE POLICY AND THE UNIVERSITY. Washington, D.C.:  Brookings Institution, 1968.  352 p.

> These papers explore the impact of federal money for scientific research and the relationships that grow out of the grants and contracts process.

1226  Ostrom, Vincent.  "Water Resource Development:  Some Problems in Economic and Political Analysis of Public Policy."  In POLITICAL SCIENCE AND PUBLIC POLICY, edited by Austin Ranney, pp. 123-50.  Chicago:  Markham-Publishing Co., 1968.

> There are numerous good reasons for the problems of water resource development to become involved in the political process.  There are problems in settling upon stable, long-term institutional arrangements for the economic development of water resources.

1227  Peskin, Henry M.  "Environmental Policy and the Distribution of Benefits and Costs."  In CURRENT ISSUES IN U.S. ENVIRONMENTAL POLICY, edited by Paul R. Portney, pp. 144-63.  Baltimore:  Johns Hopkins University Press, 1978.

> A discussion of a methodology to analyze the distribution of costs and benefits of an environmental policy.  He concludes by discussing the likely distributional consequences of alternative strategies for improving air quality.

1228  Portney, Paul R.  "Toxic Substances Policy and the Protection of Human Health."  In CURRENT ISSUES IN U.S. ENVIRONMENTAL POLICY, edited by Paul R. Portney, pp. 105-43.  Baltimore:  Johns Hopkins University Press, 1978.

> Policies designed to control the use and disposal of toxic substance may be the most difficult environmental issue to date.  While the free market cannot be expected to solve all the problems related to this area, economic incentives might be of use.

1229 Rettig, Richard A. "Science, Technology, and Public Policy." WORLD
POLITICS 23 (January 1971): 273-94.

This review essay covers five books published in 1968 and
1969 on science, technology, and public policy. Rettig
discusses the political behavior of the scientific community,
national science policy, and the use of science and technology
for social purposes.

1230 Rhoads, Steven E. POLICY ANALYSIS IN THE FEDERAL AVIATION
ADMINISTRATION. Lexington, Mass.: Lexington Books, 1974. 160 p.

Rhoads considers the extent to which policy analysts have
successfully supplied the FAA with information that would
allow the agency to engage in rational decision making. The
evaluation is made in the context of the general debate over
strengths and weaknesses of analytic theory and practices.

1231 Roessner, J. David. "Policy Issues and Policy Research in Public
Technology." POLICY STUDIES JOURNAL 5, no. 2 (1976): 205-11.

The paper discusses the nature of the issues surrounding the
application of science and technology to state and local problems. It suggests several conceptual approaches that could
be used to analyze policy issues.

1232 Rosenbaum, Walter. THE POLITICS OF ENVIRONMENTAL CONCERN.
New York: Praeger Publishers, 1973. 298 p.

This is a study of the rise of environmental politics and
the relationship between the environmental movement and the
political process. Case studies on pollution, water resources,
timber, and surface mining are included.

1233 Rycroft, Robert. "Bureaucratic Performance in Energy Policy-Making:
An Evaluation of Output Efficiency and Equity in the Federal Energy
Administration." PUBLIC POLICY 26 (Fall 1978): 599-627.

Rycroft evaluates the accomplishments of the Federal Energy
Administration by measuring its accomplishments against the
criteria of equity and efficiency. The FEA is found to be
inefficient and inequitable in its implementation of compliance
and enforcement of rules and regulations.

1234 Sabatier, Paul, and Wandesford-Smith, Geoffrey. "Major Sources on
Environmental Politics, 1974-1977: The Maturing of a Literature."
POLICY STUDIES JOURNAL 7 (Spring 1979): 592-604.

This is a review of the major works published since 1974
on the formulation and implementation of policy dealing with
air and water pollution, land use, and the protection of
natural resources.

1235 Schaller, David A. "An Energy Policy for Indian Lands: Problems
of Issue and Perception." POLICY STUDIES JOURNAL 7 (Autumn
1978): 40-49.

Issues affecting Indian energy policy and their perception
by policymakers present methodological issues for policy
analysts. They include the predictive power of policymaking,
the nature of political participation, and the capabilities of
an intergovernmental framework in explaining policy outcomes.

1236 Schooler, Dean, Jr. SCIENCE, SCIENTISTS, AND PUBLIC POLICY.
New York: Free Press, 1971. 338 p.

This is an analysis of twenty types of policy during the 1945–
1968 time period. Schooler discusses the dangers and advantages of scientific advice for indicating alternate policy choices
and proving that something is technologically feasible.

1237 Selznick, Philip. TVA AND THE GRASS ROOTS. Berkeley and
Los Angeles: University of California Press, 1949. 274 p.

This is a brief history of the TVA, its legislative history,
and the policy roles of its directors. They key is Selznick's
concern with the formulation of administrative policies and
intraorganizational conflict.

1238 Seskin, Eugene P. "Automobile Air Pollution Policy." In CURRENT
ISSUES IN U.S. ENVIRONMENTAL POLICY, edited by Paul R. Portney, pp. 68-104. Baltimore: Johns Hopkins University Press, 1978.

A discussion of the history of auto emission regulation, the
regulatory process, alternative regulatory devices, and charges
for auto emissions.

1239 Stevenson, Gordon McKay, Jr. THE POLITICS OF AIRPORT NOISE.
Belmont, Calif.: Duxbury Press, 1972. 148 p.

A systematic analysis of the participants in, and process of,
the development of noise abatement policies. The book is
especially strong on the details of policy action.

1240 Strassner, Gabor, and Simmons, Eugene, eds. SCIENCE AND TECH-
NOLOGY POLICIES: YESTERDAY, TODAY, AND TOMORROW. Cambridge, Mass.: Ballinger Publishers, 1974. 280 p.

The volume is an examination of the lack of and need for a
national energy policy concerning the role of science and
technology in national development.

1241 Tietenberg, Thomas H. "The Design of Property Rights for Air-Pollution
Control." PUBLIC POLICY 22 (Summer 1974): 275-92.

The air rights market has appeal to different groups in
society, so it might become useful as a tool for air pollution
control. Tietenberg discusses some difficulties in designing
such a market and produces an approach to combine economic
efficiency, emissions inventories, and methodological models
into a functional air rights model.

1242  Tietenberg, Thomas H., and Toureille, Pierre.  ENERGY PLANNING
AND POLICY:  THE POLITICAL ECONOMY OF PROJECT INDEPEN-
DENCE.  Lexington, Mass.:  Lexington Books, 1976.  168 p.

> This study makes two major points:  there is a U.S. energy
> policy; and it compares the utility of the analytical–rational
> and political–accommodation models of decision making.

1243  Tipermas, Marc.  "Science, Technology, and Public Policymaking:  An
Analytical Framework."  BUREAUCRAT  6 (Fall 1977):  86–90.

> This is an attempt to provide an analytical framework necessary
> if science and public policy is to establish itself as a coherent
> field of study.

1244  Utton, Albert E., and Henning, Daniel H., eds.  ENVIRONMENTAL
POLICY:  CONCEPTS AND INTERNATIONAL IMPLICATIONS.  New
York:  Praeger Publishers, 1973.  266 p.

> This is an attempt to outline a theoretical basis for the devel-
> opment of environmental quality policy.  It articulates the
> need for such a policy if humanity is to survive an ecological
> catastrophe.

1245  Wengert, Norman I.  "The Energy Boom Town:  An Analysis of the
Politics of Getting."  POLICY STUDIES JOURNAL  7 (Autumn 1978):
17–23.

> The politics of getting funds and other benefits to offset
> adverse consequences of energy boom town growth are dis-
> cussed.  While the need for action seems obvious, identifica-
> tion of the negative impacts may prove to be difficult.

1246  White, Irvin L.; Ballard, Steven C.; and Hall, Timothy A.  "Technology
Assessment as an Energy Policy Tool."  POLICY STUDIES JOURNAL
7 (Autumn 1978):  76–83.

> Technology assessment as a kind of applied policy analysis
> is described and its contribution to better informed energy
> policymaking is discussed.

1247  Winner, Langdon.  "On Criticizing Technology."  PUBLIC POLICY  20
(Winter 1972):  35–60.

> Winner attempts to determine if the debate and discussion
> regarding technology will have any lasting effect on the ways
> in which we think about technology.  There must be debate
> on the character of the technology of society.

1248  Yin, Robert K.  "Production Efficiency Versus Bureaucratic Self–Interest:
Two Innovative Processes."  POLICY SCIENCES  8 (December 1977):
381–99.

> This is a report on a study of technological innovation in
> state and local government agencies.  Two innovative processes
> can exist:  one that emphasizes service improvements and one
> that emphasizes the permanent use of innovation.

# ADDENDUM

Albritton, Robert B. "Measuring Public Policy: Impact of the Supplemental Security Income Program." AMERICAN JOURNAL OF POLITICAL SCIENCE 23 (August 1979): 559-78.

> The Title XX Amendments to the Social Security Act resulted in dramatic, nonincremental change in American welfare policy. This is important for the incrementalist theory of public policy and for future policy evaluation.

Albritton, Robert B., and Bahry, Donna. "Effects of Public and Private Sector Decisions in Health Care Costs." POLICY STUDIES JOURNAL 7 (Summer 1979): 762-70.

> The authors test the assumption that the creation of Medicare and Medicaid helped to fuel inflation by driving up medical costs. While they cannot prove a direct relationship between the introduction of Medicare and Medicaid and rising costs, federal funds seem to have had an indirect impact.

Anderson, Charles W. "The Place of Principles in Policy Analysis." AMERICAN POLITICAL SCIENCE REVIEW 73 (September 1979): 711-23.

> Anderson states that any theory of policy evaluation has to deal with the choice of values and criteria for decision making. Most criteria are derived from economic theory and use the utility-maximizing individual as a model.

Attewell, Paul, and Gerstein, Dean R. "Government Policy and Local Practice." AMERICAN SOCIOLOGICAL REVIEW 44 (April 1979): 311-27.

> The authors refute the widely held belief that federal policy becomes ineffective in the face of local realities. Using methadone treatment for heroin addiction as a case study, they show that federal actions have a major impact even at the micro level.

Baer, William C. "Empty Housing Space in an Overlooked Resource." POLICY STUDIES JOURNAL 8, no. 1 (1979): 220-26.

> Housing space in the United States is not effectively distributed. Baer discusses federal and local policies which encourage over-consumption of housing space.

Bardin, D.J. "Towards a Rational Energy Policy." ANNALS OF THE AMERICAN ACADEMY OF POLITICAL AND SOCIAL SCIENCE 444 (July 1979): 23-31.

# Addendum

Bardin claims that President Carter's energy policy is aimed at protecting the environment while increasing energy production. He asserts that we should adopt the Carter proposal while we seek technological advances and more innovative future approaches.

Baum, Lawrence. "The Influence of Legislatures and Appellate Courts Over the Policy Implementation Process." POLICY STUDIES JOURNAL 8, no. 2 (1980): 560-74.

Baum investigates the ability of legislatures and courts to guarantee the implementation of their policies. He notes that while legislatures have far greater powers than courts to control implementation, neither institution regularly has strong influence over the implementation process.

Blank, Robert H., and Ostheimer, John M. "An Overview of Biomedical Policy: Life and Death Issues." POLICY STUDIES JOURNAL 8 (Winter 1979): 470-78.

The authors provide an overview of the policy issues surrounding biomedical technology, summarize research in this area, and urge a close evaluation of the implementation of biomedical technology.

Browning, Rufus P.; Marshall, Dale Rogers; and Tabb, David H. "Implementation and Political Change: Sources of Local Variations in Federal Social Programs." POLICY STUDIES JOURNAL 8, no. 2 (1980): 616-32.

Three federal programs (Model Cities, General Revenue Sharing, and Community Development Block Grants) are analyzed as to the effects and implementation success. The specific focus is government responsiveness to black and Hispanic citizens in ten northern California cities from 1960 to 1977. The federal programs are found to have limited ability to influence the amount or direction of local political change.

Brunner, Ronald D. "Decentralized Energy Policies." PUBLIC POLICY 28 (Winter 1980): 71-91.

Local governments have made and implemented energy policies that have led to energy conservation and utilization of renewable resources. The federal government should adopt a policy which encourages such local initiatives without mandating the exact shape of local efforts.

Bullock, Charles S. III. "The Office for Civil Rights and Implementation of Desegregation Programs in the Public Schools." POLICY STUDIES JOURNAL 8, no. 2 (1980): 597-615.

A dozen variables are examined to determine the success of school desegregation efforts. Several variables are especially important in promoting successful implementation. Specifically, they are: clarity of the standards used to measure change, agency personnel commitment to reading program goals, assignment of high priority to the program by implementing agencies, and monitoring of how those affected by the program behave.

Burns, Arthur F. REFLECTIONS OF AN ECONOMIC POLICY-MAKER: SPEECHES AND CONGRESSIONAL STATEMENTS: 1969-1978. Washington, D.C.: American Enterprise Institute for Public Policy Research, 1978. 485 p.

> Most of the material in the volume is from the nine-year period (1970-1978) when Burns was chairman of the Board of Governors, Federal System. The book has five parts: free enterprise and economic growth, inflation and unemployment, fiscal responsibility, sound money and banking, and international finance.

Burstein, Paul. "Some 'Necessary Conditions' for Popular Control of Public Policy: A Critique." POLITY 12 (Fall 1979): 23-37.

> Burstein shows that traditionally held assumptions about necessary conditions for public control over public policy are not true. These conditions are: 1) candidate's stand on issues must be known; 2) voters must let the candidate's stand determine voters' choices; 3) a choice between opposing views must be available; and 4) votes must be able to count on candidates keeping their promises if elected.

Carlson, Kenneth. "Ways in Which Research Methodology Distorts Policy Issues." URBAN REVIEW 11 (Spring 1979): 3-14.

> Carlson argues that there are built-in problems with certain types of urban research that causes distorted policy issues. He focuses his attention on school finance reform and school desegregation and the experimental case study, and historical methods.

Christenson, James A., and Sachs, Carolyn E. "The Impact of Government Size and Number of Administrative Units on the Quality of Public Services." ADMINISTRATIVE SCIENCE QUARTERLY 25 (March 1980): 89-101.

> Using data from 100 localities in North Carolina, the authors find that smaller public labor forces and more administrative units per capita would likely lower the public's perception of the quality of public services.

Clark, Robert F. "The Proverbs of Evaluation: Perspectives from CSA's Experience." PUBLIC ADMINISTRATIVE REVIEW 39 (November 1979): 562-65.

> In 1946, Herbert A. Simon wrote an article titled "The Proverbs of Administration," PUBLIC ADMINISTRATION REVIEW 6 (Winter 1946): 53-67, in which he claimed that the field of adminis-tration was dominated by mutually contradictory principles. Clark provides the same sort of analysis for evaluation research. The evaluation proverbs are: 1) that the methodological standard of excellence is represented in the experimental design; 2) that credibility is assured when program managers are involved in the design, conduct, and interpretation of an evaluation; and 3) that evaluation results should affect specific and discrete pro-gram decisions.

Clark, Susan E. "Determinants of State Growth Management Policies." POLICY STUDIES JOURNAL 7 (Summer 1979): 753-61.

# Addendum

Clark examines why some states are more likely than others to
adopt a state growth management program. Using linear multiple
regression analysis, she finds that population growth in nonmetropolitan areas, the movement of higher income households
toward these areas, and the movements of nonwhite population
appear to be associated with states' adoption of growth management policies.

Conrad, Jon M. "Oil Spills: Policies for Prevention, Recovery and Com-
pensation." PUBLIC POLICY 28 (Spring 1980): 143-70.

A model of petroleum production and movement is developed to
generate policy implications for: oil spill liability, spill recovery, locational considerations, risk, and learning.

Coulter, Philip B. "Measuring the Inequity of Urban Public Services: A
Methodological Discussion with Applications." POLICY STUDIES JOURNAL
8 (Spring 1980): 683-97.

Using a technique he developed, Coulter finds that only modest
inequities in police service input and output exist in Tuscaloosa,
Alabama. Consistent with most other service equity research,
Coulter finds little systematic discrimination toward the poor
and racial minorities.

Del Sesto, Steven. "Conflicting Ideologies of Nuclear Power: Congressional
Testimony on Nuclear Reactor Safety." PUBLIC POLICY 28 (Winter 1980):
39-70.

An examination of the ideologies of pro- and antinuclear power
witnesses appearing at hearings held by the Joint Committee on
Atomic Energy in 1973-1974 in the matter of nuclear reactor
safety. Del Sesto says that much of the debate over nuclear
power safety is nontechnical and can be treated to differing
ideological positions.

Derthick, Martha. POLICYMAKING FOR SOCIAL SECURITY. Washington,
D.C.: Brookings Institution, 1979. 446 p.

Derthick divides the book into four parts. The first deals with
the evolution of the Social Security Program and the people who
were confidential in its early years. The next two sections
deal with the basic policies and goals of social security and more
recent changes in the law. Finally she addresses some of the
current problems associated with the social security program.

Due, John F. "The Revolution in Transportation Analysis and Policy."
AMERICAN BEHAVIORAL SCIENTIST 23 (January-February 1980): 353-82.

This is a general article explaining how transportation industries
operate and how public policy toward these agencies should be
formulated. He includes a discussion of railroads, air transport,
urban transportation, and trucking.

Dye, Thomas R. "Politics Versus Economics: The Development of the Literature on Policy Determination." POLICY STUDIES JOURNAL 7 (Summer 1979):
652-62.

Dye suggests that ideological beliefs have significantly affected the debate over whether politics or economics is more important in shaping public policy. He says that political science has had too narrow a definition of what is "political" and must broaden its scope of inquiry if it is to become a policy science.

ENERGY POLICY. Washington, D.C.: Congressional Quarterly, 1979. 131 p.

This book discusses the energy problems facing the country and the Carter administration's response to those problems. It includes chapters on the passage of the 1978 energy bill, the creation of the Department of Energy, and bills regulating strip mining and off-shore oil drilling.

Fairbanks, J. David. "Politics, Economics and the Public Morality: Why Some States Are More 'Moral' Than Others." POLICY STUDIES JOURNAL 7 (Summer 1979): 714-20.

Fairbanks looks at state regulations concerning liquor gambling, divorce, and birth control. He finds that the most important determinants of morality regulations were religious culture measured, not the level of economic development.

Fowler, Edmund P., and White, David. "Big City Downtowns: The Non-Impact of Zoning." POLICY STUDIES JOURNAL 7 (Summer 1979): 690-700.

This is a case study of downtown redevelopment in Toronto, Canada. The authors say that the political realities of the community determines whether zoning determines land prices or land prices determine zoning.

Gallup, George. "Cities: Unsolved Problems, Unused Talents." ANTIOCH REVIEW 37 (Spring 1979): 148-61.

The National League of Cities was asked to do a poll to find out how many citizens would be willing to serve their communities in some official capacity. He found that about 57 percent of urban residents would be willing to serve on a city advisory committee without pay; and an even higher percentage would be willing to serve on some neighborhood committee.

Game, Kingsley W. "Controlling Air Pollution: Why Some States Try Harder." POLICY STUDIES JOURNAL 7 (Summer 1979): 728-39.

This article evaluates state compliance with the 1970 Clean Air Amendments. Game determines that the main influences on clean air spending were the ability of states to delegate responsibility to substate units, the level of bureaucratization, and population levels.

Ginsburg, Helen. "Full Employment As a Policy Issue." POLICY STUDIES JOURNAL 8 (Winter 1979): 359-67.

Ginsburg traces efforts to develop a national full employment policy from the 1940s through the passage of the Humphrey-

# Addendum

Hawkins Full Employment and Balanced Growth Act of 1978. Even with the passage of the legislation, the controversy over full employment has not ended. Implementation problems may exacerbate underlying controversies over larger, inflation, price and profit controls, and so forth.

Goodwin, Leonard, and Moen, Phyllis. "The Evolution and Implementation of Family Welfare Policy." POLICY STUDIES JOURNAL 8, no. 2 (1980): 633-51.

The forty-five years of federal family welfare policy is analyzed and the complexity of the welfare issue is given considerable attention. Failure to believe desired policy implementation is due to inadequate definition of the relevant issues.

Hagebak, Beaumont R. "Local Human Service Delivery: The Integration Imperative." PUBLIC ADMINISTRATION REVIEW 39 (November-December 1979): 575-82.

Efficiency and logic demand that costly, duplicated, and fragmented human services systems be more fully integrated into an effective system. Before the self-interests that threaten to prevent any real integration can be eliminated, there must be local community-based action to put a new system into place.

Houstoun, L.O., Jr. "The Carter Urban Policy a Year Later." ANTIOCH REVIEW 37 (Spring 1979): 134-47.

Houstoun, an assistant to the Secretary of Commerce at the time of writing, identifies several urban problems which the Carter urban policy addresses. He identified these as problems of time, subject matter, and political boundaries.

Ingram, Helen M., and Ullery, Scott J. "Policy Innovation and Institutional Fragmentation." POLICY STUDIES JOURNAL 8 (Spring 1980): 664-82.

Using the committee systems of Congress and water pollution control as case examples, the author demonstrates that fragmented and decentralized policymaking structures can be responsible for major policy innovation as well as centralized structures.

Jacobs, David. "Dimensions of Inequality and Public Policy in the States." JOURNAL OF POLITICS 42 (February 1980): 291-306.

Jacobs shows how methodological approaches to defining income inequality are likely to affect substantive findings. Beyond methodological concerns, he finds that the politically most significant gap in terms of who benefits from public policies is the income gap between the law and middle income.

Jennings, Edward T., Jr. "Civil Turmoil and the Growth of Welfare Rolls: A Comparative State Policy Analysis." POLICY STUDIES JOURNAL 7 (Summer 1979): 734-44.

In 1971 Frances Fox Piven and Richard Cloward in REGULATING
THE POOR argued that government responds to the plight of the
poor with relief programs only after civil disorder of some type
has occurred. As order is restored, welfare rolls are made smaller.
This article tests several of the Piven and Cloward hypotheses.
Jennings's findings indicate that the level of urban rioting was
linked to increased recipient rates, but that spending for community action was not.

Johnson, R.W., and O'Connor, R.E. "Intra-Agency Limitations on Policy
Implementation: You Can't Always Get What You Want, But Sometimes You
Get What You Need." ADMINISTRATION AND SOCIETY 11 (August 1979):
193-215.

The authors review the traditional explanations as to why programs failed to be implemented successfully, and then present
data to show that lower level employees deliberately change
program goals to make them more compatible with overall organizational goals.

Jones, Charles O. "If I Knew Then . . . (A Personal Essay on Committees
and Public Policy." POLICY ANALYSIS 5 (Fall 1979): 473-80.

This is a first-hand analysis of Jones's experience as a member
of a study panel of the Committee on Nuclear Power and Alternative Energy Systems established by the National Science Foundation. His conclusion is that the CONAES effort was insufficient
and ineffective because time was not effectively used, study goals
were not made explicit, communication was faulty, and resources
were wasted.

Kettl, Donald E. "Can the Cities Be Trusted? The Community Development
Experience." POLITICAL SCIENCE QUARTERLY 94 (Fall 1979): 437-52.

Kettl explores increased local discretion in the federal grants
process by examining four Connecticut cities involved in the
Community Development Block Grant Program. He concludes
that cities are able to deal with neighborhood-based problems,
but are unable to cope with city-wide problems.

Keyserling, Leon H. "The Problem of High Unemployment." POLICY STUDIES
JOURNAL 8 (Winter 1979): 349-58.

Keyserling argues that the nation needs a reconstruction of its
economic policies that includes abandoning trading-off between
unemployment and inflation, attempts to balance the federal budget at the expense of the economy, establishes a monetary policy
with rising interest rates, and creates reliance on tax reductions
in lieu of increased public outlays or investment.

Kirst, Michael W.; Garms, Walter; and Opperman, Theo. "State Services
for Children in an Exploration of Who Benefits Who Governs." PUBLIC POLICY
28 (Spring 1980): 185-206.

The authors make four major points: 1) in the field of children's
social service data gathering is in a primitive state; 2) the access
of children to services varies tremendously within states; 3) accoun-

# Addendum

tability for Title XX funds is much lower than for education funds; 4) in New York, California, and Michigan, allocation of Title XX funds to localities is determined by political criteria and not need.

Klass, Gary M. "The Determination of Policy and Politics in the American States, 1948-1979." POLICY STUDIES JOURNAL 7 (Summer 1979): 745-52.

Klass develops a path model of the causes and effects of changes in taxes and spending for education in thirty-seven states. The evidence indicates that changes in party control of the legislature are important in short term change in budget priorities.

Kushman, John E. "A Public Choice Model of Day Care Center Services." SOCIAL SCIENCE QUARTERLY 60 (September 1979): 295-308.

Day care services have attributes which make it desirable to provide them via a mechanism other than by the private mandate. The public choice model offers a possible approach to the provision of such services.

LeLoup, Lance T. "Process versus Policy: The U.S. House Budget Committee." LEGISLATIVE STUDIES QUARTERLY 4 (May 1979): 227-54.

This study focuses on the House Budget Committee and the budget process in the House. The committee is a partisan, divided committee, torn between process and policy goals. It reflects the divided environment in the House concerning the budget process and fiscal policy.

Mayntz, Renate. "Public Bureaucracies and Policy Implementation." INTERNATIONAL SOCIAL SCIENCE JOURNAL 31 (April 1979): 633-45.

Since bureaucracies are not robot-like instruments but have their own goals and use their discretionary authority to realize those goals is significant because bureaucracies modify policy to the real-life situations that legislators forgot.

Mead, W.J. ENERGY AND THE ENVIRONMENT: CONFLICT IN PUBLIC POLICY. Washington, D.C.: American Enterprise Institute for Public Policy Research, 1978. 36 p.

This paper discusses the economics and politics of energy and environmental issues. Mead concludes that a comprehensive national energy policy should be developed which relies on market forces to allocate scarce resources.

Montgomery, Roger, and Marshall, Dale Rogers, eds. "Symposium on Housing Policy." POLICY STUDIES JOURNAL 8, no. 1 (1979): 204-336.

This special issue was sponsored by the U.S. Department of Housing and Urban Development. The eleven articles are divided into six sections: owner occupied housing demographic changes and housing demand, changes in the rental market, inflation, open housing policies, and low and moderate income housing.

Morgan, David R. MANAGING THE MODERN CITY: THE POLITICS AND ADMINISTRATION OF AMERICA'S CITIES. North Scituate, Mass.: Duxbury Press, 1979. 333 p.

> Morgan's purpose in writing the book was to provide some insight into what is involved in managing the modern city. His approach combines academic material and case studies to show how urban managers actually perform their jobs.

Norman, A.J. "Issues in Promoting Planning in the Human Service Delivery System: The Case of Area Agencies on Aging." ADMINISTRATION IN SOCIAL WORK 3 (Spring 1979): 79–89.

> Norman discusses Area Agencies on Aging as a human service delivery system and raises some issues that he felt are important to successful planning within the system.

Noto, Nonna A. "Tax and Financial Policies for the Housing Market of the 1980s." POLICY STUDIES JOURNAL 8, no. 1 (1979): 211–19.

> Changes in housing policies could help to offset anticipated variations in housing market demands over the next forty years. Tax and financial policies could be changed to neutralize the attractiveness of single family, owner-occupied housing.

Palley, Howard A. "Abortion Policy: Ideology, Political Cleavage and the Policy Process." POLICY STUDIES JOURNAL 7 (Winter 1978): 224–33.

> Palley reviews the U.S. Supreme Court's 1973 abortion rulings and subsequent political and policy events leading to attempts to make current abortion policy more liberal or more restrictive. He suggests that political cleavage along ideological lines will act as a major constraint on public policy initiatives in this policy area.

Radin, Beryl A. IMPLEMENTATION, CHANGE, AND THE FEDERAL BUREAUCRACY: SCHOOL DESEGREGATION POLICY IN H.E.W. New York: Teachers College Press, 1978. 239 p.

> Radin suggests that in attempting to implement school desegregation, HEW staff used administrative mechanisms that did not fit the nature of the problem to be solved. As a result, a difficult implementation task was made even more difficult. She raises a larger question for the reader: What is the role of the federal bureaucracy in social change?

Randall, Ronald. "Presidential Power versus Bureaucratic Intransigence: The Influence of the Nixon Administration on Welfare Policy." AMERICAN POLITICAL SCIENCE REVIEW 73 (September 1979): 795–810.

> Many studies claim that presidents are unable to control the bureaucracy. This study shows that the Nixon administration did change welfare policy even over the objections of agency bureaucrats. Randall claims that when used properly, the management tools available to the president are more powerful than generally assumed.

# Addendum

Rathjen, Gregory J., and Spaeth, Harold J. "Access to the Federal Courts: An Analysis of Burger Court Policy Making." AMERICAN JOURNAL OF POLITICAL SCIENCE 23 (May 1979): 360–82.

> The authors attempt to determine what motivates Burger court justices in their policy choices. They hypothesize that policy choices are a function of a belief about justice, a set of beliefs about administration and the law, and the merits of the case. They find that each justice's beliefs is unique to himself.

Redburn, F. Stevens, and Buss, Terry F. "Public Policies for Communities in Economic Crisis: An Overview of the Issues." POLICY STUDIES JOURNAL 8 (Autumn 1979): 149–56.

> This short article addresses some of the issues associated with public policy associated with communities in economic crisis. Its particular focus is on middle–sized industrial cities in the northeast and midwest. The article discusses short– and long–term effects and processes, economic development policies, corporate responsibility, community–worker ownership, and re–location policy.

Reiner, Thomas A., eds. "Toward a National Urban Policy Critical Reviews." JOURNAL OF REGIONAL SCIENCE 19 (February 1979): 67–130.

> Five original articles appear in this symposium which is devoted to an analysis and criticism of the 1978 National Urban Policy Report by President Carter. The articles focus on issues avoided, capital flow for urban economic development, the presence of an urban policy, a post–industrial perspective on the urban crisis, and federal policy and the urban poor.

Rich, Richard C. "Neglected Issues in the Study of Urban Services Distributions: A Research Agenda." URBAN STUDIES 16 (June 1979): 143–56.

> Rich reviews existing research in the area of urban service distribution; examines the limitations of current research; and suggests that future research could be improved by focusing on outcome, rather than output measures of service.

Roessner, James D. "Federal Technology Policy: Innovation and Problem–Solving in State and Local Governments." POLICY ANALYSIS 5 (Spring 1979): 181–200.

> Roessner discusses the conceptualization and analysis of public technology policy issues and the implications of recent research findings for federal public technology policy. He suggests that federal efforts should support improved analytic and evaluative capabilities for state and local governments rather than simply encouraging such governments to adopt new technologies.

Rushefsky, Mark E. "Policy Implications of Alternative Agriculture." POLICY STUDIES JOURNAL 8 (Spring 1980): 772–84.

> As a result of energy and environmental factors there has been a small change in American agricultural policy and practices. These changes may be termed organic or alternative agriculture.

Addendum

Sabatier, Paul, and Mazmarian, Daniel. "The Conditions of Effective Implementation: A Guide to Accomplishing Policy Objectives." POLICY ANALYSIS 5 (Fall 1979): 481-505.

> Five conditions are established that the authors claim will assist in effective implementation. They suggest strategies that are available to legislators to overcome the mobility to meet the condition. The conditions of effective policy implementation are: 1) sound theory characterizes the program; 2) the basic law has unambiguous policy directives; 3) implementation agency leaders have managerial and political skill and are commited to achieving statutory goals; 4) interest grows and key legislators support the program; and 5) the property of statutory objectives is not undermined by other objectives.

_____. "The Implementation of Public Policy: A Framework of Analysis." POLICY STUDIES JOURNAL 8, no. 2 (1980): 538-59.

> In the three to five years after the passage of a piece of legislation, the most important variables affecting implementation are the strengths of the legislation, the commitment of implementing agency officials, the resources of constituency groups, and a "fixer" (a political official who controls the resources important to aware actors).

Thomas, Robert D. "Implementing Federal Programs at the Local Level." POLITICAL SCIENCE QUARTERLY 94 (Fall 1979): 419-36.

> This is an analysis of how federal aid programs to local governments are modified to meet local needs and conditions. Thomas finds that federal officials are fully willing to let local officials determine their own priorities.

Welch, Susan, and Karnig, Albert K. "The Impact of Black Elected Officials on Urban Social Expenditures." POLICY STUDIES JOURNAL 7 (Summer 1979): 707-13.

> The authors find that a city having a black mayor tended to have greater increases in social welfare spending than cities with no black mayors. Their data base was 155 U.S. cities with population over 50,000 and at least 10 percent black.

Wheeler, Russell. "Judicial Reform: Basic Issues and References." POLICY STUDIES JOURNAL 8 (Autumn 1979): 134-48.

> Wheeler provides an overview of issues and references in judicial administration. He discusses court objectives, the causes and remedies of court malperformance, achieving more effective case processing, and management changes to achieve personal and procedural changes.

Williams, Bruce A. "Beyond Incrementalism, Organizational Theory and Public Policy." POLICY STUDIES JOURNAL 7 (Summer 1979): 675-82.

> There has been a long-standing debate as to whether incremental or rational models better explain the policymaking process. The author states that both sides may be present within an organization

255

and that the job of policy analysts is to predict changes from one model to another.

Williams, Walter A. "A Social Agency Implementation Strategy: Some Preliminary Ideas." JOURNAL OF HEALTH AND HUMAN RESOURCES ADMINISTRATION 1 (May 1979): 526-37.

Using data from the Community Development Block Grant Program, the author finds that the federal government has limited control over how a unit of local government chooses to implement a program using federal grant money.

# AUTHOR INDEX

This index includes all authors, editors, and other contributors to works cited in the text. It is alphabetized letter by letter. Numbers refer to entry numbers, unless preceded by "p." indicating the page number.

# Author Index

# Author Index

# Author Index

# Author Index

# Author Index

# Author Index

# SUBJECT INDEX

This index is alphabetized letter by letter. Numbers refer to entry numbers, unless preceded by "p." indicating the page number.

# Subject Index

# Subject Index

# Subject Index

# Subject Index

# Subject Index